International African Library 39
General Editors: J. D. Y. Peel, Suzette Heald and Deborah James

BEYOND THE STATE IN RURAL UGANDA

The *International African Library* is a major monograph series from the International African Institute and complements its quarterly periodical *Africa*, the premier journal in the field of African studies. Theoretically informed ethnographies, studies of social relations 'on the ground' which are sensitive to local cultural forms, have long been central to the Institute's publications programme. The *IAL* maintains this strength but extends it into new areas of contemporary concern, both practical and intellectual. It includes works focused on problems of development, especially on the linkages between the local and national levels of society; studies along the interface between the social and environmental sciences; and historical studies, especially those of a social, cultural or interdisciplinary character.

Titles in the series:
1 Sandra T. Barnes *Patrons and power: creating a political community in metropolitan Lagos*
2 Jane I. Guyer (ed.) *Feeding African cities: essays in social history*
3 Paul Spencer *The Maasai of Matapato: a study of rituals of rebellion*
4 Johan Pottier *Migrants no more: settlement and survival in Mambwe villages, Zambia*
5 Gunther Schlee *Identities on the move: clanship and pastoralism in northern Kenya*
6 Suzette Heald *Controlling anger: the sociology of Gisu violence*
7 Karin Barber *I could speak until tomorrow:* oriki, *women and the past in a Yoruba town*
8 Richard Fardon *Between God, the dead and the wild: Chamba interpretations of religion and ritual*
9 Richard Werbner *Tears of the dead: the social biography of an African family*
10 Colin Murray *Black Mountain: land, class and power in the eastern Orange Free State, 1880s to 1980s*
11 J. S. Eades *Strangers and traders: Yoruba migrants, markets and the state in northern Ghana*
12 Isaac Ncube Mazonde *Ranching and enterprise in eastern Botswana: a case study of black and white farmers*
13 Melissa Leach *Rainforest relations: gender and resource use among the Mende of Gola, Sierra Leone*
14 Tom Forrest *The advance of African capital: the growth of Nigerian private enterprise*
15 C. Bawa Yamba *Permanent pilgrims: the role of pilgrimage in the lives of West African Muslims in Sudan*
16 Graham Furniss *Poetry, prose and popular culture in Hausa*
17 Philip Burnham *The politics of cultural difference in northern Cameroon*
18 Jane I. Guyer *An African niche economy: farming to feed Ibadan, 1968–88*
19 A. Fiona D. Mackenzie *Land, ecology and resistance in Kenya, 1880–1952*
20 David Maxwell *Christians and chiefs in Zimbabwe: a social history of the Hwesa people c. 1870s–1990s*

21 Birgit Meyer *Translating the devil: religion and modernity among the Ewe in Ghana*
22 Deborah James *Songs of the women migrants: performance and identity in South Africa*
23 Christopher O. Davis *Death in abeyance: illness and therapy among the Tabwa of Central Africa*
24 Janet Bujra *Serving Class: masculinity and the feminisation of domestic service in Tanzania*
25 T. C. McCaskie *Asante identities: history and modernity in an African village 1850–1950*
26 Harri Englund *From war to peace on the Mozambique–Malawi borderland*
27 Anthony Simpson *'Half-London' in Zambia: contested identities in a Catholic mission school*
28 Elisha Renne *Population and progress in a Yoruba town*
29 Belinda Bozzoli *Theatres of struggle and the end of apartheid*
30 R. M. Dilley *Islamic and caste knowledge practices among Haalpulaar'en in Senegal: between mosque and termite mound*
31 Colin Murray and Peter Sanders *Medicine murder in colonial Lesotho: the anatomy of a moral crisis*
32 Benjamin F. Soares *Islam and the prayer economy: history and authority in a Malian town*
33 Carola Lentz *Ethnicity and the making of history in northern Ghana*
34 David Pratten *The man-leopard murders: history and society in colonial Nigeria*
35 Kai Kresse *Philosophising in Mombasa: knowledge, Islam and intellectual practice on the Swahili Coast*
36 Ferdinand de Jong *Masquerades of modernity: power and secrecy in Casamance, Senegal*
37 Charles Gore *Art, performance and ritual in Benin City*
38 Ramon Sarró *The politics of religious change on the Upper Guinea Coast: iconoclasm done and undone*
39 Ben Jones *Beyond the state in rural Uganda*

BEYOND THE STATE IN RURAL UGANDA

BEN JONES

EDINBURGH UNIVERSITY PRESS
for the International African Institute, London

© Ben Jones, 2009

Edinburgh University Press Ltd
22 George Square, Edinburgh
www.euppublishing.com

Typeset in Plantin
by Koinonia, Bury, and
printed and bound in Great Britain
by Cromwell Press, Trowbridge, Wilts

A CIP record for this book is available
from the British Library

ISBN 978 0 7486 3518 4 (hardback)

The publishers gratefully acknowledge
support received from the Economic and
Social Research Council

Photographs © Chia-Hsin Hu, 2008

For other publications of the International
African Institute, please visit their web site at
www.internationalafricaninstitute.org

CONTENTS

List of Maps, Plates and Tables vi
Acknowledgements vii
Abbreviations x
Glossary xi
Preface xiii
Maps xvii

1 Introduction 1

2 Introducing Oledai 13

3 Teso Society through the Twentieth Century 31

4 The Village Court and the Withdrawn State 63

5 The Pentecostal Church 91

6 The Anglican and Catholic Churches 111

7 Burial Societies 133

8 Conclusion 157

Appendix A: Research Methods 167
Appendix B: Interviews and Group Discussions 173
Bibliography 180
Index 195

MAPS, PLATES, TABLES

Map 1   Oledai sub-parish and its environs   xvii
Map 2   Teso district   xviii
Map 3   Uganda's Ethnic Groups   xix

Plate 1   A farm labour group (*aleya*) at work   xx
Plate 2   A farmer moves sacks of charcoal to market   12
Plate 3   The disused ginnery on the Ngora–Mukongoro road   32
Plate 4   The sub-county headquarters for Ngora   62
Plate 5   A shebeen on the outskirts of Oledai   90
Plate 6   A village church from the neighbouring sub-parish of
            Agolitom   112
Plate 7   Okello Constant, an instrument maker, working on the
            belly of a lute (*adungu*)   132
Plate 8   A woman draws water from the village swamp   156
Plate 9   A villager sells millet grain   166
Plate 10   The livestock market at Tididiek   194

Table 3.1   Declining livelihoods   57
Table 4.1   Legislated and actual work of the parish chief and village
            council chairman   68
Table 4.2   Breakdown of court cases reported by the sub-parish
            council chairman, 2002   83
Table 5.1   Committee positions of Pentecostal Christians in Oledai   100
Table 7.1   The 'tax rates' of different organisations in the village
            in 2002   139
Table 7.2   Average attendance at different sorts of meetings, 2002   151

ACKNOWLEDGEMENTS

My thanks are due, first and foremost, to the people of Oledai and Agolitom who contributed their time, energy and thinking to this study. Few villages in my home county of Shropshire would have put up with as much from an African researcher as the people of Oledai and Agolitom endured from me. I owe them an enormous debt of gratitude.

In Teso my thanks must also be extended to the staff at Vision Terudo in Ngora, a local charitable organisation that provided me with a room to work and a place to stay. In particular I would like to thank Churchill Ongole and Florence Among for their support, advice and patience during my stay in the area, and Ongit John, Isaiah Oonyu, Cuthbert Malinga and Aogon Sam for their friendship and conversation. In Kampala I would like to thank Harriet Acham and Nathan Ogwang for their hospitality and friendship, for being my Teso family. I would also like to thank my family back in Shropshire for their support and generosity. To my mother, to my brothers Robert, Matthew, Nick and Michael, to Muriel and to my late grandmother, Mary, my deepest thanks. The book is dedicated to the memory of my father.

At the London School of Economics I would like to thank the staff of the Development Studies Institute. My supervisor Liz Francis was immensely supportive of the work that led to the publication of this book. I would like to also thank my colleagues Jo Beall and James Putzel for making my stay at the Development Studies Institute a happy and productive one. Dru Daley, Sue Redgrave and Steph Davies provided much needed friendship and advice along the way. Friendship and creativity also came from my fellow musicians Paul Williams, David Ainsworth, Louisa Carney, Sean Joyce, Ruth Corbridge, Marc Verlet and James Freed. Rachel Wrangham, Thi Minh Ngo and Elliott Green provided help at critical moments in writing the book, and their input is reflected in the final text, as are the thoughtful comments of Carol Summers and Anders Sjögren. I would also like to thank my thesis examiners Paul Gifford and David Maxwell for their guidance and advice.

I would like to thank Bernard Phelan of the Mill Hill Society for Overseas Missions, particularly in advance of my first visit to the Teso region. My stay in Uganda was brightened by the presence of Father Declan O'Toole, also a Mill Hill Father, who was sadly killed by soldiers serving in the Ugandan army in March 2002. This book is informed by the memory of

Father O'Toole, and of Edotun Jackson, a young man from the sub-parish of Oledai, who was killed in August of that year.

After my stay in Teso, I was fortunate to find a haven among the research community at Roskilde University in Denmark. I would like to express my deep thanks to Edwin Rap, Wolf Dressler, Steffen Jensen, Catrine Christiansen, David Kibikyo, Birthe Bruun, Mette Gerding, Amanda Hammar, Inge Jensen, Karen Lauterbach, Holger Bernt Hansen, Roger Leys, Niels Kastfelt and Fiona Wilson. The writing seminar at the Department of International Development Studies in Roskilde was particularly helpful and I owe a great debt to the community of Africanists in Denmark. The thesis on which this book is based was revised while undertaking a postdoctoral fellowship with the Research Council for the Social Sciences in Denmark. The fellowship also allowed me to spend time at the University of Nigeria at Nsukka, a special place to stay and reflect on what I would like to say about another part of the African continent.

Writing up the book also involved a six-month stay in the Philippines, where I was given the warmest of welcomes by the School of Economics at the University of the Philippines, Diliman (a welcome that was all the more remarkable given my status as an Africanist with no presentable knowledge of economics or of the Philippines). I must extend my sincerest thanks to Emmanuel Jimenez and Odie Grajo Santos for their support in Diliman, and to James Putzel at the London School of Economics for making my stay there possible. I would like to thank the SAGA project of Cornell and Clark Atlanta Universities for the grant that made the stay of Dr Chia-Hsin Hu in the Teso region a possibility. I would also like to thank Chia-Hsin, more personally, for her wisdom and support during the long journey towards completing the book.

This book is the product of a doctoral research grant from the Economic and Social Research Council. I would like to offer my sincere gratitude to the ESRC for the tremendous support and freedom they extend to their research students. Additional support came from the LSE Research Studentship fund, the LSE Postgraduate Travel Fund and the International Development Studies department at Roskilde University. I would also like to thank the Uganda National Council of Science and Technology for making my research stay in Teso as straightforward and trouble-free as possible. The PhD thesis on which the book was based was awarded the William Robson Memorial Prize and I would like to acknowledge the support of the prize in helping towards the costs of publication.

This book is published as part of the International African Library series. I would like to express my gratitude to Robert Molteno, Stephanie Kitchen, J. D. Y. Peel and Mike Kirkwood for helping me bring the manuscript to completion. As part of the process I have also had the privilege of working with Suzette Heald, a noted Uganda scholar, and the editor responsible for

East Africa in the series. Suzette's ideas and thinking are reflected in the final text, as are the very generous comments of two anonymous reviewers.

I must divide my final thanks two ways. First, to the support of my main thesis supervisors Christian Lund and Teddy Brett. Second, to the advice and friendship of Akello Suzan, Enou Andrew Ben, Osakan Chris and Aguti Stella, my research colleagues in Teso.

ABBREVIATIONS

It is typical for texts within the field of development studies to overwhelm the reader with a long list of capital letters. These abbreviations then become the clumsy shorthand for the array of organisations, programmes and bureaucracy-speak that dominates the way aid workers, technocrats and government officials speak of development and development work. In this book I have used abbreviations sparingly. The majority appear in Chapter 3, and most there refer to the rebel and government groupings that were active in the region in the years after independence. All of the abbreviations listed below would be recognised by people living in the village of Oledai.

ACAO   Assistant Central Administrative Officers
DP   Democratic Party
FOBA   'Force Obote Back' Army
NRA/M   National Resistance Army/Movement
PAG   Pentecostal Assemblies of God
PEPFAR President's Emergency Plan for AIDS Relief
RC   Resistance Council/Resistance Council Chairman
UNLA   Uganda National Liberation Army
UPA   Uganda People's Army
UPC   Uganda People's Congress
USh   Uganda shilling(s) (USh1750 = US$1)

Dollar values in the book are based on the conversion rate of the Ugandan shilling for 1 January 2002.

GLOSSARY

abazukufu	(Luganda) 're-awakened' (a born-again Anglican)
adungu	(Ateso) a lute (pl. *adungui*)
aibok acok	(Ateso) 'to dig potatoes' (a metaphor for a way of killing)
ajon	(Ateso) beer (brewed with millet)
akogo	(Ateso) a finger piano (pl. *akogoi*)
akonye nukapugan	(Ateso) 'eye' of the government, colloq. for a village council chairman
aleya	(Ateso) a farm labour group
amisir	(Ateso) a garden (pl. *amisirin*)
apolon	(Ateso) a chief
apolon ka ateker	(Ateso) a clan leader
askari	(Swahili) a guard; soldier
atap	(Ateso) porridge (usually of cassava flour mixed with millet)
ateker	(Ateso) a clan or burial society (pl. *atekerin*)
Ateso	the language spoken in the Teso region
atesot	(Ateso) a woman from the Teso region
bakungulu	(Luganda) the men of Kakungulu
balokole	(Luganda) lit. 'saved ones' (born-again Anglicans), sing. *mulokole*
bamalaki	(Luganda) follower of Malaki (a religious leader)
boda boda	(Ateso) bicycle taxi man
ebuku	(Ateso) a county, lit. 'shield'
eitela	(Ateso) a parish, or parish chief
etesot	(Ateso) a man from the Teso region
emidir	(Ateso) a drum (pl. *imidirin*)
emorimor	(Ateso) a clan co-ordinator
emuron	(Ateso) a witchdoctor or traditional healer
erony	(Ateso) a sub-parish (*mutongole* in Luganda)
etem	(Ateso) a sub-county, lit. 'hearth'
etogo	(Ateso) a hut (pl. *itogoi*)
ggombolola	(Luganda) a sub-county; *etem* in Ateso

ikearit	(Ateso) a soldier (pl. *ikearin*)
Iteso	(Ateso) the people of the Teso region
kasanvu	(Luganda) central government labour taxation
luwalo	(Luganda) compulsory unpaid labour for local government chiefs
mayumba kumi	(Ateso) lit. 'ten houses', a tier of government in the early 1980s (from the Swahili *nyumba kumi*)
ssaza	(Luganda) a county (*ebuku* in Ateso)

PREFACE

Acclaimed by policy makers, development workers, diplomats and many academics, Uganda has been presented as a country transformed. From the nadir of Amin and the 1970s Uganda has risen to earn a reputation as one of the continent's few success stories. It has been presented as a country ahead of the curve in promoting the signature themes of development policy and programming on the continent, and was the first country in Africa both to take the HIV/AIDS pandemic seriously and to record significant declines in infection rates. In the 1989 parliamentary elections Uganda reserved a number of seats for women, making it one of the first countries anywhere to promote political equality through positive discrimination. It was also in the first wave of countries to decentralise government powers away from the centre to the regions in the early 1990s. In 1997 Uganda introduced universal primary education at a time when this was very far from being the standard policy prescription for poorer countries.

This transformation of Uganda is associated, above all, with President Yoweri Museveni, head of the National Resistance Movement. Exiled under Amin, and a failed presidential candidate in the elections of 1979, Museveni has served as Uganda's President since 1986. He is credited with bringing a new type of politics to Uganda, a politics that is less about ethnic conflict, religious division or regional opposition, and more about economic and social development. His time in office is celebrated for having brought a level of peace and prosperity to southern and western parts of the country. Uganda is now seen as a country transformed largely due the achievement of Yoweri Museveni and his government.

This book started out as one more attempt to chronicle an aspect of Uganda's transformation. Back in October 2001 I was a PhD student who wanted to look at the impact of government reforms on the lives of ordinary Ugandans. In particular I wanted to look at the impact of the government's decentralisation and democratisation reforms on the countryside. My concern was to see to what extent, a decade on from their inception, these reforms had changed the way people related to the state.

I chose to do my research in the Teso region in the east of the country, one of the poorer parts of Uganda. After arriving in the trading centre of

Ngora, I settled on the village of Oledai as the place where I would collect information and spend time. Oledai was selected as a field site because I wanted to do my research in a place that seemed typical for the area. Oledai was not a 'project village', nor was it one of those few communities where development agencies had focused their efforts and invested considerable resources. Neither was Oledai especially remote, as it is located near to Ngora, the county headquarters for that western side of Kumi District. I wanted to say something about the impact of government reforms in an ordinary Ugandan village and Oledai seemed to fit the bill. That was the theory, at least.

In practice, things did not turn out as planned. Early on during my stay it became clear that government reforms mattered little to the people living in Oledai. The village council did not meet; there were no public gatherings where people voiced their concerns in relation to government programmes. Policies on health, agriculture or education did not seem to reach much beyond the district headquarters in Kumi. The parish chief only visited Oledai twice during the eighteen months I stayed (even though he was responsible for a total of only two villages). Taxes were not collected in any serious sense (local taxes made up less than two per cent of district expenditure), while villagers contributed more to churches or to burial societies than they did to the government. The idea that there was such as thing as 'the state' which was responsible for transforming Ugandan society did not seem the best way of approaching what was going on in Oledai.

In the first few weeks of fieldwork I thought about moving to the district capital, Kumi. I knew that moving there would put me in a place where I could say something about the Ugandan state. Kumi, the district capital, was the recipient of government funds and played host to a number of development organisations and programmes, and using the district capital as a base is the usual path for social scientists who want to research rural development in Uganda. In the end, I decided to continue in Oledai and from there try to work out what was going on.

The more I stayed in Oledai, the more puzzled I became by the relationship between the village and the state. What I sensed, though I found it difficult to explain, was the feeling that the Ugandan government had withdrawn. What had once been the engine of rural transformation, at least in the earlier part of the twentieth century, had become an absence. This was paradoxical as the government's decentralisation and democratisation reforms were meant, on paper at least, to bring the state closer to the lives of the people.

Beyond the State puts forward an explanation as to why the government mattered so little. I argue that places like Oledai fall 'in between'. They are situated away from those islands of development where state activities, donor projects and international capital are concentrated in Africa. They are situated away from the places where most research on 'development' gets done. Outside of Kampala, the district capitals or a few isolated 'project communities', there is a much more general landscape of villages and communities that are marginal. The state has little interest in these places; they are under-administered and have little influence. Part of the book explains why Oledai fell 'in between', what this tells us about the actual nature of Uganda's transformation under Museveni, and what we thus learn about the way the study of development has been approached in Africa.

This book is also about those changes that mattered in Oledai. A large part of the text is taken up with a study not of the absence of the state, but of the presence of religious and customary institutions. It is through these organisational forms – churches, burial societies – that people managed their affairs. These institutions derived their legitimacy from the history of the region and from their ability to deal with people's concerns. They provided the space where disputes were managed and where people had rebuilt the virtues of politeness, deference and sociality in the aftermath of a brutal and dehumanising civil war. Religious and customary institutions which have been marginalised in the literature on development in Africa are central to the story of what had changed.

In providing a picture of life beyond the state this book contributes, I hope, towards a different way of seeing development in Africa. In pointing to the withdrawn nature of the state, and presenting a picture of what matters in Oledai this book is about how places develop in the absence of 'development'.

London, 2008

To the memory of my father

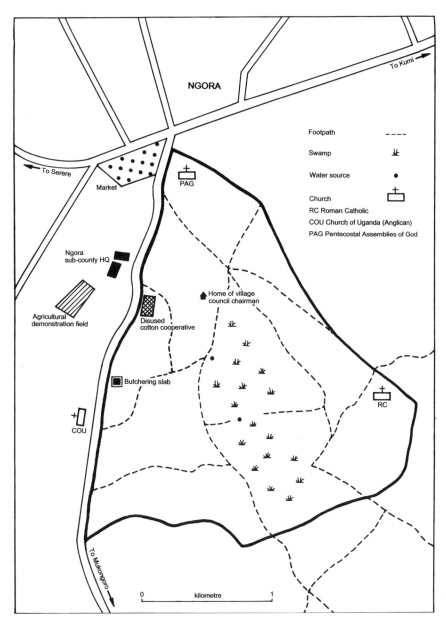

Map 1 Oledai sub-parish and its environs

Sketch map drawn by Julie Isaac, based on Map of Ngora County, Map
Collection, School of Oriental and African Studies. Government of Uganda
Survey, Lands and Mines Department. (Oledai sub-parish is within the
thick black line.)

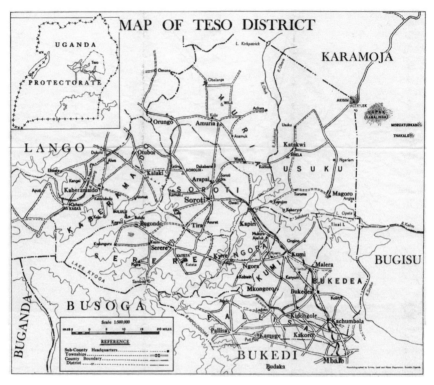

Map 2 Teso district

Source: *The Iteso: fifty years of change in a Nilo-Hamitic tribe of Uganda* (1957) by J. C. D. Lawrance. The map was drafted for Lawrance by the Director of Surveys, Uganda.

Map 3 Uganda's ethnic groups

Adapted from 'Uganda's Ethnic Groups', original version by Eva Swantz (also included in Tripp 2000: xxix), available at: https://mywebspace.wisc.edu/atripp/UGANDA-ETHNICGROUPS%20copy.jpg

Plate 1 A farm labour group (*aleya*) at work

1

INTRODUCTION

Uganda is regarded as one of Africa's few success stories.[1] Over the past two decades a consensus has been reached that the country has changed for the better. Once considered one of the continent's more tightly woven basket cases, Uganda has turned into something of a model of African development. The turnaround in Uganda's fortunes is explained, by and large, as the work of a reform-minded government in partnership with the international development community. The high rates of economic growth found in surveys commissioned by the government and its partners support the view of a country transformed. Between 1987 and 2003 the GDP growth rate was reported to be 6.3 per cent, well above the average for sub-Saharan Africa.[2] At the same time the poverty headcount – measured as the percentage of the population living below the national poverty line – fell from 55.7 to 37.7 per cent.[3]

Uganda is a poster child for liberal approaches to economic and social development in Africa. The deregulation of the formal economy and the decentralisation of government powers have pushed responsibilities away from marketing boards and ministries towards individual producers and citizens. Reforms of the civil service and the retrenchment of much of the armed forces demonstrate just how far the government has committed itself to the structural adjustment of the economy. It is an essentially liberal agenda with an accompanying language of participation, democratisation and empowerment. As one noted commentator explains:

> [Uganda is] the model country in the reconfiguration of power in late twentieth century Africa ... [a country which has] enthusiastically

---

1 See, for example, Brett 1992 and 1995; Golooba-Mutebi 1999; Hansen and Twaddle 1991 and 1998; Kanyinga et al. 1994; Kasfir 2000; Langseth et al. 1995; Mutibwa 1992; Therkildsen 2002; Tripp 2000; World Bank 1996; Wunsch and Ottemoeller 2004.

2 From Okidi et al. 2004: 60.

3 Source: Kappel, Lay and Steiner 2005: 29. Here 55.7 per cent is the proportion of the population living below the poverty line for 1992, and 37.7 per cent the comparable figure for 2002/2003. According to the more usual 'below a dollar a day' measure, however, poverty levels in Uganda were unchanged: 85.88 per cent of the population lived below $1 a day in 1992 and 84.91 per cent in 1999 (see: http://globalis.gvu.unu. edu).

adopted structural adjustment reforms, benefited from large inflows of development aid, introduced partial political liberalization, given early emphasis to human rights and popular participation at the local level.[4]

There has been much praise for Uganda's transformation, connecting the work of academics to the policies and programmes of the government. International financial institutions, most notably the World Bank, have supported structural economic change and the reform of the public sector.

At the same time the development agencies of various Western nations have helped finance the Ugandan government's commitment to social issues such as the promotion of women's rights and the fight against HIV/AIDS. A number of high-profile development schemes received some of their first outings in Uganda, including the Highly Indebted Poor Country initiative and PEPFAR (the US-financed President's Emergency Plan for AIDS Relief). The 1990s – the decade during which the Ugandan government recorded high levels of growth and a sharp fall in the numbers of people living in poverty – also saw a rapid increase in the levels of financial assistance the government received from abroad. According to the Organisation for Economic Cooperation and Development direct assistance has increased more than tenfold since 1986, with the Ugandan government receiving more than $1,157 million in overseas direct assistance in 2004.[5]

At the heart of all this there is a story of state-led transformation through which government policies and programmes have opened up the economy, made bureaucratic structures more accountable to the people, and fostered new forms of civil society. Though the changes have been criticised by some, particularly those who question the democratic credentials of Museveni and the National Resistance Movement, the broad consensus is of a country transformed by the state. Most of the available research on Uganda takes the form of 'state–society' studies where researchers examine changes in society through looking at the impact of government policies or programmes.

This book tells a very different story, one in which the government was very far from people's lives, and the welter of legislation and the rhetoric of reform did not matter. It is a story of life in a village in the Teso region of eastern Uganda. Here the state was more of a paper administration, restricted to the towns, and Uganda's 'civil society sector' was something that could be heard on the radio rather than seen in the village. Some of the most publicised reform efforts, such as the decentralisation reforms of the early 1990s, did not reach much beyond the district capital. The transformation of the countryside was limited to a few 'project communities' which had only the most tangential relationship to what went on elsewhere.

4 Richard Joseph 1999: 67, quoted in Tripp 2004: 3.
5 The figure combines bilateral and multilateral Overseas Direct Assistance. See Organisation for Economic Cooperation and Development 2005.

People spoke of decline and isolation, a situation where the material conditions of life had deteriorated and opportunities were few and far between. In marked contrast to the idea that the government was the engine of economic growth or of social transformation, there was the feeling, expressed many times during my stay, that the state had gone away. When I asked someone what the parish chief did in the area, I got the following response:

> The parish chief's work is to move from home to home to know what happens in the parish. But he does not do that here. A long time can pass without seeing him. He normally stays in the town. We get along without him.[6]

The parish chief, it should be noted, served a total of two villages. The government was likened to the dry season rains – something occasional and potentially destructive – and was remembered more for its role in putting down a violent insurgency in the late 1980s than as something that mattered in the present.[7] Oledai fell outside Uganda's 'success story'.

This book represents an attempt at making sense of why Oledai fell outside. It is organised around two basic premises: first, that the Ugandan government is uninterested in supporting an effective presence in the countryside; second, that life in Oledai is an 'open-ended' business, better understood through investigating a range of spaces and activities, rather than looking at the impact of government reforms.

MOVING THE STATE FROM THE CENTRE
The State as the Engine of Development?

In the main, what dominates studies of development and change in Africa is the study of governments, development agencies and their impact on society. There is a sizeable technocratic literature concerned with assessing the work of government in the hope of better understanding the relationship between policy prescriptions and developmental outcomes.[8] That large library of project reports, impact evaluations, household surveys, field assessments and country studies commissioned by multilateral organisations such as the World Bank, national development agencies such as the UK's Department for International Development, or charities such as OXFAM provides much of the empirical basis for understanding contemporary developments on the continent.

Alongside this technocratic literature there is a second library of academic

---

6 Interview with Amuge Immaculate, 14 October 2002.
7 The simile was used during a discussion with bicycle taxi men from the sub-parish of Agolitom, 8 May 2002.
8 Reports and evaluations from the technocratic literature used in this book include World Bank 1996; Reinikka and Collier 2001; de Weerdt 2001; Ireland Aid 2002; Appleton and Ssewanyana 2003.

studies which looks at the relationship between state and society.[9] Ranging from the detailed ethnographic studies of 'project villages' to macro-level analyses of structural economic reforms, this literature is concerned with evaluating the impact of the development system on African societies. Included within this literature are those fairly focused studies which look at the effects of a particular programme or policy. There are also accounts that take a more general perspective of the state and its relationship to society. The assumption throughout is that the state in Africa and its impact on society offer the most productive terrain for examining processes of social, political and economic change.

Considerable amounts of money have gone into looking at the implementation of schemes, projects and policies, creating something of a research cycle. A large body of data is generated, in a place where information is otherwise scarce. Alongside the technocratic accounts of projects or programmes, there develops a parallel literature which critiques development work. A sort of recycling process gets under way where researchers find it difficult to escape the rich body of data collected by development agencies and non-governmental organisations. If, for example, a researcher wants to say something about development in rural Uganda, it is very hard to avoid the 'development' literature. In other words, the funding of development produces not only projects, or a technocratic literature of reports and evaluations, but a body of academic work which frames the way processes of development and change in Africa are viewed. In the absence of alternatives a bias sets in where the state becomes the central object of study.

In the Ugandan case, state-centric perspectives dominate, and frame accounts of social change. The following is taken from a study of local politics in Uganda's market towns, and is organised around the idea that decentralisation reforms determine the way markets work:

> Since 1986, when the National Resistance Movement (NRM) government led by President Museveni took over power after five years of guerrilla war, Uganda has undergone dramatic political and economic transformation... Progress in political liberalisation is evident in a major reconstruction of politics and administration. The most significant current change in the country's transformation is the government's decentralisation program.[10]

---

9 From the academic literature see Brett 1992, 1995 and 1998; Hansen and Twaddle 1988a, 1991 and 1998; Kanyinga et al. 1994; Burkey 1991; Langseth et al. 1995; United Nations 1998; Livingstone and Charlton 1998; Golooba-Mutebi 1999; Birungi et al. 2000; Kabwegyere 2000; Okidi and Mugambe 2002; Saito 2003; Francis and James 2003; Steiner 2004; Olowu and Wunsch 2004; Kappel et al. 2005.

10 Birungi et al. 2000: 31.

The quotation is selected not so much because of the particulars of the study, but rather because it exemplifies the way researchers relate their findings to the letter of government reforms. The analytical frame is 'state-centric', in that there is a belief that government reforms are central to what goes on in society which results in an assumption that what is observed at the local level must be related to what the state says it is doing at the level of policy. Any manifestation of social change is regarded as a reflection of that category of policy or legislation being studied.

The desire to look at the impact of government policies, or the evolving relationship between state and society, frames our understanding of processes of development and change. Research is guided by the assumption that the state is the most important driver of development and change in society. Changes observed on the ground are seen as a comment on a particular government policy or development programme. So in the Ugandan case, for example, changes at the local level are understood to be no more than a reaction to the government's decentralisation efforts. In the text-book triangle of 'state', 'society' and 'market', the 'state' is always placed on top (Martinussen 1997). In visual terms, at least, the state becomes that analytical object from which social or economic changes are viewed.

Dismantling the Metaphor of the Machine

James Ferguson characterised the workings of a development project in Lesotho as an 'anti-politics machine' (1990). By this he meant that the patronage and authority of a development scheme, in the context of an income-poor southern African country, allowed a fairly weak bureaucracy to extend its power into the countryside. As the development project took hold, a number of 'side effects' could be observed in the countryside, such as increasing numbers of police and the building of roads. In these 'side effects' Ferguson sees an instrumental logic where development becomes less about meeting the needs of the rural poor, than the exercise of bureaucratic power in the countryside (1990: 254–6). The overall project of 'development' becomes one where the interests of the political class are legitimated in a process that, on the surface at least, appears apolitical.

The Anti-Politics Machine provided the template for a number of other studies in the literature on development. Ferguson's argument structures those accounts of the political externalities that flow out of the development business (Shore and Wright 1997; Grillo and Stirrat 1997; Marcussen and Arnfred 1998). Projects and programmes are presented as part of a process whereby poorer communities in the developing world are incorporated into state structures. The study of development is refracted through Foucauldian conceptions of governmentality, discourse and bio-politics, and a view is promoted where government agencies and development schemes are concerned with extending bureaucratic power in a way that dominates the countryside. In this way the pattern of politics in 'independent' post-colonial states can be linked back to the more coercive and dependent relationships that characterised colonialism.

I would argue that *The Anti-Politics Machine* offers a convincing account of what happens when a development scheme, such as the Thaba-Tseka Project, is imposed across a large swathe of a small country.[11] At the same time, however, it is important to recognise that schemes such as Thaba-Tseka in Lesotho are exceptional. They are not particularly indicative of the way governments are experienced in rural Africa. The image of an expansive bureaucracy, a bureaucracy which has essential continuities with the system of colonial administration, is not necessarily the best way of understanding what has happened to the state in recent years. Even in a place as seemingly aid-dependent as Uganda, where central and district governments have, for a long time, relied on funding from abroad, 'project communities' are few and far between.[12] In the case of Ngora sub-county, where Oledai sub-parish is located, there were, in 2003, a total of thirty-nine sub-parishes with a total sub-county population of 27,090. The Development Plan for the sub-county for 2002–5 lists only three of the thirty-nine sub-parishes as having received long-term outside assistance (Uganda Government n.d.: 49–50).[13]

Development interventions, which provide the focus for so many studies of change in rural Africa, are only occasional and exceptional variations of what can be found.[14] Development work is more erratic and marginal than the metaphor of the machine suggests. In many instances there are no projects to speak of, and the state, in its developmental guise at least, is relatively removed. There is, at times, a risk of the metaphor of the 'machine' becoming something of a machine itself, with accounts of development manufactured around the view that the countryside is populated

---

11 Ferguson is at his best in showing the way a 'development discourse' need have no relationship to observed reality. It is a discourse whose primary effect is to legitimate certain sorts of outside intervention. For example, what was communicated in the particular way development agencies wrote and spoke about Lesotho was the notion that it was a subsistence, agriculture-dependent economy (the sort of economy that would make good use of a World Bank agrarian reform package). This image of a society almost untouched by the modern world conveniently overlooked Lesotho's long history as a labour reserve for South Africa's mining industry (Ferguson 1990: 27, 69–73).

12 According to the Ministry of Finance, Planning and Economic Development, donor assistance as a percentage of government expenditure has run above 50 per cent for the past twenty years (Background to the Budget Report 2005).

13 The three communities were Kobuku (the location of the county headquarters and hospital), Angod (site of a health unit) and Agu (rehabilitation of piped water project). A number of other communities were listed as having benefited from more occasional schemes, most usually cattle or goat-restocking projects (for a comment on livestock schemes see the opening of Chapter 8).

14 Fairhead and Leach argue that the potency of development projects may be related to the erratic or uneven nature of development work (1997: 49–50).

by powerful and invasive projects and programmes, all administered by an interested state bureaucracy.

Accepting that the State Is Weak

Standing in obvious opposition to the metaphor of the machine is Goran Hyden's notion of an 'uncaptured peasantry' (1980). In *Beyond Ujamaa in Tanzania,* Hyden discusses the limits to government competence, and argues that the state was, in fact, incapable of dominating the countryside. At a time when modernising state bureaucracies seemed central to developments in rural Africa (the late 1970s), Hyden pointed to the ways in which Tanzanian society was unaffected by government reforms. One part of his explanation focused on the robustness of peasant communities which, he suggested, prevented the Tanzanian government from successfully penetrating the countryside. There was an 'uncaptured peasantry' which retarded the sorts of rational bureaucratic systems that would deliver more equitable social relations. The peasantry bypassed the ministrations of the Tanzanian government, and was able to do this because of the resilience of time-honoured customs and fairly harmonious social relations that Hyden termed an 'economy of affection' (1980: 18–19).

Hyden was criticised at the time for his rather romantic view of the Tanzanian countryside. The suggestion that people living in Tanzania in the 1970s were essentially pre-capitalist farmers, cultivating crops away from international markets and away from government structures, can be easily discredited (Bernstein 1981). His failure to account sufficiently for the role of coffee, cotton, schools, churches, courts, paper money, and all the paraphernalia of the colonial state made his book a target for historians, anthropologists and political scientists, and the reviews were less than kind (Barker 1982: 603; Thiele 1986: 541; Williams 1987; Ferguson 1990: 271). Hyden's presentation of African societies as cohesive and harmonious showed little sympathy for the fashions of the time, which favoured the study of conflict and class formation. Sally Falk Moore suggested that the penetration of capital, and attempts at codifying 'customary law' during the colonial period, were central to any reasonable understanding of what had changed in rural Tanzania in the post-colonial period (Moore 1986: 298).

The criticisms levelled at Hyden were aimed at the first half of his formulation: that the Tanzanian countryside was populated by *an 'uncaptured' peasantry.* The second half, which pointed to the persistence of *a weak state bureaucracy,* received less attention, though it posed the greater challenge to researchers interested in explaining developments in rural parts of Africa. While writers such as Colin Leys (1975) or John Saul (1976, 1979) argued that post-colonial governments played too intrusive a role in the countryside, and that their control over modes of peasant production contributed to the underdevelopment of the rural economy, Hyden pointed to the limits and incapacities of the state (see also Williams 1987).[15] I would suggest that the weakening of state structures in the years of structural adjustment, donor dependency and economic liberalisation in the 1980s and 1990s has only increased the salience of Hyden's thesis.

One way of nuancing Hyden's broad thesis about the weakness of the state is to look at the actual significance of government institutions locally. Sara Berry points to the ways in which the state in Africa is both weak in institutional terms and an object of political competition at the local level (1993). From a perspective which focuses on the history of agricultural innovation across four countries (Kenya, Nigeria, Zambia and Ghana), Berry argues that the state, in its various guises, has been important in negotiations over land and property, and hence a key arena of political competition since the early colonial period. In Berry's vision of rural Africa, government bureaucracies may be less authoritative than is acknowledged in either the 'success story' literature or the 'anti-politics machine', but perhaps more significant than is allowed for in Hyden's 'economy of affection' (Berry 1993: 45–6). Berry counts courts, councils, schools and the other paraphernalia of state authority as some of the possible arenas through which political claims can be substantiated. As well as these state-sanctioned spaces, she discusses the ways in which clans, family networks and home-town associations offer places where political actions are organised.

Berry's focus is on the history of agricultural change, and her work necessarily focuses on the way government policies and programmes affected developments at the local level. In recent years, however, the state in its developmental guise has withdrawn from much of the countryside, requiring a more ecumenical approach to the study of local politics. Thomas Bierschenk and Jean-Pierre Olivier de Sardan argue for an approach where the full range of 'public spaces and positions of eminence' are studied, whatever they may be (Bierschenk and Olivier de Sardan 1997: 441; see also Swartz 1968). In the same essay they also point to the marginal nature of the state in many parts of rural Africa, a situation where the state may be less central to developments than is often assumed. Writing of the Central African Republic they note the popular observation that 'the State Stops at PK 12' – 12 kilometres from the capital city, Bangui – and their account of state–society relations in the Central African Republic has resonances elsewhere:

> [the case of rural Central African Republic] … also reflects the more general situation in other parts of the continent where the excesses of a centralised, over-staffed post-colonial regime can coexist perfectly

15 For a criticism of this literature, see Azarya and Chazan 1987: 107–8, or Boone 2003: 18–19. The particular typology set out in the first chapter of Catherine Boone's book suggests the potential marginality of rural areas to political developments at the centre.

with the pronounced absence in the rural areas of certain functions which are commonly supposed to be provided by the state, including basic administration and justice, as well as social, educational, and health services.[16]

The above also captures popular experiences of the state in many parts of Uganda (Southall 1998, for example). Susan Reynolds Whyte's study of Banyole society notes that: 'signs of hope – new tarmac roads between the main cities, acronyms of development projects stencilled on new Pajeros in Kampala – have not dispelled the sense of impoverishment and stagnation among most rural people' (Whyte 1997: 53-4). Mark Leopold's work in West Nile tells a similar story of marginalisation and decline, while Ben Knighton describes the thinness of state administration in the Karamoja region (Leopold 2005; Knighton 2005). Something similar was also found in the village of Oledai. In concluding this chapter I would like to suggest why the state was uninterested in what was going on and the implications this has for the study of social change in rural Africa.

BEYOND THE STATE IN RURAL UGANDA

If the state is not interested in rural developments, then what is it interested in? The obvious answer is Whyte's 'new tarmac roads' and 'acronyms of development projects stencilled on new Pajeros in Kampala' (Whyte 1997: 53-4). The Ugandan state is increasingly organised around a 'development economy', where most of the funding and financing of government activities comes from outside. To use Hyden's formulation the state was 'suspended in "mid-air" over society' (1983: xii) because it lacked a relationship with the rural economy. In Kumi District, local taxes contributed less than 2 per cent of district government expenditures.[17] The economy that the state depended on came from outside, most obviously in the form of development assistance from Western governments and development agencies, but also through Uganda's interventions in eastern Congo. This development economy made the state extraverted, turned upwards and outwards by its relationship to international capital (Bayart 1993: 2000).

I would argue that instead of viewing Uganda as a country where the state involved itself in rural developments, it is more useful to think of Uganda as a sea with a few islands dotted about the place. These islands are the 'project villages', the district capitals, Kampala, a few hotels, the clinics where international pharmaceutical companies trial new drugs, and the flower and vegetable air-freight businesses situated next to Entebbe airport. Each of

16 Bierschenk and Olivier de Sardan 1997: 441. In subsequent research the authors have focused on the workings of government bureaucracies in West Africa rather than developing an understanding of politics in places like rural Central African Republic.

17 Taken from the Kumi District Development Report 2006/2007(2005): 21.

these islands depends on a relationship to outside sources of capital, rather than to the rural economy. In between these islands there is the rest of the country which, for the most part, is far from 'development'.

If we think back to the opening pages of the book, where I mentioned Uganda's status as a 'success story', it is possible to see how researchers have worked with the development sector to tell this story of success. A large part of the reason why Uganda is considered successful is because research is bound into a development economy. The project villages, district capitals, line ministries and hotels provide the entry point for most research on development. The resulting view is one where the state is at the heart of things and observed changes in the countryside are explained as the consequence of government policies.

But this book is about more than the absence of state-sponsored 'development'. In the main it is a study of those developments that matter in an in-between place. I look at religious and customary institutions and show how important these are as sites of innovation. In Oledai people invest time, energy and money into churches, burial societies and clan institutions. These institutions provide new mechanisms of social organisation and household insurance. They open up spaces where questions over land and property are negotiated, or where new social identities are formed. Moreover, the growing importance of churches and burials societies links Oledai into much wider circuits of change. The growth of Pentecostal Christianity, for example, is one of the most radical transformations in the world today, and yet is barely touched upon in the literature on African development. There is an important point to make here about the significance of religion in processes of social change.

Beyond the State offers a picture of social change away from the development machine. Instead of regarding local developments as some sort of concerted response to, or appropriation of the incursions of the state, I take a more open-ended approach that moves outside institutional confinements and studies social action in a broad landscape. I look at churches alongside burial societies and I relate the changes in village courts to what goes on in the religious sphere. There is much to be gained from this more open-ended approach, as it introduces themes and subjects which have long been sidelined in the 'state-centric' literature. Aside from studying religious and customary institutions as sites of innovation and transformation, I make a broader point about the importance of ideological and religious concerns in explaining the way poorer people organise. Developments in Oledai took hold because they meant something, a point that gets lost in the economistic and institutional approach to development that has gained currency in recent years.

THE REST OF THE BOOK

The second chapter introduces Oledai in much greater detail and discusses some of the themes and ideas that are used to guide later chapters. A vocabulary of seniority, prosperity and propriety is put forward to help define some of the more significant material and ideological concerns of those living in the village. This vocabulary captures something of the relatedness of different developments at the local level. At the same time I put forward my own view on how to think about institutional change, combining historical, structural and personal explanations.

In Chapter 3 I discuss the history of the Teso region, and show that the marginal nature of things in the present was a departure from the past. Teso's significance as a cotton-producing region in the first half of the twentieth century linked it into international markets, while tax collection and local government administration brought the state down to the village. Chapter 3 also discusses the Teso Insurgency, the most important event of recent years, a time when the social and economic fabric of Teso society broke down. Later on in the book it becomes clear how much the insurgency shapes developments at the local level.

Chapters 4 to 7 deal with different forms of organisation in the village, starting with a study of the village council. I demonstrate that at a time of 'democratic decentralisation' the council functioned mostly as a court. In discussing the unimportance of government reforms, the chapter points to the weakness of the state in rural Teso. Chapters 5 and 6 discuss the growing importance of Christianity in the village. I explain the ways in which developments in church relate both to global trends and to the experience of the Teso Insurgency. Chapter 7 offers a detailed account of the development of burial societies in Oledai. These are new organisational structures, which offer a collective system of insurance when a member of a household dies. Like churches, part of their legitimacy came from the way their work opposed the violence of the recent past.

The final chapter returns us to the discussion of the Ugandan 'success story' and its relevance to places like Oledai. I argue that the 'state-centric' approach which dominates the study of development in Africa makes it difficult to see what is going on in in-between places. Instead of putting the state at the heart of things, I argue for a more open-ended and ecumenical approach to the study of development and change.

Plate 2 A farmer move sacks of charcoal to market

2

INTRODUCING OLEDAI

The sub-parish of Oledai is located in the Teso region of eastern Uganda. As of 1 January 2002, the sub-parish numbered 126 households, and had a total population of 862.[1] The majority of these households were extremely poor.[2] People made a living mostly through cultivating foodstuffs – cassava, groundnuts, millet and sorghum, as well as sweet potatoes. Much of this production was used to feed the family, though some of it was sold on at the market in nearby Ngora. Eighty of the 126 households listed farming as their main occupation.[3] Women did the bulk of farmwork and housework. Men were responsible for cattle, while women had charge of smaller live-stock, mostly chickens and goats. *Atap*, a claggy and heavy porridge of cassava flour, flavoured with millet, provided the staple food. *Ajon*, a beer brewed from millet or sorghum, was the most popular drink.[4]

Households lived in the middle of the land they farmed, making for a dispersed pattern of settlement. Oledai was not a nucleated village and this geographical fact is worth bearing in mind when reading the rest of the book. Even though I repeatedly use the word 'village' to describe it, Oledai did not look like a village in the usual sense of the word. Each home would be located in the middle of the piece of land that the family farmed and would be made up of a number of grass-thatched huts (*itogoi*) providing room for

1 The breakdown of this figure by age and gender is 192 women, 168 men, 256 girls and 246 boys.
2 From what we can tell from the national poverty survey, the eastern region, which includes Teso, was ranked third out of four in terms of income poverty (Okidi and Mugambe 2002: 10). The Uganda Human Development Report of 2001 (UNDP 2001) lists Kumi District as the sixth poorest in Uganda (ahead of Moroto, Kotido, Kitgum, Arua, and Adjumani) out of fifty-one districts. In 1998 the district was ranked twelfth poorest out of forty districts.
3 Of the 126 household heads in Oledai sub-parish the breakdown for main source of employment goes as follows: 82 listed farming as their main occupation; 12 listed casual employment; 8 said that they ran a market stall in Ngora; 14 said that they were able to draw regular income (as teachers, watchmen, bus drivers, etcetera); 8 collected state pensions; 2 households had no members able to work (due to old age or disability).
4 For further studies of the lifestyle of the Iteso, the importance of *atap* and *ajon*, and the meaning and form of household relationships see Lawrance 1957; Uchendu and Anthony 1975; Karp 1978; Heald 1991; Henriques 2002.

sleeping in and for storing grain and household goods.[5] (Of the 126 house-holds a total of twenty-six functioned as polygynous units.)[6] Twenty-four of the households in Oledai were female-headed, many of them widows from the Teso Insurgency. Marriage was something that continued to be negotiated by the extended family. Brideprice was paid in cash or in kind, and the children of the marriage would be regarded as the property of the man and his lineage.

A number of households offered a place to stay for grandparents, though this was a matter of choice rather than obligation. The land farmed by the household was nominally the property of a lineage group, known as an *ateker*, typically numbering between twenty and thirty households who owned a given piece of land. Land transactions – for rental purposes – involved the *ateker* and were meant to be limited to members of the same lineage (although land sales outside the *ateker* were not unknown). Inher-itance among the Iteso (the dominant group in the region) was patrilineal, and settlement patterns patrilocal, meaning that land and livestock passed from father to son, and that the son, once married, was expected to farm land near to his father.[7] In theory, all of the sons of a home were entitled to land and livestock when they graduated into manhood. This meant that land ownership tended towards a pattern of fragmentation, with plots being divided and sub-divided as new generations came up.

Life in Oledai could be categorised around a fairly modest hierarchy of activities. These activities generated some sort of income for the different households. Day-labouring for a neighbour, farming one's land, or, in the case of women, brewing and selling *ajon*, offered the most regular sources of income for the majority of homes.[8] A much smaller number of households expected some money from working in the schools or through casual work in the trading centre of Ngora. An even smaller number received money or support in kind from relatives in the towns, though it should be added that the habit of sending money back home or bringing gifts to the family was not a particularly important part of life in the Teso region, when compared to neighbouring societies. Instead, the difficult business of making a living was largely confined to the home. Incomes were also augmented by gaining

5 An *etogo* (pl. *itogoi*) refers specifically to the compound of a wife. In polygynous house-holds the number of *itogoi* would denote the number of wives (Karp 1978: 24).
6 Of the twenty-six, seventeen were two-wife and nine were three-wife households.
7 Of the population of Kumi District, 98 per cent were categorised as 'Iteso' in the 2002 census (Uganda Government 2007 (volume 1): 21). This ethnic homogeneity is due, in part, to the 'cleansing effect' that the violence of the insurgency had in the late 1980s. By contrast, Vincent's ethnography from 1968 was focused on a poly-ethnic community on the shores of Lake Kyoga. The household survey carried out as part of the research found that all the 126 households in Oledai identified themselves as Iteso.
8 Labouring in another person's fields, or casual work in the trading centre, though never guaranteed, could expect to earn USh1,500 ($1) a day.

positions of prominence in the sub-parish, with court fees, burial fees and church collections offering opportunities to those who managed them. Gaining a position of influence could also make it easier for the person involved to get a favourable decision from the village or *ateker* court.

Poorer homes would have one or two huts for sleeping in, and a more dilapidated hut for cooking food. The huts were made of dried earth, the floors smeared with cow dung and the roof thatched with rushes. One or two of the richer households had a more permanent structure with a cement floor, brick walls and an aluminium roof. Such homes were usually built by sons living in Jinja or Kampala and were occupied by parents, wives or children. In terms of the geography of the sub-parish, about a third of Oledai was on swampy ground. The swamp was used for grazing cattle, as well as providing the main source of water for drinking and cooking (pictured on page 156). Water was drawn from an open well that grew thick and dirty as the swamp dried out in the long dry season, which lasted from December to March.

The lack of clean water, the poor economic prospects for those living in the village, and the unimportance of the local government in the day-to-day life of the area all suggested that Oledai had benefited little from Uganda's reputed success. 'The state' as an agent of development did not matter that much in Oledai, and what struck me on first arriving was the sense that Oledai was on the margins. Not much seemed to be going on; those aspects of the government which should have mattered most – the office of the parish chief, the village council, and the provision of public services – were absent. There was, in fact, much more connection to Joan Vincent's description of 1960s Teso as a 'backwater' (Vincent 1968: 27). Though it has been usual to emphasise the importance of government reforms in recent years, the state seemed to be somewhat removed from life in the village.[9]

And yet, despite the sense of marginality, it is important to understand that Teso did not always belong to the nether reaches of Uganda's political economy. Oledai's marginality went against its own history. The longer I stayed in the area, the more I got to see the remnants of a different sort of economy, and a different sort of relationship with the wider world.

A disused concrete shell sitting east of the Ngora–Mukongoro road turned out to be the remains of a ginnery, a place where villagers had sold cotton for export to the international market as late as the 1970s. A piece of bushy land next to the sub-county headquarters had once been a site for agricultural demonstration. Until recently the Iteso were respected as cotton growers; Teso was the first region in Uganda to adapt successfully to the cattle plough. In the earlier part of the twentieth century, their adap-

---

9 Some of the better accounts of Uganda's 'transformation' can be found in Mutibwa 1992, Langseth et al. 1995, Villadsen and Lubanga 1996, and Reinikka and Collier 2001.

tation to the crop helped transform the fortunes of the Uganda Protectorate
(Thomas and Scott 1935: 448–9; Vincent 1982: 170). Cotton also brought
in a large number of Asian traders.

There were also the remnants of a cattle-keeping society. A bloodied
concrete slab surrounded on all sides by bushy ground was still used as
the place where livestock were slaughtered for sale at the market in Ngora.
As well as having established a reputation as cotton growers, the Iteso
are remembered as a pastoralist people. Ivan Karp describes cattle as 'an
important nexus of value for the Iteso' and, during the years when cotton
was king, many growers had channelled their profits into acquiring large
stocks of cattle (Karp 1978: 13). Up to the 1970s it was not uncommon
for the richest man in a sub-parish to own two or three hundred head.
Such a man would also retain a number of younger men as cattle herders,
often outsiders from the Karamoja or Ankole regions. Cattle were a way
of signalling social status, a way for boys to become men, providing the
most important part of the brideprice paid during marriage negotiations
(Lawrance 1957: 202–7; Vincent 1968: 119–25).

In the trading centre of Ngora, as well as in the villages, there were
churches which ranged from the imposing Roman Catholic parish church
on the outskirts of the town, with its stained-glass windows and clay-tiled
roof, to the grass-thatched and mud-walled churches serving village congregations in Oledai. There was also an Aga Khan community of Muslims
in Ngora which worshipped at the local mosque. The presence both of
church and mosque reflects a fairly long history of engagement with the
world religions. Ngora was a centre for Christian mission activity in the
Teso region in the early years of the twentieth century, with the Anglican
Church Missionary Society setting up in 1908, and the Mill Hill Missionaries of the Roman Catholic church following soon after. There was also the
more recent addition of Pentecostalism, a version of Christianity which had
become popular in the late 1980s. All of the households in Oledai claimed
affiliation to one of the Christian denominations: Anglican, Catholic, or
Pentecostal (Islam was limited to the towns).

Talking to the older men in the sub-parish I learned there were also past
connections to the military. When I was introduced to one older man, Okurut
Gereson Nairobi, I asked him to explain the meaning of the various parts of
his name.[10] He explained that 'Okurut' was his 'clan name', one of a number
of Ateso names available to members of a particular *ateker*; 'Gereson' was
his Christian name (an indication of the influence of Catholic missions in
the region).[11] 'Nairobi' was the nickname given to Okurut Gereson as a

10 Throughout the book I follow the custom of listing the *ateker* name first and the
    Christian name second.
11 For those with an interest in such matters, Gereson is a corruption of Gershon.
    Gershon was the oldest of the three sons of Levi; his brothers were Kohath and
    Merari (Genesis 46: 11; Numbers 3: 17).

way of remembering his years of service in the King's African Rifles, which included a spell in Kenya in the late 1940s.[12] As late as the early 1980s, Teso had served as a recruiting ground for much of Uganda's military and security forces (Omara-Otunnu 1987: 35–8, 67).[13]

But the military connection, like cattle and cotton, had gone away. The expulsion of the Asian community in the early 1970s had helped bring an early close to the production of cotton, which was already on its way out in the 1960s (Young 1971: 141; Vincent 1976: 94–5). Cattle had gone in the late 1980s, the result of the widespread cattle raiding that accompanied the Teso Insurgency. The military connection fell away when the National Resistance Army (NRA) of Yoweri Museveni seized power in January 1986. In other words, the landscape of the village reflected a more complex history of engagement and withdrawal, of transformation and dissolution.

What was harder to detect in the village was the impact of HIV/AIDS. Though Uganda has been studied for its success in dealing with the epidemic, HIV/AIDS was not a subject that provoked much comment or discussion in Oledai (cf. Epstein 2007: 134–5).[14] The impact of the virus, which may explain the growing significance of burial societies, was not something that framed people's discussions of health or well-being. This was not because people felt unable to talk about the subject; the work of non-governmental organisations and churches in making HIV/AIDS a social and moral issue had had an impact at the village level. Rather it would seem that the absence of any major health initiatives in the Teso region meant that the virus lacked the sort of political or economic weight that had elevated it above other health concerns in neighbouring regions. Teso in 2002 and 2003 was not a focus for development projects and community interventions dealing with HIV/AIDS. Funding had been concentrated in central and western parts of Uganda, the epidemic's early epicentre (Sjögren 2007: 149–50; Hooper 1987). It may well be that the subsequent introduction to Teso of HIV/AIDS programmes, such as the the US-backed President's Emergency Plan for AIDS Relief or the AIDS/HIV Integrated Model District Program, has worked to make HIV/AIDS more central to the political economy of the region. The flow of funds has encouraged a number of community-based and faith-based organisations to re-orient their work towards prevention and treatment.

12 From an interview with Okurut Gereson Nairobi, 23 August 2002.
13 The importance of the colonial army to the history of the people of the Teso region could be seen from the fact that the Ateso word for soldier, *ikearit*, is a vernacularisation of 'KAR' (short for King's African Rifles).
14 UNAIDS estimated the national prevalence rate to have fallen from between 10 and 20 per cent in 1991, to an estimated 5 per cent at the end of 2002 (Parkhurst 2002: 574).

THEMES THAT CUT ACROSS DEVELOPMENTS IN THE
VILLAGE: SENIORITY, PROSPERITY, PROPRIETY

Subsequent chapters deal with different sorts of village organisation. Chapter 4 explains the work of the village council, while chapters 5 and 6 detail the increasing influence of churches in local affairs. Chapter 7 looks at the growth of burial societies. Through each of these chapters I try to piece together an understanding of how each type of organisation relates to other local-level institutions. Changes in the Anglican and Catholic churches need to be understood in relation to the growing influence of Pentecostalism, which I discuss before looking at developments in the historic mission churches (even though Pentecostalism was a newer phenomenon). For not dissimilar reasons, I look at burial societies after the chapters on churches and the village. Burial societies were built, in part, out of existing practices and social arrangements and it is useful to have a prior knowledge of these.

There is a certain artificiality to this structure, with each giving the impression that there are different spheres to life in the village; this is not really the point I want to make. One of the ways in which I have tried to cut through this somewhat categorical, chapter-by-chapter approach is to link different chapters through using a common analytical vocabulary. Consequently, the analysis is organised around three themes: seniority, prosperity and propriety, which give the text a greater level of coherence than it would otherwise achieve. I look at the attempt by older men to reclaim their political influence in the years after the insurgency (seniority); at the ways in which individuals have tried to improve their material condition in recent years (prosperity); and at the growing emphasis on respectability in public life (propriety). While the first two are stand-in terms for notions of status and wealth, propriety is a more interesting term as it suggests that there was a particular ideological project in the village, and I discuss it in greater detail.

Seniority

Seniority is hereafter meant to refer to the role of political status based on age. In the particular case of Teso, seniority mattered for those men, in their forties and fifties, who were able to command respect in the sub-parish. These were the men who expected to dominate the various sorts of organisations to be found in the village: the 'big men' of Oledai. The question of who was becoming a 'big man' was something that dominated the way people spoke of and thought about politics (as was the more interesting subject of who was losing 'big man' status).

Joan Vincent, writing on life in Teso in the 1960s, describes a similar sort of politics. Men came to prominence in the parish of Bugondo through gathering together supporters. Having assembled a group around him, the would-be 'big man' would find it easier to assert his influence in a debate

(Vincent 1968: 211–30).[15] On those occasions where conflicts reached boiling point, 'loyalty' typically prevailed over 'voice' or 'exit', to borrow from Hirschman's terminology (1970). The weaker party was more usually prepared to accept the settlement put forward, only on occasion resorting to criticism. 'Exit', which I would take to mean leaving the village, was a path rarely trodden. The gerontocracy of 'big men' was maintained through its involvement in continuous negotiations, and had to piece together a consensus rather than having the authority to impose a decision. As D. H. Okalany describes in his essay on judicial and legal principles in Iteso society:

> The ideal clan elders were men of understanding and impartial judgement who saw themselves not as rulers but as the arbiters and mediators of their people ... if a son lacked the quality of leadership, another among the sons, fulfilling the requirements of leadership, was chosen by the clan to take over. Courage and generosity, coupled with a sharp sense of good and impartial judgement were the ideal qualities of a leader. (Okalany 1973: 129)

What is important to recognise in all of this is the fairly open-ended way in which things worked. You became a 'big man' through your initiative and entrepreneurship, rather than because it was something that you inherited from your father or uncle. It was a status that was earned (and taken away). Teso, populated by acephalous, or 'chiefless', societies, has a politics, at the village level at least, which remains essentially egalitarian and competitive.[16] There was none of the hierarchical or courtly politics of the monarchical societies to the south and west. Mechanisms for managing conflicts were instead focused on the evolving community of 'big men'. Major crises were negotiated, and political authority was demonstrated. What you did, more than who you were, was the basis of authority.

The sort of 'big man politics' observed during my time in the village was, to a very large extent, the same as that witnessed by Joan Vincent forty years earlier. 'Big men' achieved their positions of influence through partici-

15 Vincent's analysis focused on the rise of 'big men', a local elite, in what had once been a relatively prosperous port and cotton ginnery on Lake Kyoga, but had, by the 1960s, become something of a backwater. *African Elite* was based on many months of fieldwork, and the book was significant at its time for its ability to demonstrate the degree to which political leadership could be contingent and competitive in a community that claimed affiliation to a variety of ethnic groups.

16 For people of the Teso region 'there was no institutionalisation of hierarchical office or ranking of groups – apart from that to be found in all small-scale societies where elders, youth and womenfolk are set apart by the specialisation of their labour and their opportunities for social power' (Vincent 1977: 143). The absence of fixed and extensive hierarchies meant that being a 'big man' could be a precarious position, particularly when compared with the relative stability that lineage hierarchies provided in the more centralised, Bantu societies to the south and west.

pating in a range of political and institutional spaces. At the same time, it is important to remember that what I was observing was in many ways a restoration, rather than an uninterrupted continuation. The Teso Insurgency – of the late 1980s and early 1990s – meant that established mechanisms for negotiation and compromise had been suspended during that period. Rebels had targeted and killed older men, while the loss of cattle meant that the means through which older men negotiated their influence over younger men, particularly with their sons, had been weakened. The insecurity that characterised the insurgency period resulted in a retreat from public life, and the public forums which were necessary to demonstrate or make one's 'bigness' were not available.

The sort of violence that took hold during the insurgency necessarily gave a different flavour to notions of seniority in the years after. The restoration of peaceable relations in the early 1990s saw older people trying to revive the 'big man' politics of the past, though this had to be done in ways that reflected on the actual experience of the insurgency. One way of shoring up the authority of 'big men', was to have a much more explicit discourse concerning seniority.[17] Later on in the book I show how, in a number of court cases ostensibly centred on other topics, there was a preoccupation with whether or not a young man involved in the case had been wilful in his actions. If such a charge could be made the case would go against him, in part, because his actions reminded people of the insurgency, and disciplining younger men put that experience in the past. On one level, then, the insurgency produced a political discourse which disadvantaged younger men and promoted the importance of seniority.

At the same time, the memory of the insurgency worked in the opposite direction. Rather than promoting the seniority of older men it undermined their authority. In trying to deal with the perceived wilfulness of youth, there was also an acknowledgement of their potential political power.[18] A common topic of discussion was the fear that the sorts of violence that had taken hold during the insurgency could return, and that this would overturn social hierarchies yet again. As one *ateker* leader observed:

> If insecurity should return to the region, then the place will become worse, because those young men who are now quiet will bring

17 The cultural politics of seniority and its reassertion after a period of violence has also been discussed in Mikael Karlström's essay on moral community in Buganda (Karlström 2004). The means through which morality and gerontocratic authority have been renegotiated in Ganda society – largely through the institutions of kingship and kinship – can be contrasted with ways in which they have been managed by the Iteso — through the conduct of politics and more contingent forms of social interaction.

18 The restoration of the different *atekerin* was seen as the main guarantor of peace in the area: 'the biggest change in recent years has been peace in the *ateker*. When there is a problem it is easy to handle and settle'. Interview with Okiria Fastine, *ateker* leader of Ichaak (29 August 2002).

trouble. They can bring trouble to the place and spoil the name of the *ateker*.[19]

This meant that 'big men' had to be more careful than before. Those who gave judgements or who occupied positions of authority had to be mindful of the decisions they made, and how these decisions were perceived. They were wary of provoking controversy when settling cases. If a 'big man' developed a reputation for making contentious judgements, then he could expect to be at the top of the list of targeted individuals should insecurity return. There was, in a very real sense, an aversion to publicity (making the sort of open and public politics demanded by the government's democratisation efforts a practical impossibility). Many of the 'big men' I spoke to suggested that they were happy to deflect conflicts by keeping a relatively low profile. There was a tendency to move disputes from court to court, and many of the more difficult cases were concluded through exhaustion rather than through the imposition of one man's judgement.

All of which reminds us of the insurgency and its importance in shaping developments in Oledai. Many of the changes in the village were a reflection on, or a reaction to the experience of the insurgency. The need to discipline younger men was driven by the knowledge that youths had done most of the killing. In terms of the politics of seniority, this meant that judgements had to be put together carefully. The easy sort of 'big man' politics described by Joan Vincent was no longer possible.

Prosperity

The significance of becoming a 'big man' was measured in terms of livestock and household goods, as much as by the shadow the individual was able to cast over political debates (Vincent 1968: 6; Karp 1978: 13). And those debates were largely concerned with access to and control over land. In a place where people had very few resources at their disposal, small differences in personal or household wealth mattered. A house with six goats and four gardens was understood to be very different from one where there was only one goat and three gardens. As the population increased, and with little diversification in the economy, conflicts over land persisted, and in some ways intensified. Land mattered not only because it was the thing that best survived, but also because making a living in the village was, by any measure, a modest affair.

The politics of land was played out in the courts and the various customary institutions, and, to a surprising degree, in the different churches. The different organisations provided places where conflicts were negotiated, and where one's status and reputation could be brought to bear. While a limited

19 Interview with Ichodio Stephen, *ateker* leader of Ipagitok (30 August 2002). Similar comments were made in interviews with Odongo Emmanuel, *ateker* elder in Ipagitok (22 August 2002).

number of households had access to other sources of wealth – coming from relatives in town, from working in the schools, from petty trading in the market centre in Ngora, or from court fees, church collections or burial dues – this should not disguise the fact that the wealthiest homes had to invest time and money in ways that secured their hold over land.

If we reflect on the modest changes in wealth that had taken place in Oledai, one observation that can be made is the ability of relatively better-off homes to restore their economic position after the insurgency. This was in spite of the levelling effect of the cattle raiding, and the looting of property and household goods. By my count, of the ten wealthiest homes prior to the insurgency, six had re-established themselves in the top ten afterwards.[20] Ogwapit Joseph, owner of eighty cows, forty bulls, twenty-five goats and forty chickens before the insurgency, was once again the wealthiest man in the sub-parish. Even though the insurgency was a time when Ogwapit lost his cattle and saw his home burnt to the ground, he had managed to acquire six bulls and six cows, as well as two bicycles, by 2002. In other words, he was a man who had been able to restore something of his earlier prosperity.[21]

It follows that those villagers who were poorer before the insurgency tended to remain poor afterwards, and a large part of the restored inequality can be related to the persistence of certain social differences. Ogwapit's relative prosperity was due to the sorts of networks he belonged to, to the fact that he was a man and not a woman, to his relatively high level of education and to his acumen as a businessman. He was also able to hold on to some of his wealth during the insurgency (he managed to store goods in the lock-ups in Ngora market). In other words, one can appreciate that Ogwapit had certain sorts of capital – social, cultural, human, economic – that made him better able to engage in the field (*champs*) of politics (Bourdieu and Wacquant 1992).[22]

This study does not offer a comprehensive account of individual strategies of wealth accumulation. That said, I do explore the relationship between wealth and participation. I focus less on individual stocks of capital, but rather on the ups and downs that came through participating in different institutions. The increasing complexity and number of organisational forms in the village – the setting up of burial societies, the advent of Pentecostalism, the introduction of charismatic groups to the historic mission churches –

20 Two homes had been dissolved, two homes had not recovered.

21 Also reflected here is the reluctance of villagers to store their wealth in something that could be easily looted in future raids. Joanna de Berry observed something similar to this in the efforts of villagers in Nyadar parish (north-east Teso) to have a more diverse set of assets (de Berry 2000: 139–49; see also Henriques 2002: 116).

22 To Ogwapit's other 'capitals' one could add the capital embedded in the statuses he acquired after the insurgency as committee member of his burial society, and a member of the School Management Committee of St Aloysius Primary School, and an *ex officio* member of the village council.

could be understood, in part, as a way for certain homes to restore some of their wealth. The efflorescence of institutions after the insurgency was not without an economic logic. While this could be said to produce a somewhat circular argument – in terms of whether leadership made the person rich, or rich people made for popular leaders – when set against the flattening effect of the insurgency the advantages of having been a leader become clear. The renewed interest in becoming a 'big man' could be understood as an indication of the benefits to be had from taking up positions in churches, courts, and *atekerin*. Such positions brought the person closer to membership funds and ensured more influence when disputes over land were being settled.[23]

And yet, wealth needs to be understood in absolute as well as relative terms. Ogwapit's case tells us of the material hardships villagers endured at a time when Uganda was supposed to be an economic 'success'. The recovery from the mid-1980s was very modest indeed. After losing one hundred and twenty cattle Ogwapit had only got together a herd of twelve by 2002. Survey work, discussed in the following chapter, suggests that Ogwapit's story was typical, with the average household recovering a fifth of the wealth that had been lost during the Teso Insurgency. Though Teso's case may be extreme, my argument links up with the observations of other ethnographers working in northern and eastern Uganda. Susan Reynolds Whyte and Mark Leopold, in their respective studies of Bunyole and West Nile, have similarly observed the way people speak of impoverishment and diminishing opportunities rather than economic growth or increasing prosperity (Whyte 1997; Leopold 2005).

Propriety

But perhaps the most talked-about change in the sub-parish was the increasing importance of a certain sense of proper behaviour in the conduct of public life. A central concern, not only of this book, but also of the religious, political and moral debates that circulated in Oledai during my stay, was to work out why notions of proper behaviour had become so important. There was an understanding that there was a correct way of doing things, which needed to be demonstrated through public displays in formal institutional settings: in church, at court, or during a burial service.[24] The value

---

23 It is also important to appreciate that within this overall pattern of restoration, there was the possibility for individuals to do something new. The growth of burial societies, and, more importantly, the rise to prominence of the Pentecostal church opened up new arenas through which political careers could be built.

24 Notions of respectability and propriety have preoccupied a number of social historians, particularly those with an interest in the mid- and late Victorian periods. A number of scholars have sought to link personal codes of behaviour with broader institutional and political transformations. See Thompson 1988; Best 1971; Harrison 1982; Harris 1994. There are also a number of fairly new studies detailing the relationship between respectability and public politics (see Goodhew 2000; West 1997).

attached to having a decent burial, to attending church, or to demonstrating other outward signs of religiosity, seemed to matter more. Those interviewed stated that 'rules are more important now'; 'the dead are now buried in a proper way'; 'only those who go to church get prayed for when they die'. Whether this was objectively the case is, perhaps, less important than the need to express the idea that things had changed. Certainly when compared to what has been written of the region in earlier ethnographic work, there would seem to have been a considerable shift towards attaching meaning and value to religiously inflected notions of proper behaviour (cf. Lawrance 1957; Vincent 1968).

The increasing concern with propriety related, most obviously, to the growth of Pentecostal forms of Christianity in the region.[25] Pentecostalism as a version of Christianity places considerable emphasis on inner conversion. This inner conversion then needs to be displayed outwardly through certain spiritual gifts: speaking in tongues, healing ceremonies, prophesying. Although it is difficult to generalise about Pentecostalism, given that it places the super-rich congregations of Lagos and Houston alongside gatherings under grass-thatched roofs in the east of Uganda, it is a version of Christianity which necessarily stands in opposition to older, more established churches (which in Oledai meant the Catholic and Anglican churches). Those attending the Pentecostal Assemblies of God church in Oledai accepted new rules and adopted new behaviours which marked them out from others, and this marking out was done in public, as well as at home. The prohibitions on drinking beer, on smoking, or on taking more than one wife had implications for how one behaved on public occasions such as weddings and burials.

Alongside the influence of Pentecostalism, there were other developments which promoted a similar emphasis on proper behaviour in public. Propriety, as an idea, was something which brought together new ways of burying the dead and new ways of arguing cases in court. In either institution there was a growing concern with institutionalising respectability and ceremony. When compared with the way funerals were organised in the past, burials were better-organised and more elaborate affairs. Burial societies offered those who joined them a more institutionally bound structure, with elected committees, codified by-laws, membership dues, and a list of punishments for those who failed to behave properly. They were not dissimilar from Pentecostal churches. Notions of propriety also mattered more in court (as evidenced in the punishment of 'wilful' younger men).

In this growing emphasis on propriety there was, of course, a reaction to

25 See Meyer 2004 for an overview of the literature on Pentecostalism in Africa and Gifford 1998 for the changing relationship between church and state. The literature on contemporary changes in burial patterns is less complete, though studies by Whyte and Higenyi 1997 and Whyte 2005 provide a discussion of the role of burial societies among the Banyole of eastern Uganda.

the violence and collapse of the insurgency. The memory of that time was an organising principle of life in Oledai. The work of burial societies was regarded, in part, as a public demonstration of how much things had moved on. That burials had become ceremonial and public stood in sharp contrast to the disorganised and lonely deaths of the insurgency years. Similarly the commitment to a more expressly religious life was understood in terms of the distance put between the past and the present. Becoming a 'born again' Christian or joining a group of charismatic Catholics meant a conversion to a new way of life, one that was respectable and peaceful. New forms of Christianity and new ways of burying the dead emphasised the importance of breaking with the past, and in the Teso region that past was framed by the memory of the insurgency. If we can speak of the relationship between the institutional and the ideological, the institutions which mattered in the years after the insurgency were those which contained the idea that their work made a symbolic break with the past.

EXPLAINING CHANGE IN THE VILLAGE

In talking about churches, courts or burial societies it should be clear by now that much of this book is concerned with explaining how various forms of organisation in the village came to be as they were, and how they had changed over time. In understanding what developments there were in Oledai, it is necessary to understand what I term the 'institutional land-scape' of the village. It is through looking at different sorts of institutions that I understood the relative unimportance of the state in the life of the village. Looking at the range of institutions in Oledai also encouraged me to understand the significance of ideas and meanings in the work of different forms of social organisation. Throughout the book I fall back on a fairly broad vocabulary to explain how institutions develop and evolve. In what follows I would like to explain my particular perspective on the ways institutions come to be and how they change over time. It is a perspective which points to the way different organisations are shaped by their past, by their relationship to one another and by the interests of those who use them.

Institutions Borrow from the Past

In *The State in Africa* Jean-François Bayart points to the historicity of societies in Africa. By this he means that there are certain logics, structures and practices which are embedded in African societies and that these are reflected in the way social and political institutions work. Rather than explaining political culture in Africa as a straightforward response to external interventions – slavery, colonialism, the Cold War, the development apparatus – Bayart shows that the way politics is practised in Africa is rooted in a longer durée. There are fundamental continuities between pre-colonial, colonial and post-colonial societies which need to be understood. Changes are likely to be incremental, and developments more a reflection of that past history as well as a reaction to reforms imposed from above.

This emphasis on historicity also tells us something about the way institutions work. Structures are relatively resilient and practices persist over time. Instead of external interventions – a government reform, or mission enterprise – transforming local institutions, existing forms of social organisation are relatively resistant to change. A useful way of thinking about this is to imagine that social and political institutions have a sedimentary character. They are built up over time through a process of accretion rather than transformation. Each superficial change gets laid on top of what is already there, and what was already there helps determine the overall pattern of development and change. Institutions can be thought of as an accumulation, or accretion, of logics, structures and practices, and in order to understand a particular institution it is necessary to excavate these layers (Bayart 1993: 15; see also Harsch 1997). Though a somewhat conservative argument, the notion of 'sedimentation' offers the best explanation as to why institutions are rarely reformed by government legislation.

An example of this can be found in the way village councils worked. Village councils have, in theory, been radically reformed by the decentralisation and democratisation legislation of the 1980s and 1990s. What was written on the statute book, however, was much less important than the way council structures had worked in the Teso region over several decades. The work of the village council chairman was largely a continuation of the work of his predecessors. His job was to listen to cases and settle disputes (rather than organise development projects or petition the district government). Like his predecessors, the chairman worked in conjunction with the *ateker* courts and the churches, and he adjudged cases. The institution which he embodied borrowed from its own history. The only obvious change was the growing emphasis on disciplining young men, which was related to the particular experience of the Teso Insurgency. In many ways this is a direct comment on the weakness of the government bureaucracy in Teso; on another level, it should be seen as a comment on the way logics and practices persist in any form of organisation.

Or, to put it another way, institutions change with one foot in the past. Where legislation is introduced, such as in the village council reforms of the 1980s and 1990s, it is laid *on top of* what has gone before – offering, at best, an addition to what already exists.[26] Parker Shipton and Mitzi Goheen express this point particularly well when discussing the complex world of competing norms and rules in relation to land reform programmes:

26 Or, as Monique Nuitjen comments, in relation to the local political of *ejido* reform in rural Mexico: '[w]hen a legal procedure is initiated with the Ministry of Land Reform, this does not simply mean that the law will be enforced in a straightforward way. It only means that other negotiators and "interpretations" are brought in, and that the dispute is extended into a different arena' (Nuitjen 1992: 196).

the embeddedness of land-holding in ecological, social, cultural and political life means that one tenure regime can seldom be legislated away in favour of another. To try to do this is to add layers of procedures or regulations on to others unlikely to disappear, and to add possibilities of manipulation and confusion between the multiple opportunities, and conflicting constraints, of older and new land-holding regimes. (1992: 316)

Even when institutions change, they change in ways that reflect on past versions of themselves. In places where the state bureaucracy is weak or uninterested in what goes on, institutions at the local level will necessarily bear only a passing resemblance to current policy or formal legislation.

Institutions Borrow from Each Other

At the same time, institutions, whether old or new, bear more than a passing resemblance to one another. Although we like to divide institutions into discrete categories – religious, customary, government – churches, courts, councils and burial societies had certain similarities. Institutions are complex, lived-in arrangements, and the way one institution works can be seen to inform the workings of others. The bric-a-brac of what is around the place helps explain what comes to be established. Even radically new ways of organising are partly the result of *bricolage*, a process where the logic and structure of something new is, to a considerable extent, a composite of existing arrangements.[27]

To put my point about institutional *bricolage* in less abstract terms, I will say something about the setting up of the Pentecostal church in Oledai. Pentecostalism was, on the surface of things, a radically different kind of Christianity. It had become important in the region only in the late 1980s, and an active congregation had been in Oledai for about a decade by the time I arrived. I have already suggested the ways in which Pentecostalism was a distinctive creed, when compared with the historic mission churches. With an emphasis on salvation through conversion, and church members required to adhere to a fairly long list of rules and prohibitions, there was a purposeful difference in being 'born again'. Prohibitions on alcohol, polygamy, cigarettes and 'marrying out', and a much greater emphasis on sin and personal responsibility, made the church a somewhat marginal presence, particularly in the early years, both more isolated and more oppositional than other institutional arrangements. Pentecostalism seemed to be an entirely original and antagonistic development in the village.

27 Where Claude Lévi-Strauss regarded *bricolage* as the reconstruction of myths from cultural debris, it can also be argued that this idea has its uses in more historically and politically informed approaches. The 'debris' of past experiences can be seen to form part of an evolving political and institutional landscape (Lévi-Strauss 1966: 19–20).

And yet, much of the logic and structure of the church borrowed from what already existed. The particular structure of the church committee, the schedule of Sunday services and weekly meetings, the collection and handling of funds, and the types of punishments meted out all borrowed from other institutional forms in the village. Many of the more mundane practices that sustained the church were appropriations from other local organisations. Even though Pentecostal Christians wanted to claim that their church stood in opposition to the norms and conventions governing the lives of unsaved villagers, as a form of organisation the church borrowed from the existing institutional landscape.

In a way, then, the Pentecostal church did much of the organising itself, as an institution. It borrowed structures and practices from other parts of the sub-parish, without necessarily requiring conscious 'crafting' on the part of individual actors. It was the church as an institution, as much as the individual church members, who developed and institutionalised the church in the village (Cleaver 2002: 16). This is an important point as it suggests the extent to which institutions are related to the broader institutional landscape. They are rarely an easy translation of a piece of legislation or a simple reflection of people's material needs. This line of thinking can be contrasted with much recent political science writing, particularly in the area of 'new institutional economics', where the approach has been to assume that individuals are rational actors capable of crafting precise structures (Ostrom 1992). In my view this is an overly unrealistic understanding of how things work. Instead, as Mary Douglas suggests, there is an often *ad hoc* or approximative process through which new forms of social organisation develop (Douglas 1987: 46–7).[28]

Individuals Change Institutions

And yet the degree to which institutions 'do the thinking', or the extent to which the past finds itself in the present, has to sit alongside some sense that individuals are able to improvise or innovate. What changes in a society remains contingent on the actions and ideas of individuals. Although the structures that underpin any society are important in defining or delimiting the possible range of outcomes, there is debate and there is discussion. As John Gledhill notes, there is a tendency among sociologists to emphasise the non-cognitive – the pull of the past, *bricolage, habitus* – and to regard such processes as determinate in explaining social or political developments. This emphasis on the non-cognitive makes individuals seem passive when, in reality, debates are aggressive and strategising conscious and political (Gledhill 1994: 138). The sorts of debates and discussions that accompanied

28 In similar vein Richard Werbner takes issue with Lévi-Strauss's conception of *bricolage*, arguing that it carries 'too structuralist a stamp', decontextualised and uninterested in historical narratives of change (Werbner 1986: 151).

a burial or a meeting of the village court in Oledai were important, and had a significant impact on the development of that particular institution.

One way of dealing with an over-emphasis on the structural is to bring in the 'actor-oriented' approach of Norman Long. Long has studied the ways in which individuals and groups mediate and transform externally directed changes, based on perceived interests and prevailing social structures.[29] His methodological approach has been to study the interface, or encounter, between the different worlds of social actors, and he is interested in exploring the politicking, strategising and discussions that go on when different worlds collide.[30] (The usual collision is that of a development initiative, where project workers encounter the social logics and practices of a different society.) Long writes against those who view the developing world as no more than a repository for externally determined transformations – the position taken by the more reductive of the dependency theorists. He points up the need to study social change in ways that explain the variety of responses. Or, as Long argues it: 'all forms of external intervention necessarily enter the existing life-worlds of the individuals and social groups affected, and in this way are mediated and transformed by these same actors and structures' (Long 1992: 20; 2001: 13–14).

Given my own interest in balancing individual actions against institutional or historical constraints, I am somewhat resistant to adopting Long's 'actor-oriented approach'.[31] That said, I am interested in retaining a vocabulary which explains innovation, and tries to make sense of it in a given social context. The question is how to balance the influence of individual with historical and institutional considerations. In the case studies placed throughout the book, I try to remain open to individual interests while understanding the ways in which cases relate to broader changes in the social landscape. Individuals, or groups of individuals, are seen to use their relative power; their capacity to argue for certain outcomes; or their desire to privilege certain discourses; and are thus able to draw on past experiences in bringing new things into being. The careers of individual villagers, the trajectory of a court case, or the establishment of something new should

29 An 'actor' may be an individual, though more typically the term refers to a group, category or class.
30 Norman Long has gathered a number of scholars and students around his particular way of thinking about the sociology of rural development at the Agricultural University in Wageningen in the Netherlands. This gathering has produced something of an actor-oriented paradigm.
31 In much of the work coming out of this actor-oriented tradition there is too much emphasis on the ability of individuals or groups of individuals to structure or subvert institutionalised power. This is partly a problem of semantics: when people with few material assets are labelled 'actors', they appear more capable and influential than they actually are (Olivier de Sardan 2005: 13). At the same time it should be added that Long's own agenda was paradigmatic in that it wanted to oppose earlier more structuralist explanations of social change; adopting his approach runs the risk of a return to the rather stale dichotomy between structure and agency.

be seen as relying on individual skills, competencies and personalities. But the extent to which individuals are able to drive changes through needs qualification.

If we think about the setting up of burial societies in the years after the insurgency it is possible to see the importance of individual initiative. Burial societies are organised around earlier burial practices and borrow from already existing institutional forms, such as the various *atekerin*. At the same time, however, burial societies are also the outgrowth of conscientious and concerted efforts on the part of individual villagers. Those who had been in exile during the insurgency made a conscious effort to bring back what they had learned from neighbouring societies. In the setting up of a burial society in Oledai there is Long's appreciation of the agency of actors and networks, and an emphasis on the way new institutional structures are embedded in past histories and other sorts of organisation. Of course, these analytical distinctions bleed into one another at the level of experience. What is borrowed from one institution finds its reflection in the history of another, and that history can itself inform the arguments of individuals in the context of another institution. And whether one writes of sedimentation, *bricolage*, or individual action in describing how it is institutions change, the reality is likely to be less clear-cut than the language of social science analysis allows.

3

TESO SOCIETY THROUGH THE TWENTIETH CENTURY

No portion of the Protectorate has displayed more spectacular progress. At the beginning of the century the district was almost completely unknown, much of it appearing on maps as a blank, inscribed 'Natives rich in flocks, herds and food, but reported treacherous'.[1]

Thus Thomas and Scott, in their 1935 survey, on the transformation of the Teso region. The survey came twenty-eight years after Teso was granted district status within the Uganda Protectorate. Their commentary suggests the rapid speed with which colonial government established itself in what was considered a 'backward' region. Cotton, the driver of change, was introduced in the first decade of the twentieth century and transformed not only the social and political geography of Teso, but also the fortunes of Uganda. The revenues from cotton made Uganda self-financing. Cotton, which comprised only 10 per cent of exports in 1906–7, made up 90 per cent of exports in value terms in 1926–7 (Vincent 1982: 170).[2] Teso came to serve as a by-word for development, a sign of how much could be achieved through colonial government.

This faith in progress, so central to the view of colonial administrators, contrasts sharply with the accounts of more recent visitors to the region. Joanna de Berry, writing in the 1990s, spoke of Teso as a place 'all but destroyed' by violence and economic collapse, and I myself have described the sub-parish of Oledai as underdeveloped, poor and marginal (de Berry 2000: 25; Jones 2005: 503).[3] The decline of cotton offers one possible explanation for the collapse in the region's fortunes. The collapse of Teso must also be related to the violence and insecurity of the years of insurgency from 1986 to 1993. These years saw not only further economic deprivations but

1 Thomas and Scott 1935: 448.
2 This observation is also contained within Ehrlich's paper on 'Cotton and the Uganda economy, 1903–1909'. By 1913 the value of Uganda's exports had increased twelvefold. The share of cotton as a percentage of exports rose from near to nothing in 1903 to near 60 per cent in 1913 (Ehrlich 1957: 162–3).
3 Joanna de Berry is careful to ground her study in practices which describe the importance of economic and social activities, but her avoidance of the politics of the insurgency tends to construct the rural population as passive and disengaged (and consequently requiring the active efforts of development agencies on such questions as gender sensitisation, human rights promotion and empowerment).

Plate 3 The disused ginnery on the Ngora–Mukongoro road

Chapter 3 details the declining rural economy.

also the destruction of social and political structures at the local level. If Joan Vincent writes of the early years of the twentieth century as years of transformation, reflecting the radical and often violent changes wrought by colonialism, the closing years of the century were a time of decline and dissolution.

As a reflection of this divided history, this chapter is divided. I begin by looking at the first half of the twentieth century, with a particular focus on new kinds of institutional arrangements that developed in response to colonial administration. Clans as well as courts, councils, churches and schools were formed out of the experience of colonialism. Second, I look at the insurgency period, a time when most of these institutions came under attack. The first half of the chapter relies on a number of historical accounts drawing mostly from the archival and ethnographic works of Joan Vincent, and the writings of the one-time district commissioner J. C. D. Lawrance (Vincent 1968, 1976, 1982; Lawrance 1957; but see also Vail 1972; Uchendu and Anthony 1975; Karp 1978). The second half of the chapter attempts to reconstruct the history of the insurgency through a synthesis of newspaper articles, academic analyses and a number of oral testimonies given by villagers, government officials and missionaries. Before going further, it should be noted that though religious and customary institutions are mentioned in this chapter, their influence is discussed more fully in Chapters 5–7.

FROM STATELESS TO SUB-COLONIAL

In their myth of origin, the *Arionga*, the people of the Teso region came to the area at the end of a long history of migration from the east (de Berry 2000: 381; Emwamu 1967).[4] The *Arionga* speaks of a time when the ancestors of what came to be termed 'the Iteso' migrated from what is presently north-east Uganda into the regions bordering the Lake Kyoga basin to the south-west (see Map 1).[5] As they moved between these two regions, there was a gradual accumulation of people speaking the various dialects that constituted the Ateso language cluster. This age of migration is dated to the seventeenth and eighteenth centuries. The migrations would eventually extend further south into what is currently north-west Kenya, where there

4 According to Pirouet, W. A. Crabtree was the first person to use the word 'Teso'. The term was found in a 1901 report in the *Church Missionary Intelligencer* (Pirouet 1978: 172).
5 The 'Iteso' are one of the largest 'tribes' in Uganda and have been classified as Nilo-Hamitic, after Driberg (Driberg 1939: 20–1). They share a linguistic base with the Jie, Dodoth, Toposa, Karamojong, Turkana, Murle and Suk, all living to the north or east of the region, indicating the direction of their migratory movement (Dyson-Hudson 1966: 260). More recent work rejects the baggage of the term Hamitic (implying that Hamites were the descendants of Ham, one of the sons of Noah); the people speaking the dialects categorised as Iteso have been characterised, less romantically perhaps, as part of the 'phylum' of the Nilo-Saharan group of languages (Bender 2000).

remains a population of Ateso speakers, separated from the 'northern Iteso' by the Bantu-speaking populations of south-east Uganda (Karp 1978: 9–10; Heald 1991). The *Arionga* period was followed by the *Asonya*, the time between roughly 1800 and the late 1890s, which ended when the *bakungulu* (literally 'the men of Kakungulu') arrived in the area (cf. Webster 1973). In their oral history the Iteso are remembered as a pastoralist people.

Pre-colonial Economy and Society

Up to 1900 Teso was intersected by trade networks, notably the Swahili and Arab caravan routes, which traversed their way to Bunyoro to the north-east (Tosh 1978: 85). For the people living in the Teso region, the caravan routes involved the trading of a range of goods – ivory from the northern and western parts, millet from the southern areas – in exchange for cattle and ironware (Vincent 1982: 71–4). Joan Vincent describes the rich and diverse pre-colonial economy: 'at least three different types of spear, made with iron and wood, as well as bows and arrows ... bird and fish traps made of woven basketry. Wicker work and coiled basketry ... hay forks and small weeding hoes were made of wood. Shell weeding tools were also used. Hoes, finger knives, and hooks, digging spears, and slaughtering knives were of iron' (1982: 65–6).[6] Those living in the region were increasingly integrated in a more extensive regional economy; though the fragmented nature of Iteso society meant that they were at a disadvantage in their dealings with caravan traders.

The peoples of the Teso region have been described as comprising a number of acephalous or 'stateless' societies, with a pattern of social organisation small in scale and contingent in form. Political authority was not ordered in the manner of more hierarchical or centralised societies found in the southern or western parts of Uganda, nor did it appear to be organised into well-structured age-sets, as has been the case for a number of other acephalous societies. Thomas and Scott go so far as to state that 'among the Teso alone, there is no evidence to show that clans have ever existed' (1935: 283). Social organisation in the southern portion of the region – where Oledai is located – was relatively unpredictable or amorphous (Tosh 1978: 35).[7] In many instances it appeared that there was no established pattern of

6 The people of the Teso region, despite their (self)-representation as pastoralists and cattle keepers in the period prior to colonialism, depended on cereal production as well as stock-rearing. The idea that colonialism introduced arable cultivation to the region is something of a myth, though it persists in the literature (cf. Zistel 2002: 99).

7 The studies of the Nuer of southern Sudan by E. E. Evans-Pritchard, or the Tallensi of northern Ghana by Meyer Fortes, caused anthropologists to conclude that acephalous, or 'stateless', societies could nonetheless be ordered around age sets. Elizabeth Colson put forward the view that acephalous societies need not adhere to age-set structures. Societies could persist through time without predictable patterns of political organisation (Colson 1969: 48).

leadership, and leadership typically implied neither permanence nor inheritance (Vincent 1982: 89–95).[8] Who got to lead depended on the crisis at hand and the level of confidence an individual could muster from the people around him.[9] The Iteso region provided an absolute contrast to the more centralised societies of Buganda to the south. With its monarchy, military forces, tax collectors and territorial integrity Buganda offered a complete contrast to the blank spot on the map where the people speaking the Ateso dialects had managed to establish themselves (Reid 2002; Hanson 2003). Before colonial agents arrived, cartographers labelled the region around Teso as 'Bukedi' – literally 'the land of the naked people' (Vincent 1982: Chapter 2).

What should be apparent, then, is the considerable disjuncture between the pattern of pre-colonial society, and the type of society and economy that developed around cotton production in the early twentieth century. Though others have sought to tease out the continuities between pre-colonial and colonial societies in other parts of the continent, it is important to understand the degree of transformation in Teso (cf. Bayart 1993). There were none of the indigenous forms of chiefly authority that would have melded with colonial bureaucratic institutions. In the religious sphere there was nothing to compare to those societies who already believed in a creator-god. Instead entirely new ways of organising and new ways of thinking had to be imposed. A society whose value system was based on cattle had to learn about paying taxes and cropping cotton. The early colonial period was a time of intense activity when bureaucratic structures were built up. As we shall see, clans, as much as courts, were invented in response to the ministrations of colonial government. People had to adapt to the new dispensation. That these new institutions never managed to erase the egalitarian inheritance of the Iteso should not disguise the profound transformation that took place.

---

8 Pirouet, following Lawrance, argued that the Iteso were organised around a 'highly complex system of age-sets by which authority was vested in the more senior members of the clans who had slowly worked their way up the grade, and who were closely bound together as a group' (Pirouet 1978: 171). In my view this represents an overly structured account of Teso society, and Joan Vincent's description of Teso society as 'amorphous' comes closer to the open-ended and contingent approach to social and political organisation that I was able to observe (Vincent 1982: 76–80).

9 Age-sets and accompanying initiation ceremonies are more likely to have persisted in the parts of the Teso region bordering Karamoja, notably the Usuk area (see Map 1). Lawrance argues that age-set ceremonies were only brought to an end with the arrival of Kakungulu, though he also concedes that 'it is a curious fact that no early observers of the Iteso mention even the existence of the age-set system, and there is scant reference to it in official documents and published works' (Lawrance 1957: 248). C. P. Emudong suggests that many societies in the Teso region had a distinctly different history from the Karamojong and that the people of the Teso region were arable farmers who may never have had an established age-set system (1973: 88).

The Bakungulu

The 1890s, the decade immediately prior to the colonial encounter, was a decade of crisis. As is often the case in places on the eve of a revolution, the shadow of that revolution was felt in advance. Apart from the decline of the caravan economy, due to the disruption of trade networks by wars of conquest, there were a number of crises that affected the Teso region directly. Competition over land intensified, as people from neighbouring societies sought to escape the violence that accompanied the expansion of colonial government (Vincent 1982: 80). The 'Great Famine', or *ebeli*, lasting from 1894 to 1896, had weakened the social and economic basis of life in the Teso region.[10] At the same time outbreaks of rinderpest were killing many cattle, a disaster shared with the rest of east Africa at the turn of the twentieth century (Berry 1993: 78; Lawrance 1957: 31).

In 1899 Kakungulu, a Ganda chief, was authorised to explore the territory east of Lake Kyoga on behalf of the British (Twaddle 1993: Chapter 5). This form of colonialism – in effect a form of sub-colonialism – reflected the admiration British officials had for the people of Buganda, as well as the shortage of Europeans on the ground. The Baganda – described by Lugard, the author of indirect rule, as 'probably the most civilised of any native state in Africa' – were deployed throughout the Protectorate to advance British interests (cited in Vincent 1982: 32). A man such as Kakungulu was given the freedom to act as a sort of colonial entrepreneur, a leader who could further British interests in the region. By 1901 Kakungulu's men (*bakungulu*) had led a number of assaults on the people living in southern Teso, including raids on settlements around present-day Mukongoro, Ngora and Kachumbala. The historian Michael Twaddle suggests that the *bakungulu*, like their colonial backers, regarded the people of the Teso region as backward and deserving harsh treatment:

> Iteso captives as well as their cattle [were] herded into huts, which were then fired. 'This was an act of excessive cruelty', admitted one of the Baganda responsible for the atrocity at a later date; 'but it served its purpose in dealing with a primitive community'.[11]

The expansion of Ganda influence combined with a number of ongoing conflicts over inheritance and personal authority at the local level. In certain instances the force of arms represented by the *bakungulu* proved transformative. In 1901 Ijala of Ngora sought out Ganda agents to assist him in a succession dispute with his father that involved only a small number of households. And yet, after the defeat of the father, Ijala, with the help

---

10 The term *ebeli*, Webster explains, suggests that the famine of the mid-1890s was severe and widespread. *Etengei* (hunger) refers to a shorter and more localised famine (Webster et al. 1973: 52).
11 Twaddle 1993: 142.

of some '250 Ganda rifles', was set up as a sub-county, or *ggombolola*, chief from his base at Ngora (Pirouet 1978: 176).[12] Such dramatic promotions became commonplace, even though the conflicts in which the *bakungulu* found themselves caught up were relatively insignificant. Ijala achieved something akin to 'chiefly' status, and from Ngora the *bakungulu* extended their authority over southern Teso, elevating local men to the positions of sub-county, parish, or *muluka* chiefs.[13] In doing this the *bakungulu* introduced something akin to an idea of chiefly status into what had been a mosaic of smaller societies.

As it turned out, even with the appointment of men such as Ijala, the *bakungulu* needed a number of allies in the villages if they were to achieve anything approaching control over the countryside. P. H. Gulliver argued that 'the indigenous clan and community system was heavily overlaid with a Baganda-like political structure'. This overstates the competence of Ganda administration. In fact the hierarchical structures of Ganda authority had great difficulty building on the fragile foundations of the smaller societies found in the Teso region (Gulliver 1952: 1). The expansion of Ganda influence in the area was piecemeal, and relied not only on men such as Ijala of Ngora but also on allies in the villages, the *erony* chiefs. What is worth noting is the way chiefships were associated first and foremost with service to the colonial administration. To be a chief was to be the client of the new government, and the higher up the chiefly hierarchy you were, the more distant from Iteso society.

Vincent describes the mode of government during the days of the *bakungulu* as a 'paper administration', a weak sort of authority not helped by the absence of European mission societies. Missionaries, who had done much to educate or establish chiefly elites in other parts of the Protectorate, stayed out of Teso in the years that followed the arrival of the *bakungulu*.[14] At the time of the colonial conquest of Teso, missionary organisations in Uganda were at full stretch and the Mill Hill Missionaries of the Roman Catholic church and the Church Missionary Society of the Anglican church only began serious evangelisation in the Teso region in the 1910s. It was

12 In Teso the position of sub-county chief gained the ascription *apolon lo etem* (literally 'chief of the hearth'), because it happened to correspond to certain geographical boundaries, such as the divisions produced by swamps, which defined areas such as Ngora, Nyero and Kobwin. The counties, which were run by Baganda agents, rather than Itesots, retained the Luganda title *ssaza*, though they later acquired the ascription *obuku* or *ebuku* (from the Ateso for 'shield').

13 N. Egimu-Okuda makes a similar point about the influence of men such as Ijala at the time of the *bakungulu* (1973: 169–70). D. H. Okalany argues that the pacification of the Teso region came because of the fear of guns and the *bakungulu*'s reputation for violence (ibid. 129–42).

14 W. H. Crabtree led the call to annex the Teso region in a 1901 article in the *Church Missionary Intelligencer*. It is an indication of the religious rivalries that shaped early colonial Uganda that his main enemy was not ignorance so much as Catholicism (Vincent 1982: 107).

Ganda agents, inspired by military rather than religious considerations, who opened up the Teso region (Vincent 1982: 122n). Christianity played 'catch-up' in Teso, with conversion rates lagging far behind other parts of the Protectorate. The Catholic and Anglican churches, which Kevin Ward later described as the 'folk churches' of Uganda, in the sense that they were popular, lay-led organisations, were at their weakest in places like Teso (Ward 1995: 72; Pirouet 1978: postscript). Again, the particular context of Teso society was important. The informal and contingent social arrangements found across the Teso region at the time represented an obvious disjuncture with the religious hierarchies and bureaucracies of the missionary societies (Pirouet 1978: 169–72).

Early Colonial Administration: 'Development' from Above

Kakungulu's career went into eclipse around the time of the establishment of the Mbale Collectorate in 1908 (Twaddle 1993: 233).[15] The Collectorate was responsible for gathering the peoples of eastern Uganda under Protectorate administration so that they could pay taxes, and Collectorate officials were keen to bring Teso into line. The northern boundaries of the region were established through military campaigns and expeditions at about the same time (Vincent 1982: 124–34). This was all part of an attempt to formalise British control. In the southern half of the region, where Oledai is situated, a bureaucratic system was developed that resulted in a radically changed economy and society. Cotton, it had already been decided, would be the cash crop for the region, and required more than the skeletal and militarised bureaucracy built up by the *bakungulu*. The local government system had to be sophisticated enough to sedentarise the population, instruct small-holders in new agricultural techniques and collect taxes (Brett 1973).

Cotton required close supervision, and a system of chiefs was introduced. A troublesome crop to grow, it demanded more in the way of clearing land, digging and weeding, and was not always that profitable (Young 1971: 143).[16] Chiefs were responsible for forcibly imposing the cultivation of this difficult crop on a population that retained its acephalous and pastoralist inheritance. This made for a very particular form of politics organised around the tension between the hierarchies of colonialism and the egalitarianism of Iteso society. There were none of the deep-rooted indigenous bureaucracies that were available elsewhere. Above the level of the village, local government structures related to the countryside through a series of coercive relationships. Chiefs were typically appointed away from their home areas. Positions of authority were in the gift of the colonial adminis-

---

15 The term 'Collectorate' was meant to imply the collection of taxes, not people, though in this case the distinction was somewhat academic.
16 Vincent herself noted that 'it has long been one of the least rewarding cash crops for the peasant cultivator', hence its association with slavery (Vincent 1982: 210).

tration and chiefly office depended on good relations with one's superiors. Chiefs had to prove themselves capable of contributing to the running costs of district administration and the export economy. Cotton production and tax collection served as the markers of state engagement in the countryside (Vincent 1968: 68). As well as ensuring that cotton was grown throughout the region, the local government system also had to find a way of paying for itself.

The tax system was both unfair and difficult to administer. The Poll Tax Ordinance introduced in southern Teso in 1909 involved the payment of a head tax by all adult men (Vincent 1982: 142). This was the first proper indication that the colonial state wanted more than a paper administration. With the transfer of political control from the *bakungulu* to the British, taxes became a way of binding the interests of appointed chiefs to the colonial state. Chiefs were paid through a cut of 10 per cent of the taxes they collected. As late as 1919, Africans paid the same head tax as Europeans and Asians, despite their exclusion from all but the lowest levels of economic activity. Those who wished to escape this system had to migrate to under-administered areas in the north and east, or accept the threat of dispossession and violence.[17]

At the heart of the colonial enterprise there was also a sense of mission. As Sara Berry observes in her overview of colonial government in British-administered Africa, taxes were the necessary corollary to 'progress' (1993: 26). There was a profound concern with making colonial government self-financing. In 1901 Sir Harry Johnston, Special Commissioner for Uganda, suggested that, in exchange for an administration that would promote 'the interest and welfare of the inhabitants of the soil',

> the natives must meet us by taking up their burden, and furnishing that share of the revenue which is adjusted to their means. Even this moderate taxation comes far below the amount of property they were formerly accustomed to give or to lose them wholly at the mercy of the Chiefs, or of conquerors of negro race.[18]

Though Johnston's view of 'native' society was a poor fit with Teso, the presumption that taxation was the measure of development suggests something of the zeal with which new forms of administration and organisation were imposed on Teso society.[19]

17 D. H. Okalany's interview with Okiria, an elder from Mukongoro, describes the consequences faced by those who opposed colonial policies. Agi, a chief, 'was killed because he resisted the Baganda by refusing to lead his people to dig a ditch at Mukongoro' (Okalany 1973: 156).
18 Report by H. M. Special Commissioner on the Protectorate of Uganda, presented to both Houses of Parliament by Command of His Majesty, July 1901, p. 17.
19 Johnston is instead alluding to Baganda society, which had a monarchy and an extensive administrative bureaucracy.

The expansion of colonial administration was also accompanied by the first serious attempts at missionary work. In 1908 the Catholic Mill Hill Missionaries and the Anglican Church Missionary Society established sites on the edge of the administrative centre of Ngora. Though late to enter the area, these mission societies were, in many respects, the most important catalyst of change. In particular mission schools provided a way of acculturating chiefs in the business of government administration and cotton production. Ngora High School, set up by the Anglicans in 1912, provided the first such place for instruction. J. C. D. Lawrance documents the importance of mission societies in introducing the plough, an innovation that set Teso apart from other parts of Uganda (1957: 25). In terms of ideology, missions provided places where the economic and political practices required of a 'progressive' society could be given religious narratives: the seven day week, the special status of the Sabbath, new modes of dress and conduct, the value of literacy and numeracy.

A listing of the cumulative developments through this decade does much to convey the rapid speed of the transformation. In 1908 the trading centre of Kumi was established as regional headquarters; in 1909 the Kyoga Marine Service came into operation; in 1910 the land on either side of the road from Mbale to Gondo – via Kumi – was opened for cotton cultivation; in 1911 the first ploughs arrived in the district.[20] The year 1912 saw the rapid expansion of public works in the region; sod-cutting in the swamps, in particular, required a rapid increase in the amount of forced labour, *luwalo*, demanded of the rural population. By 1914, Soroti, in what had once been the hinterland of the northern half of the region, was made the district capital (Vincent 1968: 41–5). Acreage of cultivated land in the Teso region increased thirteenfold in the years between 1910 and 1920 and the proportion of land given over to cotton rose from a negligible figure at the start of the decade to something close to a third of the total cultivated land in the region by the decade's end. During the same period cotton production increased from 1,100 tons to 9,400 tons (Vail 1972: 146, cited in Vincent 1982: 193).

These developments were achieved despite outbreaks of rinderpest in 1914, three years of crop failure in 1916, 1917 and 1918, instances of smallpox, Spanish 'flu and the plague, and a famine in 1919 which resulted in 2,067 (recorded) deaths (Vincent 1982: 185–92). Even in places blighted by famine, plague and rinderpest, the end of the 'development decade' saw

20 In Mahmood Mamdani's earlier work there is an almost cavalier inaccuracy which
    dates the introduction of cotton to the 1920s and the introduction of the plough to
    the 1930s (Mamdani 1976: 133). Vincent uses the term 'Gandaphilia' to describe
    the outlook of the Imperial British East Africa Company. 'Gandaphilia' also seems to
    apply to the biases of much of the available historiography of Uganda, where histories
    of northern and eastern Uganda have been marginalised and treated carelessly by
    scholars working in central parts of the country (Vincent 1982: 29).

a year of bumper poll tax receipts, totalling 351,200 rupees, up sevenfold from the 1910 figure (Vincent 1982: 153; Vail 1972: 146). Within these numbers there is an idea of a system built on compulsion, where a rural population was subjected to a form of colonial rule without the political or legal rights afforded to those in the towns (Mamdani 1996: 52–4).

The colonial government had to rely on a degree of coercion and centralised authority which had not been experienced in the region before.[21] Hut taxes were paid, mostly in kind or with labour, while the production of cotton relied on a class of Asians who were important in the running of ginneries and the provision of agricultural tools, seed, fertilisers and pesticides. The African population was confined to the roles of producer and chief, essentially a system of agricultural production and self-administration (Ehrlich 1957: 169). As E. A. Brett points out, the exclusion of entrepreneurial Africans from the commercial sector made it difficult for Ugandans to reconcile economic weakness with political power in the years after independence (Brett 1973: 243–59). The granting of monopoly powers to non-natives in the early years, and the dominance of cooperative societies in later years, underlined the gap that developed between those who were educated and non-native, and those who remained in the village.

Many of the above developments are incorporated into Mahmood Mamdani's thesis on 'decentralised despotism' (1996). In *Citizen and Subject* Mamdani shows those instances where chiefs, as agents of the colonial state, subjected rural populations to forms of authority that made political administration more rigid and conservative. Power in the countryside was legitimated through the codification of 'customary' laws which favoured a 'chiefly' class within the population (men such as Ijala of Ngora). Where, in the past, there had been a plurality of social structures and institutions, and negotiable forms of custom and convention, colonial administration required a more organised and bureaucratically rational system of government.

Early Colonial Administration: Developments from below

Although this would appear to be a story of the complete subjugation of one society by another, there were limits to the reach of the transformation brought about by colonialism. In 1911 the number of Europeans in the district totalled only three, and by 1921 only sixty-six. This can be compared to an indigenous population totalling 270,211 (Uganda Protectorate 1921:

---

21 To give some indication of the reach of the colonial state, the provision of cotton seed in Teso was organised around the Cotton Ordinance of 1908, and enforced with typical success. The ordinance was designed to prevent mixed harvests and consequently lower prices on the global market, and Ehrlich records that the ordinance was 'ruthlessly pursued in a country which had barely become accustomed to the crop' (Ehrlich 1957: 171), a point also made by A. R. Morgan, a retired cotton inspector (1958: 110).

1). In other words, though the use of guns and the deployment of client chiefs produced a coercive system, it was a system that had, to some extent, to find an accommodation with the pre-existing logics of Iteso society. At an intermediary level, there were those who were willing to engage in the educational and religious structures as a way of gaining some advantage over their neighbours. There were also those who accepted positions of local authority as a way of protecting those around them from the worst excesses of colonial government.[22] What came to be established in institutional terms in the village was, by necessity, a version of colonialism that was refracted through existing social and political patterns.

Past forms of social organisation, which had been more *ad hoc* or temporary in nature, were, to some extent, reorganised around the requirements of colonial government. Alongside the establishment of bureaucratic institutions like the parish chief or the sub-county chief, there developed a number of more informal positions of authority around familial and kinship networks which made use of some of the changes brought about by colonial government. Kinship structures became more obviously formalised, providing a setting where new conflicts over land or property could be negotiated. The development of judicial spaces at the village level responded to the increasing importance of land, as Teso made its transition to a society of small-holders. All this meant that the 'informal' sector of kinship relations, as much as the more formal aspects of bureaucratic administration, shifted towards greater fixity. It was not so much that colonial administrators 'invented' the traditions of the Iteso, but rather that there was a reaction to the economic and political implications of colonial expansion (an argument best outlined by Berry 1993: Chapter 2). At the local level the effect was to produce a number of new institutional spaces around clans, courts, and public moots.

At the same time aspects of the acephalous inheritance of the societies that made up the Teso region did not necessarily disappear simply because they did not dovetail well with the interests of the cotton economy, nor did the conditional nature of leadership give way entirely to the bureaucratic hierarchies of colonial administration. As Richard Werbner suggests, in more general terms, there was, amidst the story of colonial expansion, a

---

22 The story of Omiat of Kumi offers an insight into the tensions inherent in the workings of the new system. In a case study put together by N. Egimu-Okuda, this story tells of a local man who made considerable gains during the early colonial period. Through collaborating first with the Baganda and then with the British, Omiat amassed great wealth and political power – 'almost all the first *eitela* or parish chiefs were Omiat's appointees' – and his family was one of the richest in Amuria (1973: 182). Egimu-Okuda also points to the popular hostility towards such men. Omiat failed to find an accommodation between his status as a parish chief and those who were opposed to the colonial regime. Though Omiat negotiated with enemies and accepted a relatively lowly position, his work was as 'oppressive as that of any Muganda chief' (1973: 183).

certain resilience to existing social forms and logics (Werbner 1984: 70). In the Teso experience rather contradictory ways of doing things had to muddle together, coinciding at certain points, pulling away at others. While the more centralised societies of the Uganda Protectorate elided their own institutions with those of the colonial system, the notions of sub-county, county or district remained on the margins of political meaning for those who lived in rural Teso. Those who served at these higher government levels grew away from their own society, and this division made for a style of politics that was at odds with the sort of patron–client system found in other places. What Fred Burke would later describe as the 'parochialism' of the Iteso, their limited interest in national politics, and the relative detachment of rural communities from hierarchical, bureaucratic structures, indicates the resilience of pre-colonial forms and logics (Burke 1964: 164–8, 229). To return to the metaphor of sedimentation, the seismic shift of colonial rule was nonetheless built on top of the residual geology of more localised societies.

TESO THROUGH THE POST-COLONIAL PERIOD
Independence and the Military

Uganda gained independence in October 1962. In many respects the appearance on the national stage of Ugandan politicians, and the withdrawal of colonial administrators, had little obvious impact on rural politics in Teso. While politicians from the region participated in the Constituent Assembly of 1958, the main difficulties facing Uganda as it moved towards independence involved others more directly. Colonial administrators assumed that those Ugandans who lived in the historic kingdoms of Buganda, Busoga, Bunyoro, Ankole and Toro should receive greater powers of self-administration. The acephalous or non-monarchical societies to the north and east were seen as less capable of self-government. In the years after Independence these regions would increasingly come to be characterised as 'underdeveloped'.

The Constitutional Agreement, established on the eve of independence, contained within it differing degrees of centralisation and decentralisation. The kingdom of Buganda, Uganda's most 'developed' territory, was granted considerable autonomy. There were considerable variations in regional integration and disintegration, and this made for a less than unified structure of national government, one which would later be regarded as flawed (Mutibwa 1992: 25–6; Doornbos 1978: 8–11). The new government also inherited a number of very political problems, notably a dispute over some counties that had been transferred to the kingdom of Buganda from the neighbouring kingdom of Bunyoro in the nineteenth century (Mutibwa 1992: 2–3, 24).[23]

---

23 The 'lost counties' consisted of a stretch of land that was considered part of the pre-colonial kingdom of Bunyoro-Kitara. The land had been awarded to Buganda by

At a remove from debates on Bunyoro's 'lost counties', and less able to forge a strongly factional presence in the Constituent Assembly, politicians elected to represent the Teso region came to achieve positions of prominence on a case-by-case basis, rather than as a collective. The elevation of certain Iteso 'big men' at the national level did not necessarily mean that their rural constituencies benefited. The pattern of patron–client relationships that forms such a strong feature of politics in West Africa – where national politicians are seen as patrons because they are bound to their constituencies through an elaborate network of obligations and relationship – was not a feature of Teso politics (see Boone 2003: Chapter 1). Instead rural areas were cut off from the sorts of patronage networks that tied Teso's 'big men' into the national political drama. Government money 'trickled down' in a rather desultory fashion, in the form of projects and programmes. Though Teso showed consistent support for the Uganda People's Congress (UPC) of Milton Obote, the ruling party after Independence, this did not mean that the benefits for the rural population were very great.

The one area where the region's population was more obviously a part of Uganda was in terms of service in the military and police force. Men such as Okurut Gereson Nairobi (mentioned in Chapter 2) were part of this history of service. The military was, and remains, the most important political actor in Uganda, and authority in the army continues to be organised around the regional and ethnic loyalties of the officer corps (Brett 1995: 149). Up until Museveni's seizure of power in 1986, people from the Teso region had been well represented at all levels of the armed services. In his history of the Ugandan military, Amii Omara-Otunnu identifies Okuni Opolot and David Livingstone Ogwang, both Itesots, as two of the four 'big men' of the Ugandan army at Independence (the others were northerners: Tito Lutwa Okello, an Acholi, and Suleiman Hussein, a 'Nubian') (Omara-Otunnu 1987: 36). Omara-Otunnu explains the reasons for this bias towards the north and east in terms of the prejudicial policies of the colonial administration, which required, after 1939, that all soldiers should be at least five foot eight inches tall; a way of promoting northerners and easterners, who were felt to have a more martial bearing than their Bantu neighbours (Omara-Otunnu 1987: 35). The Protectorate made a concerted attempt to conscript soldiers from these regions also because they were felt to be less educated, less well-organised than their southern neighbours, and consequently less likely to oppose colonial rule (Leopold 2005: 73–5).

---

the British in recognition of the support Ganda soldiers provided in the subjugation of Bunyoro and other parts of western Uganda, and was formally annexed by the kingdom of Buganda in the Uganda Agreement of 1900. The six counties remained a point of division throughout the colonial period, and Uganda's first constitution provided for a referendum on their status. The 1964 referendum went in favour of the counties being restored to Bunyoro, meaning that the 'lost counties' were lost for a second time, this time by Buganda (Green 2008).

Independence exaggerated these biases. At the time of the 1966 constitutional crisis, 137 of the army officer corps came from either the northern or eastern regions; a mere thirty-four officers came from the central or western regions (Omara-Otunnu 1987: 36).

In 1966, Milton Obote used the army to resolve the dispute between the Bunyoro and Buganda kingdoms, and set about diminishing Buganda's power within Uganda. In what was essentially a *coup d'état*, Obote, as Prime Minister, seized executive powers, deposing the Kabaka of Buganda, who had served as Uganda's ceremonial president since Independence (Mutibwa 1992: Chapter 5).[24] Obote's actions would never be forgiven by the Baganda, and the coup weakened his hold on power considerably. The Baganda were prominent in the civil service and had risen to positions of prominence in the historic mission churches. Even though the crisis had little direct effect on the Teso region, it further ethnicised the military. After August 1966 those identified as 'Iteso' formed the second largest group in the army officer corps (only the Acholis were represented in greater numbers) (Omara-Otunnu 1987: 80). In the police force 'Iteso', who made up 8.1 per cent of the national population by 1966, provided 15.2 per cent of the police recruits for that year. The government's security apparatus took on greater significance after Major-General Idi Amin deposed Obote in a second *coup* on 25 January 1971 (Mutibwa 1992: 78).

The Amin Years

For many, Uganda will always be shadowed by Idi Amin. One of only a handful of Africans to have gained name recognition outside the continent, Amin personifies the African dictator. The image of Amin, the laughing 'buffoon tyrant', is complemented by a number of startling images: the expulsion of Uganda's Asian population in 1973; the harbouring of hijacked Air France Flight 139 in 1976; and the assassination of Archbishop Janani Luwum in 1977. A reputation for excess and abuse lingers on in the popular imagination. And yet, Amin's time in office was experienced very differently in some parts of the country.

The most obvious disaster for the Teso region in the 1970s was the collapse of the economy. This can be attributed to Amin's assault on Uganda's Asians, his economic isolation, and falling global prices for Uganda's main export crops (Southall 1980: 631–2).[25] Cotton, which had been the cash crop in

24 The imposition of a one-party state, which, in effect, meant the end of federalism in Uganda, affected the four kingdoms of Ankole, Buganda, Bunyoro and Toro more directly than the Teso region, which had much less autonomy from the centre. That said, the message of the crisis of 1966 – the ascendancy of the military in domestic politics, and the entrenchment of grievances between different ethnically based regions – also had consequences for the Teso region in the longer term.

25 Despite the overall decline in the terms of trade for Uganda's main exports in the 1970s, the spike in coffee prices in 1976 served as a stay of execution for Amin's government, bringing in much needed foreign exchange (Southall 1980: 630).

the Teso region since the 1910s, depended on a system of ginneries, whole-salers and agricultural input vendors, and international markets. Aside from a few government cooperatives, most of the infrastructure was Asian-run and Asian-owned, and Amin's 'Economic War' elided with a policy of 'Afri-canisation'. The available system for exporting cash crops was dismantled, and what remained of the cotton and coffee industries was concentrated in the hands of a few of Amin's supporters. The massive decline in production from 78,100 tonnes of cotton for export in 1971 to just 1,200 tonnes by 1981 indicates the scale of the collapse (Edmonds 1988: 102).[26] Beyond the collapse of cotton, which was already on its way out, there was a more general economic crisis. The absence of basic commodities such as soap, salt and sugar made life in the town and villages particularly hard. Teso, unlike Bugisu to the south-east, did not have the international borders over which goods could be smuggled, and was unable to circumvent the collapse of the formal economy by setting up parallel markets (Bunker 1987: 22–5). Instead, the rural population had to rely on their stocks of cattle and wait for the marginal improvements that came later in the decade.

What marked out Amin's rule in the 1970s most famously was the level of violence the state bureaucracy was prepared to use against civilians. As Saul suggests, Amin's grip on power was consistently unsteady and violent (Saul 1976), and Amin presided over the militarisation of the state. The centralisation of government powers, which had already begun under the first Obote government, took a more sinister turn during Amin's rule (Brett 1995: 218–33; Gertzel 1980: 470). As early as November 1971 Obote's internal security apparatus, the Special Police Force, had been replaced by Amin's Public Safety Unit and State Research Bureau, which were little more than paralegal death squads. The highly political nature of the violence under Amin can be contrasted with the violence of later governments, which tended to affect the poor rather than the wealthy (Mutibwa 1992: 112–13; Gifford 1998: 114–15).[27] The Anglican Archbishop Janani Luwum and cabinet ministers Charles Oboth-Ofumbi and Erunayo Oryema were murdered, and many professionals and academics were targeted and killed. Religious institutions came under particular attack: only the Anglican, Catholic and Greek Orthodox churches, along with Islam, were recog-nised by the state. Numerous independent churches, as well as the Bahá'í

26 The monopolisation of marketing boards in the cash-crop sector, and control over the right to trade through licences and the Departed Asian Custodian Board, led to the creation of what Brett has termed 'a statist siege economy' (Brett 1992: 18). Districts were run by military commissioners rather than civil servants, and the rhetoric of local government was increasingly tied to questions of security and loyalty to the ruling regime (Golooba-Mutebi 1999: 100).

27 As Adrian Hastings later commented, a religious figure like Luwum represented possibly 'the only alternative political figure with national significance to that of the President'. Amin managed to emasculate not only the civil service, but also Ugandan society (Hastings 1979: 263).

movement, were banned, even though some of these religious groups had been active in Uganda since the 1930s (Southall 1980: 634).

And yet, for the Teso region, the political violence of the Amin government was not quite the disaster it was for other parts of the country (Brett 1995: 138–9; Zistel 2002: 113). Teso has been described as 'one of the areas least involved in specifically political conflict' (O'Connor 1988: 90). After the initial shock of the departure of Asians from the towns, the region was relatively peaceful, if impoverished. In the political sphere the subversion of the Ugandan state was felt more obviously among the Acholi and Lango populations to the north and the Baganda to the south (Southall 1980: 633; Brett 1995: 138–9). These were the regions where the army and security services were most violent. Only the flight of Amin's soldiers after his fall in 1979 affected Teso directly. Their desertion of the Moroto barracks allowed cattle keepers from the Karamoja region to arm themselves, after which a period of cattle raiding ensued along Teso's eastern border (de Berry 2000: 66; Ingham 1994: 170–1).[28]

After the fall of Amin in 1979 came the lull years of the early 1980s. The Iteso spent the five years of the second Obote government (1980–5) set apart from the conflicts waged in the other parts of Uganda. The civil war in the Buganda region was at a certain remove from life in Teso. Relatively good security in the east of the country and the continuing value of cattle meant that those living in Teso fared better in the early 1980s. In the higher reaches of the government the more important division appeared between the Langi and the Acholi. The second government of Milton Obote, a Langi, was brought to an end by the duumvirate of Tito Lutwa Okello and Basilio Okello, both Acholis. Opposition from outside government came from central and western Uganda. The National Resistance Army, one among a number of rebel movements which sought to depose Obote, and later the Okellos, from power, drew the bulk of its support from the Ankole region to the south-west.

This means that the story of the Teso region needs to be told outside the dominant narrative of post-colonial Uganda. While Mikael Karlström speaks of Uganda's 'postcolonial disaster' as 'the twenty years from 1966 to 1986', he is not really speaking for the east of the country (Karlström 2004: 597). His is the view from Buganda, where the collapse started with the constitutional crisis of 1966 and ended with the arrival of the NRM in 1986 (see Mutibwa 1992: Chapter 10; also Hansen and Twaddle 1988a).

28 Interestingly, the people of the Teso region, despite their reputation as supporters of Obote, made up only a small percentage of the Uganda National Liberation Army (UNLA) that removed Amin from power. Omara-Otunnu claims that only 1 per cent of recruits to the UNLA belonged to the Nilo-Hamitic language group (Iteso, Kumam, Karamojong) by November 1979 (Omara-Otunnu 1987: 150–1). Bantu and Luo groups (mainly Banyankole, Bakiga and Acholi) made up 98.5 per cent of the recruits.

For those living in northern and eastern Uganda the story was somewhat different (see also Vincent 1999; Behrend 1999; Southall 1998). For Teso the post-colonial disaster started in 1986.

THE TESO INSURGENCY

In 1986 the cattle stocks, on which the region's economy had come to rely, began to be looted by warriors from the neighbouring Karamoja region (the same people who had gone cattle-raiding in 1979).[29] The raiding began in what is presently Katakwi District, and spread through the region, reaching the Ngora area in early 1988. After each raid there was, as a matter of course, a newly formed group of cattle-less people prepared to raid their neighbours, and by the time cattle were taken from villagers in Oledai the looters were a mixture of men from Karamoja and eastern Teso.[30] Estimates put the number of cattle lost at 500,000. For the people caught up in the raiding the numbers were of less importance than the overwhelming nature of the losses. As soon as cattle raiders hit a particular area the local economy foundered (Henriques 2002: 18).[31] The raiding involved not only the stealing of cattle, but also the burning of huts, the theft of ploughs and hand hoes, and the looting of stores of grain and flour (Mudoola 1991: 244). The loss of cattle also represented a heavy blow to the social identity of the people of the region. Cattle formed the key element in marriage negotiations, judicial compensation, and the means through which youths became men (Zistel 2002: 126; Henriques 2002: 114).

The cattle raiding started at about the same time as Museveni's arrival in power. Museveni was a military man who had acceded to the position of head of state after a long and bloody guerrilla war against the government of Milton Obote. When the National Resistance Army (NRA) took power in January 1986, people living in the Teso region found themselves in a difficult

---

29 Seeing these developments from the other side of the border, Mirzeler and Young suggest that the raiding was the result of the militarisation of Karamojong politics and a response to the effects of drought (2000: 416–17).

30 This makes it difficult to give the raiding precise dates. Peter Henriques, working in Mukura, dates the Karamojong raiding to early 1986, reflecting on the point at which the raiders entered the Teso region from Karamoja, rather than the time when they reached Mukura (when the raiders were a mix of Iteso and Karamojong) (Henriques 2002: 209–19). Zistel and de Berry both date the raiding to the end of 1986, and 1986 makes sense for de Berry's work in Nyadar parish, along the Teso–Karamoja border. Usually there is a tendency to limit the raiding to that year, giving the false impression that cattle raiding was a singular event, rather than an extended series of raids lasting into 1989 (cf. Zistel 2002: 118; de Berry 2000: 67). I am grateful to Okiror Ben Isaac and Fr Bernard Phelan for suggesting the graduated nature of the raiding chronology in Teso.

31 An article in *New Vision* dating from 1997, and based on veterinary records, puts the decline in cattle stocks at the figure of 452,000 head of cattle in 1985 down to just 32,000 head in 1997 ('Teso Commission risks loss of 270m/-' by Anne A. Mugisha, *New Vision*, 30 June 1997).

position. Many had served in the army or the police force of the defeated government, and were worried that they would be targeted by those who had taken power. At the same time, the return home of many of these former military and security personnel destabilised the region (Henriques 2002: 212–13).[32] There had already been something of a political vacuum after the internal coup that removed Obote from power six months earlier. The spread of lawlessness across the Teso region was not helped by the accession to power of Museveni's military government (Brett 1995: 144–6).

In July 1986 roughly three-quarters of the national police force were dishonourably discharged, losing their entitlement to severance pay and pension (Omara-Otunnu 1987: 178; ILO 1999).[33] This appeared to give credence to the rumour that Museveni's government planned to punish those who had worked for the army or police. Men and women who had served under earlier administrations left the towns and sought refuge in rural areas. Such people brought guns and grievances to the countryside (and also the expectation that Museveni's government might turn out to be as short-lived as that of the Okellos) (see also Allen 1991: 371–2). To make matters worse, local militias, which had been set up in the Teso region to fend off Karamojong raiders, had been disbanded by the new government as they were felt to be possible sites of rebellion (Zistel 2000: 118; Pirouet 1991: 201). It must be remembered that this increasing insecurity coincided with cattle raiding. Cattle raiding and Museveni's accession to power were bound together in the memory of villagers:[34]

> The people say that it was Museveni who stole the cattle… If Museveni had wanted to, he could have stopped the raids. The government could have stopped the Karamojongs from reaching Teso. We asked for security, but Museveni refused to bring soldiers in. We believe that Museveni sent the Karamojong to steal the cattle.[35]

32 As the village council chairman noted: 'by the time the President came to power there were so many guns in the place, and they are still there today. That is where so many problems have come from.' Interview with Akorikin John Vincent (21 August 2002).

33 Major Abadi Ayeko, a one-time rebel leader, recalled: 'when the issue came of rounding up those who had been in the army, I was one of the victims'. When his cattle (270 head) survived the Karamojong raids only to be taken by government soldiers, he was provoked into rebellion, or so he claimed' ('Former Kumi rebels state their case', by Asuman Nakendo, *New Vision*, 24 April 1992).

34 In a *New Vision* article in February 1995 the Minister of Local Government, Jaberi Bidandi Ssali, accepted that the NRA had been complicit in the cattle raiding ('Iteso to be compensated – Bidandi' by Nathan Etengu, 14 February 1995).

35 This point was put forward by Tukei Gerald in a discussion with older men in the sub-parish, 11 December 2002. The other men present at the meeting, though highly critical of the rebels, agreed with Tukei's basic assertion that the NRA failed to protect the Iteso, and that this failure was one of malign intent, rather than benign neglect.

As early as January 1986, political leaders from the Teso region began visiting trading centres to mobilise support for a rebellion (de Berry 2000: 67). Rebel leaders argued that their movement would bring about the restoration of law and order, and, given the cattle raiding and growing insecurity in the region, their arguments found a receptive audience (Ocitti 2000: 342; Ingham 1994: 210). Popularly called the Force Obote Back Army (FOBA), this rebel group drew on popular opposition to Museveni.[36]

But popular support for the rebellion began to fall off as soon as the insurgency started. At the time of FOBA the region's economy was in free fall. The continuous cycle of cattle raiding included not just Karamojong warriors, but also bands of 'rebels'. There were those who were prepared to use the cover of the insurgency for personal gain:

> What came at that time was the revenging of conflicts. Over land and women ... one man could run to the rebels with a story, and the rebels would come and settle that dispute with a gun. You asked me what rebels did for this place. They got revenge on their own disputes.[37]

The rebellion quickly fragmented into a confusing array of groups and alliances. According to those I interviewed, any veneer of military management from the leader-in-exile Peter Otai, or the nominal commanders of FOBA or the Uganda People's Army (UPA) on the ground, failed to correspond to the lived experience of the insurgency.[38] Instead the actions of rebels aggravated the already chronic problems of insecurity and impoverishment, and helped promote an environment where long-standing conflicts were mediated through the actions of insurgents. Within a sub-parish of little more than a hundred homes, villagers could recall at least four different rebel groups working in the area and, as the rebellion progressed, various militias turned their fire on elements in the rural population.

The war's recurrent theme, one which cuts across the different accounts collected during my time in Oledai, was the particular and political nature of the violence. Rebels targeted local politicians. The political dimensions of the rebellion were parochial rather than regional in orientation, a point not really developed in the literature on the Teso Insurgency (de Berry 2000; Henriques 2002). Those targeted were not so much government soldiers, or district officials, but rather those who had positions of authority.[39] The

36 The analysis contained within this paragraph is particularly indebted to Okiror Ben Isaac of Agolitom sub-parish, who gave an extended interview on the chronology of the insurgency (14 January 2003).

37 Agama Pascal made this point in a group discussion, 12 December 2002.

38 Whereas the literature in the national press focused on the role of certain 'big men' such as Peter Otai (a former defence minister under Obote), the rebellion as experienced in the village was explained as much more the result of young men 'going to the bush'.

39 The village council chairman, Akorikin John Vincent, observed the following: 'some people went to the bush with the aim of killing certain men, claiming they were the

killing of 'big men', such as the village council chairmen, the parish chief, or the leaders of an *ateker*, was the remembered theme of the rebellion. Although the war was meant to be a war against the central government, it is more accurately looked on as a civil war:[40]

> The rebels were always looking for the village chiefs. How could those people survive in the villages? The rebels did not want them. If the rebels saw a village chief he would be dead soon after. They would take him to 'dig his potatoes' (*aibok acok*), or to be buried in the swamp. Within a short time they would cover his eyes and face with his shirt and they would move him to the swamp, while singing:
>
> mam idaete eong ne, koyangarai eong da ore neja ikatunga
> (don't bury me here, take my body home to my people)
>
> That was their song, their song for killing. [41]

As if to underline the political nature of these attacks, the above song refers to the intentionally disrespectful way in which those who were killed were buried. 'Big men' were typically murdered away from their home compound, and taken to the swamps or the bush. They were denied the sort of burial that would have allowed their spirit to rest.

In Oledai the parish chief, Angatia, was killed, as was Abwot, one of the leaders of Ogoria *ateker*. The deaths of these men were symptomatic of the way the violence of the insurgency had a political dimension. Oberei Fastine, who has since been elevated to the position of chairman of the Atekok *ateker*, spoke of his own situation during the insurgency:

> I was one of those they tried to kill. It was only God who made me to survive. I was at gunpoint, but I somehow had the courage to run. They burnt all of my property and my home, they wanted to shoot my wife also ... they said we were collaborating with government, that we were informers.[42]

Behind all of this violence there was the loss of cattle. The loss of cattle signalled not only the collapse of the region's economy, but also a crisis of social identity. Cattle were intrinsic to Iteso culture. The giving of cattle, from father to son, demonstrated the son's graduation into manhood. Cattle formed the major part of the brideprice a man would need in order to get a

---

ones who had brought trouble to the area. Men joined the rebellion not so much because they wanted to fight the government but because of conflicts and jealousies. Land was a big issue at the time.' (Interview, 30 September 2002)

40 This micro-political aspect to the conflict is marginalised in the literature, where rebels are usually presented as aiming at government targets, rather than settling scores in the village (cf. Zistel 2002; de Berry 2000).

41 From a discussion with Angejet Jennifer Loy, a widow from the sub-parish of Agolitom. Interviewed 7 November 2002.

42 Interview with Oberei Fastine (30 August 2002).

wife. The slaughtering of a cow or bull was a celebrated part of ceremonies such as a burial or a marriage. While cotton was the crop that transformed the region's economy, cattle remained the asset with which people most obviously identified. With the loss of cattle the culture of the Iteso became practicably impossible, and this placed considerable stresses and strains on relationships, particularly those between younger and older men. The process through which youths became men was closed off because there was nothing to inherit. The loss of cattle meant that younger men lost much of the need to defer to older men:

> Some of the old men did not care so much that they had lost their cows. It was the boys who felt it the most. They thought that cattle would be their route to marriage and to education. Our sons were just told that the cows had gone. At first they did not know what it was to lose them. But after a time a young man becomes angry, he knows there is nothing the old man can do to get back the cattle. So the young men were resentful.[43]

A final point: it is possible to see the rebellion as a conflict that expressed, in fairly desperate ways, the competition between hierarchical and non-hierarchical forms that had been institutionalised in the early colonial period.[44] This probably explains why the insurgency was increasingly defined in terms of local political disputes. 'Big men' were killed in ways that attacked their claim to political and social status. Their killing can be seen as a revolt against those institutions that had entrenched authority and hierarchy (Gluckman 1952, cited in Welbourn 1961: 4).

Internment

Even at the height of the Teso Insurgency, when much of the countryside appeared to be under the control of one or other group, the government was never entirely absent from life in the village. One of the difficulties in retelling the history of this period is to balance the sense of disorder with the continuation of seemingly mundane aspects of village life and local government administration. Village council elections were held in 1988, and village council chairmen continued to participate in government-run training on the rules of the new Resistance Council system (see also de Berry 2000: 68). The army usually had control of the roads, and this meant

---

43 From an interview with Akol James, 21 November 2002.
44 There are parallels with the pattern of resistance during the early colonial period. C. P. Emudong's fieldwork from the late 1960s records the divisions between those who accepted the colonial system and those who opposed it. Interestingly, Emudong suggests that the division was largely generational, with older men supportive and younger men against. Men in positions of leadership 'preferred to collaborate with the invaders' while the people who were most inspired to resist and fight 'were the young men' (Emudong 1973: 113).

that those who had the means to travel from one town to another required proof of identity, usually in the form of tax receipts:

> if you did not have graduated tax tickets you were considered to be a rebel. Some people had those tickets but they were few. People were killed by the soldiers because they lacked a ticket. But the sub-counties were not working at that time so you could get neither your tickets nor a photo.[45]

For most of the insurgency, in most parts of Teso, the government retained control of the roads and the towns.

Control over the countryside was a different matter, however, and the army set about interning the rural population as a way of emptying rural areas. Internment, the government argued, would force those rebels who chose to remain in the bush out into the open, and would cut off civilian support for the insurgency, allowing the army to sweep through the countryside. Vincent later termed government actions at the time a 'scorched earth policy', a course of government action that was characterised by extreme and unforgiving violence (Vincent 1999: 122).[46] This overstates the capabilities of the National Resistance Army in the countryside; where the new government was more obviously unforgiving was in its treatment of the interned rural population. Those who did not have access to accommodation in the towns were put into hastily assembled camps. They were interned for nine months, starting in February 1990. Estimates put the total interned at well over one hundred thousand people, roughly half the population of the region (Henriques 2002: 223–4; de Berry 2000: 72).[47] The camp at Ngora, to which villagers from Oledai were sent, interned around 35,000 people over a few square miles (Amnesty International 1999: 21).[48] From the start, the government made no attempt to meet the needs of the villagers they had forcibly removed from their sources of livelihood.[49]

---

45 The comment comes from an interview with Ikara Patrick, a Roman Catholic catechist, 4 December 2002. It is a point echoed in Margaret Davies's collection of interviews, *Iteso Voices*. Pastor Matthew recalled that: 'If you wanted to go from one place to another you had to have a letter' (Davies n.d.: 50).

46 Ingham overstates his case when he criticises the 'protection afforded to people of Teso by the NRA' as little better than the UNLA tactics in Luwero (Ingham 1994: 210).

47 The population of Kumi District, according to the 1991 census, was 236,694, and that of the Teso region 670,000. The 2002 census put Kumi District at 389,665 and the Teso region at 1,190,054. The share of the national population living in the Teso region had fallen from 5.6 per cent in 1980 to 4.8 per cent in 2002 (Uganda Government 2002: 46).

48 The area where the camp was sited can be seen on Map 1, as the striped area of land near to *ebuku* (the sub-county headquarters).

49 Alito Fastine, who was a young man at the time of his internment, observed the following: 'In the camps life was not easy, people slept outside, under trees at the start. There was not really anything like pit latrines or clean water, and that gave

There was a lack of adequate food, shelter and water. A missionary later recalled:

> The internment camps, which we at the time called concentration camps, which is what they were, concentrating people in certain areas … that was a terrible blow to those who were caught up in it …

> … The mortality rate was quite high in most of the camps … there was a big camp in the centre of Ngora next to the county headquarters, at one point there were about 20 people a day dying in that camp. You could not travel past the camp without meeting people carrying bodies. That was quite a severe punishment, that's the way people saw it.[50]

The experience of death and dying is taken up in detail in Chapter 7, as it provides a large part of the reason why villagers established new ways of organising burials in the years after the insurgency.

Yoweri Museveni came under increasing pressure from the churches to do something about the desperate situation in the camps. Two months into the internment, the government allowed in relief agencies, including the Red Cross and OXFAM. After their entry, conditions in the camps improved. The introduction of basic sanitation measures, better food, clean water, and the provision of cooking utensils and medicines made the camps a more tolerable place to live.[51]

Aside from the degrading experience of internment, it is useful to note that the camps helped to maintain something of the institutional structures of the local government sector. The interned population was organised along fairly regimented lines, where the sleeping and living arrangements were mapped out according to where people lived. The handing out of food was coordinated by resistance council chairmen who used village elders to organise sub-parishes into 'cells' (an inheritance of Obote's *mayumba kumi* system of local government).[52] This sense of divisional organisation was further maintained by the social practices of villagers, as internees from one sub-parish would often avoid socialising with villagers from another. The

---

us problems. We had to share one well, sometimes you would find that people had stepped in faeces on the way to the well and that would get into the water. The maize meal the government brought was not good: that gave people dysentery, and so problems added to each other, like that' (20 December 2002).

50 Interview with Father Bernard Phelan, Mill Hill Mission, London, 20 August 2001.

51 This point was put forward in a group discussion with older women (10 and 18 December 2002).

52 'In every parish you would be divided into "cells", so that when it came to distributing relief it was done like that. The RC would divide the people and he would appoint the cell leader. When they brought relief you would stand up in your cells. Your leader would be given food as he would be standing at the front and then he would hand out the cooking oil, maize meal and beans.' A comment from Adongo Christine from a discussion with older women, 19 November 2002.

uneven presence of rebel groups in the countryside meant that the rural population was divided into 'pro-government' and 'pro-insurgency' areas within the camps.[53]

As I have mentioned, the main rationale for putting people into camps was to isolate the rebels from their supporters in the general population. The nine-month internment was meant to clear the rebels from the bush, drawing the insurgency to a swift conclusion and bringing peace, if not prosperity, to the countryside. Despite a number of military actions, rebels remained, and when internees returned home they faced increasing violence and hardship. Those rebels left in the bush were distrustful of the civilian population, and regarded many villagers as sympathetic to the government. The growing hostility between rebels and the rural population was aggravated by the food crisis that greeted internees when they returned to the countryside. The nine months of internment made it impossible for villagers to plant foodstuffs, and the spread of a mosaic disease in the cassava crop meant that food was in short supply:[54]

> The time when people came back home they found that all the food in the granaries had been eaten or burnt [by the rebels]. The cassava we had left could not be eaten. There was no planting, no harvest, and then there was that disease. That is what brought famine to us on our return from the camps.[55]

> It was hard to start life here again. We could not satisfy the few rebels still in the place with what we had.[56]

By the end of 1993 most of the rebels had formally surrendered or had simply stopped fighting.[57] The Amnesty Statute of 1987 and the presidential

53 Oledai, located near to the army detachment in Ngora trading centre, was thought of as a government area and was not called upon by rebel groups to pass on some of the food or household goods that were being given to internees in the camps (this observation was made by Ongole Israel in a group discussion with villagers from the neighbouring sub-parish of Agolitom, 20 November 2002).

54 Cassava mosaic began to affect the region in early 1991 ('Famine hits Soroti', *New Vision*, 18 April 1991; 'Soroti famine bites', by Alan Zarembo, *New Vision*, 8 May 1991). 1991 was also a year when the 'wrong' sort of rains fell, leading to further hardship in 1992.

55 Comment by an older woman from the sub-parish of Achinga, in a group discussion held in Oledai sub-parish, 20 December 2002.

56 Those who had been interned returned with utensils, household items, agricultural equipment, and basic foodstuffs that had been donated to them by the various relief agencies. Many of these items were looted by rebels after the return to the countryside.

57 As if to underline the hostility that developed between the rural population and the rebels, 1991 saw the first large-scale transfer of rebels to the government's side, according to the *New Vision* newspaper ('Kumi rebels give up', by Fidel Omunyokol, 20 May 1991; '300 UPA rebels give themselves up', by Fidel Omunyokol, 24 May 1991; 'Okiror gives up', by Henry Epolu, 12 July 1991; 'UPA splits up', 14 November 1992).

pardons that followed provided guarantees of safety and a certain level of compensation for those who crossed over to the government side (Zistel 2002: 174). The Presidential Commission for Teso, an important forum for the region's more prominent politicians, helped a number of the elite negotiate their way into government jobs. A number of rebel commanders took up positions in the ruling National Resistance Movement. Hajji Omar Okodel, a one-time rebel leader from Atutur, went on to become chairman of Kumi district council and head of the NRM secretariat for the region, while the Resident District Commissioner for Soroti District, Max Omeda, had also been a rebel commander. At the level of the village, however, ordinary rebels attempted to melt back into village life, chose to serve in the government army, or relied on the relative anonymity of the towns (Henriques 2002: 22).

The end of the Teso Insurgency has been presented in the literature as another case study in the art of conflict resolution, an example of how state and civil society actors work together to move a region towards peace (cf. Zistel 2002). This overstates the case. The defeat of the rebels should be understood more as a consequence of the limited availability of arms and the exhaustion of the rural population (Brett 1995: 144–9). The winding down of hostilities in Teso was an outgrowth of the demoralisation of the rural population and the increasing confidence of the military. Growing disillusionment with rebel groups, particularly after the months of internment, resulted in increasing cooperation with the government army. As a retired school teacher put it, 'it ended because our boys decided not to fight any more' (Davies n.d.: 132). The early 1990s was the last time the state exerted a strong and authoritative presence in rural Teso. The insurgency ended, in symbolic terms at least, with an open-air Mass presided over by Pope John Paul II at the diocesan seat of Soroti in February 1993.

1993 to the Present

A word should be said on the divided nature of the Teso region. The Ugandan government, which has done little to develop the region in terms of providing economic or social infrastructure, has made an obvious difference in the realm of security. Katakwi District and the eastern parts of Soroti, Amuria and Kumi districts have been destabilised continuously by cattle raiding from the neighbouring Karamoja region and, more recently, by the Lord's Resistance Army. Many people living in this half of Teso have been re-collected into displaced persons' camps, and the rural economy has foundered as farmland has become bush (de Berry 2000; Isis–WICCE 2002).[58] More educated people from these eastern and northern parts have

58 The problems of internment were not eased by the incursions of insurgents from the Lord's Resistance Army into the northern and eastern parts of the Teso region, starting in June 2003 ('LRA displaces 80,000 in Teso', *Monitor*, 21 July 2003).

moved to the towns, and speak of their resentment at the way the National Resistance Movement has allowed their home areas to regress into a sort of impoverished dependency. Oledai sub-parish, which falls in south-western Teso, has not had it so bad. Here, at least, the threat of cattle raiding has subsided and farming has been possible.

But apart from maintaining a basic level of security in southern Teso, the influence of the government has become less than overwhelming. Despite the emphasis on decentralisation and democratisation at a formal level, the state, as a bureaucratic structure, was fairly uninvolved in developments in the countryside. The return of farming meant that a majority of households were better off in 2002, in terms of livestock and assets, when compared with their situation ten years earlier (though much worse off when compared with their situation pre-1986), and although cotton has not recovered since the collapse of the 1970s, the diversification into other marketable crops has continued. By 2003, cassava and millet flour, as well as groundnuts and sweet potatoes, were being sold in Ngora, or were bought up by market traders from Kampala.

If we look at the data collected during fieldwork, it is possible to see the stunted nature of the recovery that had taken hold since the insurgency period. In survey work conducted late in 2001 those who were household heads back in 1985 (at the tail-end of the Obote government), were asked to list their assets from that time, from 1991 (the year of internment), and from the day of the interview in early 2002. Assets included not only live-stock (cattle, goats, sheep, chickens, etcetera) but also household items, such as mattresses, bicycles, sewing machines and iron boxes. Table 3.1 can

Table 3.1 Declining livelihoods*

Year	Combined asset wealth of the 88 households surveyed**	Asset wealth per household
1985	USh287,594,525 $164,340	USh3,268,120 $1,867
1991	USh35,588,900 $20,337	USh404,419 $231
2002	USh58,390,575 $33,366	USh663,529 $379

* The eighty-eight households that responded for all three years were included in the table (eighty-eight out of 126). Asset data were collected through the household survey. Household assets were given a shilling value based on market prices for January 2002.

** Measured by average household assets and livestock for 1985, 1988, and 2002

be taken as a crude indicator of the economic change in the village since the mid-1980s. The table translates the responses of those eighty-eight heads of households who had been household heads for all three reporting years (1985, 1991 and 2002). Assets are converted into shilling values, based on market prices for 2002. The table shows that average household wealth in 2002 was only one fifth of what was reported for 1985.

There are problems with survey work of this kind, particularly as the responses rely on the ability of individual villagers to recall things they owned in the past (and on the assumption that market prices for these goods remained fixed over time). That said, those interviewed had a strong memory of what they had lost; the dramatic nature of the cattle raiding meant that people could recall with precision what their livestock situation had been before the raids took place. The answers given to the survey questionnaire indicate something of the collapse of the region's economy (and were much more in line with popular opinion than national survey data).

For villagers in Oledai, the modest economic recovery of the 1990s could be said to be focused on the household rather than on kinship networks, or the wider community. The various donor-funded programmes that sought to promote a more collective, communitarian approach to farming did not appear to have translated, in any successful way, into new patterns of collective economic organisation.[59] If anything the reverse was the case, with economic relationships becoming more the preserve of the individual. The 'reporter projects' – where ex-rebels were given hoes, ploughs, cattle and seed to manage a piece of land as a shared enterprise – were quickly reorganised so that the assets were divided and used by each 'reporter' separately. In terms of the seemingly expansive non-governmental sector, popular encounters with development projects were occasional and erratic. The Presidential Commission for Teso, which was meant to rebuild the region's economy, proved no better suited to improving the lives of the rural population than more conventional government programmes. The money granted to the Commission in the early 1990s was diverted to officials in Kampala, or was appropriated by the few families involved in the Commis-

---

59 Local non-governmental organisations working in the region tend to have a confessional basis and include the Soroti Catholic Diocese Development Organisation (SOCADIDO), Vision Terudo (Church of Uganda), and the PAG Development Secretariat (Pentecostal). International non-governmental organisations working in the region include ActionAid (UK), Tear Fund Australia, Christian Engineers for Development (UK), VECO-Vredeseilanden Coopibo (Belgium), Strømmestiftelsen (Norway), Red Barnet (Denmark), 'Send a Cow' International (UK), and SNV (Netherlands). Bilateral agencies that have worked in the region over the past decade include Ireland Aid, DFID, JICA, DANIDA and USAID. Multilateral or inter-governmental agencies include the World Bank, the African Development Bank, the European Union and various arms of the United Nations bureaucracy.

sion's work.[60] Where external funding was more obviously useful was in the rehabilitation of physical infrastructure through the Northern Uganda Reconstruction Programme, which financed the building of a number of schools, hospitals and roads.

What Does This Tell Us about the Ugandan 'Success Story'?

Without wishing to take issue with the particular authors of the next two paragraphs, they offer a basic shorthand for the way Uganda has been represented to the outside world:

> Uganda, that [so] enchanted Winston Churchill as the Pearl of Africa, got independence in 1962 with a vibrant economy and a strong civil service. The great potential and promise was soon lost when Uganda was engulfed in a constitutional crisis in 1966 that was to last twenty years. This resulted in two decades of destruction of physical and institutional infrastructure. The pearl ceased to shine: Uganda entered the dark age of political, economic and moral degradation.
>
> These were decades for a contestation between forces of autocracy and those bent on establishing democracy. The democratic struggle triumphed in 1986 when Yoweri Museveni led a popular guerrilla rebellion to State House. At that moment began daunting efforts to rebuild Uganda's shattered economy and institutions ... It was in recognition that a positive change was going on in Uganda, and that it needed to be systematically observed, recorded and explained that a team of scholars began the study of development efforts in Uganda since 1986.[61]

For a picture of what had changed in terms of the state's role in the countryside, it is, perhaps, more instructive to look at Map 1 (page xvii). The map is a combination of my own sketch of the sub-parish and a government map from the mid-1950s. What is found on it captures not only what has remained of the state since the 1950s, but also what has been lost. The cotton ginnery was an empty shell, and is shown in the photograph on page 32. Also gone is the fenced-off land near to the sub-county headquarters which was originally used for agricultural demonstration. The sub-county headquarters functioned mostly as a court, rather than as an administrative centre.

---

60 Established in October 1990, the Presidential Commission for Teso was mandated to help with bringing an end to the insurgency, as well as promoting development and reconstruction. In 1996 a committee of the Ugandan parliament was set up to investigate the work of the Commission. The findings showed that the Ministry of Finance failed to disburse funds to the Commission. In one example a USh270 million ($157,000) grant from the Swiss government was diverted to the Ministry of Agriculture instead. (Source: *New Vision*, 30 June 1997; 26 February 1998; 3 September 1998)

61 Langseth et al. 1995: x.

Teso more closely resembled Susan Reynolds Whyte's more cautious assessment of life in the neighbouring Bunyole region (to the south-east of Teso):

> The economic and social consequences of fifteen years of misrule [under Amin and Obote's second government] have not been alleviated in ten years since the NRM took power ... Everyday life in Bunyole is as much or more concerned with the struggle for prosperity and health in 1995 as it was in 1970.[62]

What Whyte suggests is the gap in interpretation that divides the limited number of ethnographies of social or political change, and the more numerous accounts of administrative changes and their 'impact' on the countryside.[63] While the former point to the sense of impoverishment, the latter invariably point to the successes and transformation brought into being by the government bureaucracy.

The gap that divides ethnographic studies from writings on state-led 'success' becomes most glaringly apparent when authors working on the state – usually political scientists – validate claims that would be better grounded in more detailed research. Nelson Kasfir has argued that 'most Ugandans, and especially the rural dwellers, clearly believe that Museveni and the NRM have made fundamental contributions to improving life in Uganda' (1998: 62). Aside from the fact that his assessment is unsupported by the work of those who have spent time among 'rural dwellers', the assertion is based on very partial sorts of data: interviews with district politicians and the popular vote for Museveni in the 1996 presidential election.

In place of Kasfir's desire to place the state at the heart of things, it is useful to return to Whyte's more measured position. Though Whyte does not wish to argue that nothing has changed since the 1970s – she writes of major changes in terms of the security situation, and the experience of ill-health and disease – it is important to appreciate that the changes taking place in the countryside went on in the context of a weak and disinterested state bureaucracy. It is not quite, as Hyden earlier argued, that the peasantry was 'uncaptured' by the ministrations of the state; rather that the state was less than authoritative and engaged in what went on in rural areas. This meant that developments in the countryside were less a reflection of government policies, and government policies less a reflection of what went on in the countryside. The belief that the government bureaucracy has been the main developmental actor tends to exaggerate the ability, and the desire, of civil servants and elected politicians to enforce directives or to carry

---

62 Whyte 1997: 53–4.
63 For other ethnographic accounts of political change at the local level in Uganda, along a more sceptical line, see Southall 1998; Leopold 2005: chapters 1, 2 and 3; de Berry 2000: *passim*; Karlström 1999.

through reforms. It is a belief that would appear to be more a reflection of the desire of social scientists to say something about the state than an attempt to understand what has changed.

CONCLUSION

While it is usual to trace continuities between pre-colonial and colonial societies in Africa, I have emphasised the breadth of Teso's transformation in the early part of the twentieth century. The institutionalisation of clans, courts and village councils represented a radical change in the way political, economic and social relations were organised. Though the form of new institutions reflected pre-colonial patterns of organisation, they developed in response, and in reaction, to the transformative experience of colonial administration. Tax collection, cotton cropping, and a concern with public order meant that the state built up coercive structures that were bureaucratic and hierarchical. At the same time, new institutions developed at the local level, around kinship or community relations, as a way of mitigating some of the coercion that was embedded in formal government structures.

If the early twentieth century was the high water mark of government involvement, then more recent times have seen years of political violence, and a more general experience of marginalisation within Uganda's political economy. The 1970s saw the cotton economy collapse, alongside the expulsion of Asian settlers by Idi Amin. The 1980s saw the breakdown in law and order around the time when Yoweri Museveni and the National Resistance Army seized power. Extensive cattle raiding, and the removal of the last vestiges of government authority in the region, dragged the region into a long period of rebellion, and the insurgency pointed back to the essentially fragmentary character of local politics in the absence of a coercive and extensive state bureaucracy. The rebellion was not really a coordinated attack against the central government, nor was it an assault on the region's elite; rather, it was a time when local conflicts took centre-stage – a moment when young men from a given area trained their fire on village 'big men'.

What was striking about Oledai a decade on from the end of the insurgency was the unimportance of the much-touted policies and programmes of the national government. Despite the view of Museveni's Uganda as an example of a society successfully transformed by a reform-minded government, the state was increasingly withdrawn from the countryside. The local government system had become uninterested in rural developments, a paradox given that decentralisation and democratisation have been the signature reforms of the past twenty years. What this says about the state and its relationship to society is taken up in the next chapter.

Plate 4 The sub-county headquarters for Ngora

Chapter 4 discusses the work of the village council in Oledai sub-parish, and focuses on its primary function as a village court. The sub-county headquarters appears later on in the chapter, as a place where court cases were occasionally referred.

4

THE VILLAGE COURT AND
THE WITHDRAWN STATE

Since the late 1980s the Ugandan government has produced a raft of reforms aimed at moving power away from the centre.[1] Decentralisation, or the transfer of decision-making powers closer to the point of delivery, was the signature reform of the 1990s, and links Uganda into a much larger story of political reform across the African continent. Over the past decade a number of African governments have reorganised themselves in similar fashion. The 1995 Constitution enshrined the decentralised system of government in Uganda, while subsequent reforms have transferred more and more political and economic responsibilities to district and local governments. Uganda is regarded as a model, its decentralisation programme as 'one of the most far-reaching local government reform programs in the developing world' (Francis and James 2003: 325). Decentralisation is predicated on the notion that the transfer of powers from the centre to the regions makes the government bureaucracy more responsive and accountable to the general population, while the general population becomes more engaged with the workings of government.

Alongside this programme of administrative decentralisation there has been a process of democratisation at the local level.[2] Village councils –

1 In terms of decentralisation and democratisation, the first priority of the government was to institutionalise the resistance council system developed by the National Resistance Army during its years of armed opposition. These councils were established throughout Uganda after the seizure of power in 1986 and were given a basis in law with the statutes of 1987 and 1988 (the Resistance Councils and Committees Statute 1987, the Resistance Committees [Judicial Powers] Statute 1988). The Local Government (Resistance Councils) Statute of 1993 ushered in a clearer commitment to the decentralisation of government powers to district bureaucracies, and the decentralisation of political powers to the local council system. The Constitution of Uganda (1995) enshrined the present version of the local council system.
2 Established initially as a five-tier system of councils (sub-parish, parish, sub-county, county, and district) there are currently three tiers of local council (sub-parish, sub-county, and district). In earlier versions, all of the members of the village council were elected. After this, all of the sub-parish committees within a parish would form an electoral college, which would then vote a nine-member parish committee. The parish committees would then form an electoral college for the sub-county and elect a sub-county council committee, and so on up until the district council was formed. The current three-council system has replaced this indirect electoral-college system with direct ballots. The sub-parish council chairman and the sub-county chairman are elected directly, as are all of the district councillors.

nine-member committees – form the basic building block of the system. They are the first in a series of institutional spaces that connect villagers to the state.[3] In their ideal form these councils are supposed to serve as public forums where elected figures plan and debate development work. District and sub-county councils are also voted for in direct election and are responsible for the delivery of public services such as education, water, roads, health and sanitation. The decentralisation of powers combined with the democratisation of the local government structures is meant to produce greater participation and a more effective bureaucratic state.

These reforms did not matter that much in Oledai. What could be observed instead was a situation where the state bureaucracy and the local government system had withdrawn from the life of the village. There was little evidence that the projects and programmes which the district government was meant to implement existed in anything other than paper form. Villagers collected water from an open well in the middle of a swamp (see the photograph on page 156) while the school at Kaderun had to meet in the church because the government had not managed to build a separate structure. In terms of local government administration this story of withdrawal was repeated. The parish chief (the bureaucratic counterpart to the village council) was absent; and there were only half-hearted attempts at collecting taxes. Churches and burial societies collected more money, and demanded higher levels of participation and political activity. Lack of engagement on the part of the district bureaucracy was mirrored by a lack of interest in the newly decentralised governance structures on the part of villagers. The sub-parish council did not meet (at least not in its ideal nine-member form) and there were no public gatherings that related to the local government system.

The one aspect of the state that mattered was the village court. The court was an arena where concerns could be debated, and the main work of the village council chairman was to listen to cases and see that they were settled. Much of the work of the court was supported by the work of *ateker* courts and churches and, as such, the court was embedded in the institutional landscape of the village. The village court was a more parochial version of the Ugandan state than the district government bureaucracy and its persistence requires a different explanation.

In this chapter I shall argue that the continued presence of the court is

---

3 Throughout Chapter 4, I use either 'village council' or 'sub-parish council'. The official name for these councils is Local Council Schedule 1 (LC1), a title that was instituted following the 1993 local government statute. I favour the general terms village council and/or sub-parish council because this is simpler English, and also because it avoids the suggestion, common in the literature, that renaming village councils as something else constitutes meaningful change.

best understood in relation to the underlying history of the Teso region.[4] The court was not an outgrowth of the reforms introduced in the 1980s and 1990s but had been in existence, in some form, for several decades. Much of its authority depended, paradoxically perhaps, on the idea that the court represented an idea of governmental authority in the village. The village council chairman, Akorikin John Vincent, was referred to as 'the eye of the government' (*akonye nukapugan*) and his authority was drawn from his relationship with authoritative aspects of the Ugandan state (he could, if he felt it necessary, refer cases on to higher courts or to the police post). In other words, the village court was maintained because it was understood in relation to the coercive history of the state in the Teso region.

The village court in Oledai also mattered because it offered villagers a way of dealing with the memory of the Teso Insurgency. Later on in the chapter, I discuss the particular pattern of arguments and judgements that emerged in court. Cases were framed by political debates about violence and indiscipline. Young men who were felt to be stubborn or wilful found decisions going against them, even if the evidence went in their favour. The village court was a space where ideas of seniority and propriety were developed. In this the work of the court connected up to the work of burial societies and churches. These not only settled private disputes, but also articulated public concerns. All of this meant that the village council evolved more in relation to the experience of the Teso Insurgency than in response to the government's decentralisation agenda.

AWAY FROM DECENTRALISATION

Decentralisation is the dominant concern in the current wave of writings on the significance of the state in rural Africa. It is the key supposed to open many doors: the creation of political space at the local level; the overthrow of past experiences of authoritarian rule; the emancipation of developmental forces at the local level (Bierschenk and Olivier de Sardan 2003: 145). In the early days of the decentralisation reforms in Uganda there was considerable optimism that these reforms would refashion the relationship between the central government bureaucracy and local civil society. Most notable among the supporters was Mahmood Mamdani (a member of the commission responsible for proposing the reform of local government in the late 1980s). Writing in 1988, Mamdani considered the abolition of chiefly authority, and the democratisation of village councils, as a significant step

4 David Apter notes that Teso was the first district in Eastern Province to introduce a conciliar system of local government. For present-day readers his work, published nearly half a century ago, provides one indication that democratic decentralisation has had a longer history than the memories of most studies of local government. Apter evaluates the degree to which these councils adhered to a 'representative principle', and the extent to which this principle was likely to reform the workings of the Ugandan state (Apter 1961: 217–26).

forward for Uganda: 'Resistance Councils were the first attempt to crack the regime of dictatorship introduced by the colonial power into village society at the turn of the century.'[5]

Anthony Regan, writing a decade on, noted that 'NRM decentralisation policy *has had a remarkable impact on the state in Uganda* [emphasis added]' and argued that local government reforms dominated the experience most Ugandans had of the state (Regan 1998: 170). Mikael Karlström in his discussion of the local council system in the Buganda region has suggested that village councils had become part, not only of the Ugandan state, but also of Buganda's civil society (Karlström 1999: 111–15). E. A. Brett, in his overview of government policy in Uganda, commented that: 'the *most important* political change since 1986 has been development of a local government system which operates at five levels, from the village to the district, and has been given increasing degrees of authority' (Brett 1998: 32, emphasis added). Wunsch and Ottemoeller declare: 'it is difficult to overstate the importance of the change from a system based on appointed administrators to a system based on elected committees' (Wunsch and Ottemoeller 2004: 193). In other words, decentralisation is seen as having transformed the relationship between state and society.

A number of recent studies suggest that the reach and results of Uganda's decentralisation programme have been less successful than was earlier imagined. Fred Golooba-Mutebi contends that the reforms failed to take into account the pull of culture, and his analysis of decentralisation in Mukono and Rakai districts leads him to claim that rural populations lack the attributes required for participation in a democratic government system (Golooba-Mutebi 1999: *passim*). Tarsis Kabwegyere (who would later serve as Minister of Local Government) explains his disappointment with decentralisation, as it relied on the engagement of villagers who were uninterested, he felt, in the possibilities of political participation (Kabwegyere 2000: 7). The problem of political accountability has led a number of authors to comment on the weakness of civil society in Uganda, particularly at the 'grassroots' level. Aili Mari Tripp suggests that the policies of the National Resistance Movement, notably the ban on political parties which remained in place until the 2006 elections, squeezed out 'societal autonomy', making it difficult for ordinary Ugandans to engage with the state on their own terms (Tripp 2000: 55–67). In an echo of the literature more generally, Geoffrey Tukahebwa argues that the failings come not only from government policies but from ordinary Ugandans: 'On the ground, particularly in rural areas, where a majority of the population lives, civil society hardly exists ... meaningful participation is lacking.'[6]

The study of decentralisation frames research on local political devel-

---

5   Mamdani 1988: 1173.
6   Tukahebwa 1998: 29–30.

opments in Uganda. There is the analytical assumption that government reforms offer a way into an examination of the impact of the Ugandan state on society (Langseth et al. 1995; Brett 1998; Sjögren 2003; Saito 2003). In many instances there is an understanding that local developments represent, first and foremost, a response to the logic of decentralisation. Wunsch and Ottemoeller, for example, produce survey data to show that the provision of 'problem solving' and 'peace and security' are regarded as the best things about the elected council system introduced by the National Resistance Movement (Wunsch and Ottemoeller 2004: 193). As I later argue, it is also possible to regard 'problem solving' and the provision of 'peace and security' as a reflection of the practice of government at the local level over a number of decades.

In making sense of developments in Oledai it is more useful, I would argue, to borrow from perspectives which focus on the history of institutions, and the continuities in political and social practices over time. Mahmood Mamdani and Jean François Bayart, for example, point to the way the past informs the present (Mamdani 1996; Bayart 1993). Mamdani focuses on the colonial encounter, seeing this as the foundational moment for African politics, a time when the institutional and ideological infrastructure that dominates present-day African societies was formed. The system of chiefly rule, or the codification of legal systems, are central to understanding the evolving story of rural politics in the post-colonial period. Bayart points to the way colonialism was itself a reflection of pre-colonial social and political practices. The idea of extraversion, in Bayart's reading, suggests an extension into the present of the way African elites have depended on their relationship to the outside world.

In the case of Teso the legacy of colonialism is particularly strong. Much of the institutional infrastructure of Teso villages, from the household to the court, was transformed by the experience of colonial rule. At the same time, it is also possible to see institutions, and village life more generally, as accommodation between pre-colonial patterns of social organisation and colonial political systems. The particular nature of chiefly authority in Oledai, the attack on local political institutions during the insurgency, or the present-day weakness of the linkages between village and district are a comment not only on the weakness of the Ugandan state bureaucracy, but also on the acephalous and egalitarian inheritance of Iteso society.

Uganda's local government system is complicated, and this chapter limits itself to looking at what aspects of the state bureaucracy mattered in the sub-parish of Oledai. The simplest way to think about the state at this level is to imagine two individuals: the village council chairman and the parish chief. The village council chairman is elected by the adults living within the sub-parish, and is styled, rhetorically, at least, as the 'policy-making' arm of the local-government system. The parish chief is a civil

Table 4.1 Legislated and actual work of the parish chief and village council chairman

	Legislated role	Actual role
Parish chief* (appointed by the district)	• Tax assessment and collection • Justice • Project implementation • Local development work	
Village council chairman (elected by villagers)	• Justice • Designing development schemes • Community mobilisation	• Justice

* In the case of Ngora sub-county the parish chief typically covered two parishes. The sub-parish of Oledai was paired with the neighbouring sub-parish of Nyamongo (the parish was also called Nyamongo). The parish level had little administrative significance, as parish councils (LC2s) had been abolished.

servant appointed by the state and is meant to be the 'implementing arm' of the policies developed by the village council chairman.[7] In contrast to many other parts of rural Africa the chief is the government's man, while the council chairman is the man from the village. The work of the two institutions can be divided into their legislated and actual roles (Table 4.1).

THE HISTORY OF THE STATE IN TESO VILLAGES

In order to understand the differences that separate the village council chairman from the parish chief, it is important to consider the history of state structures in rural Teso. People's experiences of local government predate the arrival of Museveni and the National Resistance Movement in 1986, and much of what could be observed in Oledai reflected this longer history. While the previous chapter discussed in some detail the general experience of colonial and post-colonial government, the following section outlines the particular history of these two forms of political-administrative bureaucracy. The first, in chronological terms, is the parish chief, established in the area in 1909. The second is the local council system, first established in 1937. The system of national representation, which came into being with elections to the Constituent Assembly in 1958, is also discussed.

The Parish Chief

In 1968 Joan Vincent was able to offer the following judgement on the office of the parish chief:

> The parish chief, the administration's representative living within the community and a potential political broker for the parish in its wider

7   The government statute of 1993 attempted to clarify the division between civil and political administration.

political setting, does not perform this role ... His office is one of clientship, not of traditional leadership. (Vincent 1968: 50)

This description also holds true today. The parish chief has always been an unpopular figure in Teso, associated with tax collection and public works. Iteso society with its acephalous inheritance and relatively egalitarian social structures lacked the hierarchies so popular with colonial administrators. This meant that chiefs in Teso had none of the legitimacy of their counterparts in the 'kingdoms' to the south and west, and a considerable amount of violence had to be embedded in the system of administration. Chiefs were further alienated from the rural population by the policy of posting them away from home (a convention which continues up to today).[8] As if to underline their dependence on the colonial administration, the 1920s and 1930s saw two purges of chiefs in the Teso region (Vincent 1982: 251–9). Throughout the local government system, chiefs were destined to be outsiders, whose careers were closely aligned with the interests of the district government, rather than with the interests of their parishioners.

Parish chiefs were established by the colonial government in Teso in 1909. Prior to this a more *ad hoc*, but essentially similar structure was introduced through the Ganda agents of Semei Kakungulu (Twaddle 1993: 137–42; Roberts 1962: 440–2). From the outset, each chief, whether a Ganda or local man, was responsible for maintaining law and order, collecting taxes, extracting compulsory labour and forcing every household with access to land to grow cotton. Aside from the income the chief derived through the taxes collected from his parishioners, he was also entitled to extract labour from men and boys in the parish – a practice which persisted even after the formal abolition of *luwalo* in 1934.[9] The level of brutality was such that, even in the 1950s, parishioners could be killed by parish chiefs (a reminder that the arbitrary violence of the state was not an invention of the Obote or Amin governments).[10] Egimu-Okuda, drawing on oral testimonies from Northern

---

8   Fred G. Burke also observed this tendency: 'in 1956 only seven of Teso's forty three sub-county chiefs were serving in their home counties' (1964: 154).

9   *Luwalo* was one month of compulsory unpaid labour, and was to be used for public works at the local level, such as the upkeep of roads. Vincent noted that 'although it was intended that *luwalo* corvée labour be used with discretion, most chiefs made use of it as a personal labour force' (Vincent 1968: 68–9). *Luwalo* was formally abolished in 1934, though Burke noted in the 1960s that 'its legacy still lingers', with chiefs, particularly sub-county chiefs, continuing to extract unpaid labour from the rural population (Burke 1964: 175). There was also *kasanvu*, 'a form of labour taxation imposed by the central government throughout Uganda ... [that] involved the forced migration to tasks at which the labourer was paid below market rates' (Vincent 1982: 69). *Kasanvu* was formally abolished in 1923.

10 Colin Leys, in his review essay on *African Elite*, was struck by the degree to which the parish chief in Teso was 'not an intermediary figure but a frankly feared and hated representative of higher, outside authority' (Leys 1973: 288).

Teso collected in 1969, offers the following judgement of the system of chiefs:

> It was autocratic and demanding. As elsewhere in Teso the main resentment fixes upon the forced labour system of the early colonial period and all the early chiefs, whether Iteso or Baganda, were identified with it. (Egimu-Okuda 1973: 183–4)

The relationship between parish chiefs and parishioners was contingent. The work of parish chiefs depended on what was required of them by the district bureaucracy. Taxes and the basis of the rural economy signalled the level of engagement, and can be thought of as the basic measure of the state's involvement in the countryside (Vincent 1968: 152). That district government was self-financed during the colonial period. That cotton persisted as the dominant cash crop, despite the high inputs and poor returns, suggests the level of coercion involved in the local government system in the first half of the century.

By the 1950s there were changes which began to affect the workings of this system in the countryside. Cotton began its long decline, both as a share of agricultural activity and as a means of generating income (Vail 1972: 171). At the same time a not unrelated development was the declining importance of locally generated tax revenues as a way of financing district administration.[11] Though the Native Administration Tax Ordinance, dating back to 1938, allowed local governments to levy an administrative tax from the population – instead of sending tax revenues to the central government and then waiting for the budget allocation to return – the costs of district administration were increasingly met by central government subventions (Golooba-Mutebi 1999: 90). Burke notes the fall in the share of local government revenues raised through taxation, with grants-in-aid providing 30 per cent of district revenue in 1962–3 in Teso; the comparable figure for 1940 was only 7 per cent (Burke 1964: 176).[12] The present-day irrelevance of the countryside to the funding of the state bureaucracy in Uganda has a fairly long history.

If the logic of local government, under which the parish chiefs laboured, was of an extraverted sort (focused on political relationships beyond the parish), then the centralisation of government power after Independence further encouraged the withdrawal of the state from the countryside. The 1967 Local Administrations Act abolished democratically elected district councils and formed part of a more general policy of asserting government

---

11 Teso was not exceptional in this regard. Grants-in-aid to the region were lower in Teso than those received in Bunyoro to the west, where they actually exceeded tax revenues for most of the 1960s (Burke 1964: 176).

12 This was despite the express commitment, in the Local Administrations Ordinance of 1962, that local governments should collect taxes to cover their expenditures (Golooba-Mutebi 1999: 93).

control over regional elites. Positions of political influence were appointed through the Ministry of Local Government, and the attention of district leaders was turned away from more local concerns. One consequence of this policy, as Sathyamurthy has argued, was the retreat of parish chiefs from the countryside (Sathyamurthy 1982: 61; see also Heald 1989: 246). Parish chiefs became ever more removed figures, whose presence was felt through occasional acts of brutality. One of the few occasions villagers were able to recall when asked about district government activities in the later years of Idi Amin was when they were rounded up, to work unpaid, on the land of the sub-county chief.

This past history of coercion and violence makes it less surprising that when regional security structures broke down in the Teso region in the late 1980s, much of the violence was directed at what remained of the state bureaucracy. The killing of Angatia, the parish chief, was not only a consequence of his personal reputation but also the price paid for the unpopularity of the office he held.

Despite the return of peace to the Teso region in the 1990s, parish chiefs had not returned to administer the countryside. They were infrequent visitors during my time in the region, intervening only on those occasions when higher-level officials passed through the place. They were unimportant in court cases and appeared to have little work assigned to them. Their withdrawal was signalled, most obviously, by non-residence. Government-built homes, which were meant to house parish chiefs, were either gutted during the insurgency or disposed of through land sales under earlier administrations, while villagers likened the parish chief to the seasonal rains: unpredictable and potentially capricious.[13] A senior civil servant spoke of the local-government system in Kumi District thus:

> The office of the parish chief is a dead structure. It is only that it is still within the structure of Government and that there is a salary that people occupy those posts ... Perhaps if they were residing there, like in the past, they could walk out in the morning and do something ... They only go [to the parish] when there is a visitor, to accompany them. They do not go to monitor work. That is the system, all the way down.[14]

The three-year development plan for Ngora sub-county makes essentially the same point: 'the parish chiefs do not stay with the people they govern in their areas of work, so there is no effective mobilisation and collection of resources' (Uganda Government n.d.: 7). The tenuousness of the relationship between state and society was also apparent in the considerable

---

13 This rather elegant simile was used during a discussion with bicycle taxi men from the sub-parish of Agolitom, 8 May 2002.
14 Interview with a member of the planning committee for Kumi District, 23 January 2003.

gap that had developed between hoped-for revenues and actual funds. The 2002–5 Ngora Sub-County Development Plan noted that in 1998–9 the estimated revenues were USh77 million, while the actual revenues were just USh25 million (ibid.).[15]

To return to the question of tax revenues, tax collection rates can be used to signal the changing pathology of local government.[16] Ole Therkildsen has argued, drawing on the work of Mick Moore, that the amount of taxes collected should be seen as a reflection of the relationship between the government bureaucracy and the rural population in Uganda (Therkildsen 2006: 3; cf. Moore 2004).[17] If this is so, then the relationship between state and society in the Teso region must be tenuous. Graduated Personal Tax – which continued to be collected as a tax on households rather than on individuals (a further indication of the gap between what had been legislated and what is actually practised) – was unimportant.[18] In 2000/2001 a typical household head would be assessed at USh4,000 ($2), with the actual amount eventually paid averaging about USh2,000 ($1), considerably less than was contributed to churches and burial societies. Actual tax revenues from the parish of Nyamongo in 2000/2001 were USh525,000 ($300), meaning that the parish chief earned more from the state in salary than he collected for it in taxes.[19] This was the case for all of the parish chiefs in Ngora sub-county, and Ngora sub-county has been considered one of the better-administered parts of the Teso region.

The contrast between past and present is also thrown into sharp relief when contrasting the differing dispensations concerning what could be thought of as the moral economy of taxation (see also Guyer 1991). Compare the above situation with the 1920s, when 'an unskilled labourer earned 5 shillings a month and paid an annual tax of 21 shillings' (Iliffe 1987: 154), or F. G. Burke's earlier observation that tax collection in the 1960s absorbed 'a considerable part of the farmer's limited cash income' (Burke 1964: 53). In the early years of the Uganda Protectorate the question of how to make the territory self-financing was paramount in the thinking of government officials. Fiscal independence was seen as a sign of the spiritual as much as the economic well-being of the colonial enterprise. Cyril Ehrlich cites

15 Interestingly, Nyamongo sub-parish scored somewhat better than the average with a 48 per cent collection of the estimated total.
16 The recent literature on taxation in Uganda has dwelt mostly on the regressive nature of the tax system, with the burden of taxation falling too heavily on the poorer sections of society (Therkildsen 2006; Tidemand 1995; Livingstone and Charlton 2001). I would argue that the more striking aspect of Uganda's tax system is the absence of any meaningful attempt at basing government expenditure on available revenues.
17 As of 2001, Therkildsen estimates income taxation, as a share of central government revenue, to be 20 per cent, remaining fairly constant since the 1960s (Therkildsen 2006: 5).
18 See also Mamdani 1991.
19 Source: Uganda Government 2003.

the following from Harry Johnston, appointed special commissioner of the British Government in 1899, in answer to an inquiry from Bishop Tucker of the Church Missionary Society, as to whether the churches could be aided in their endeavour:

> the Imperial Treasury cannot go on many years longer supporting the Protectorate at so vast a cost to the British taxpayer ... When we have something like a revenue, the Government might be able to subsidise education ... Pending this development you cannot render a greater service to your converts than to teach them English and ... useful industries by which they may earn good wages ... I cannot tell you how eagerly I look forward to a fair return from native taxation during the current year.[20]

Sara Berry frames the view of British officials in the colonial period in similar terms and relates Earl Grey's conviction that 'the surest test for the soundness of measures for the improvement of an uncivilised people is that they should be self-sufficient' (Berry 1993: 24, citing Pim 1948: 226).[21]

In the past decade or so, state structures in the Teso region, as with those of the Ugandan state more generally, have shifted further away from the sort of political economy necessary for effective tax collection. The more coercive aspects of the colonial state, which had helped foster extractive forms of agricultural production and public works, as well as the collection of taxes, had given way to a withdrawn bureaucratic system. Despite the rhetoric of grassroots accountability or 'bottom-up' development, the local government bureaucracy was less a part of the life of the village than it had been in earlier decades. The declining relevance of the countryside to the maintenance of the government is well illustrated in the account books for Kumi District. For the year 2003/4 tax receipts collected within the district (including market dues as well as head tax) provided only 1.5 per cent of district revenues. The other 98.5 per cent of revenues came in the form of grants-in-aid from the central government and direct budget support from foreign governments.[22] In such numbers the logic of extraversion becomes clear.

20 Quoted in Ehrlich 1957: 165.
21 The importance of fiscal solvency to the business of colonial government was also laid out in E. A. Brett's *Colonialism and Underdevelopment in East Africa* (1973). Brett has argued that in the inter-war years 'Britain's central concern [in the area of financial policy] was to ensure colonial self-sufficiency ... [with] the first objective of any administration to pay for all its services out of recurrent revenue' (Brett 1973: 141). By the late 1920s Uganda faced a collapse in the export price of cotton, coffee and tea (the time of the Great Depression). Even so, the Protectorate administration fought off any attempt to utilise the surplus balance of £1.3 million that remained from the boom years of the 1920s to ease the tax burden on the general population (Brett 1973: 147).
22 Taken from the Kumi District Development Report 2006/2007 (Uganda Government 2007): 21.

In their essay 'Reconstructing the Ugandan state and economy', Himbara and Sultan put this point in more general terms. They argue that Uganda's political economy under Museveni had come to resemble that of a South African Bantustan: a peripheral, dependent region, where the government bureaucracy, nominally managed by Ugandans, is subject to the developmental visions of foreigners.[23] The reliance on donor assistance, they argue, has extended beyond questions of donor funding, and, over time, has resulted in the re-colonisation of the state. The deployment of foreign personnel in key administrative positions has produced, in many ways, a number of arrangements worse than colonialism, for 'not even a direct colony was as acutely reliant on external forces' (1995: 85). It is important to understand, however, that the 're-colonisation' that Himbara and Sultan speak of is based on a much less involved relationship between state and society, with the Ugandan government, like a South African Bantustan, dependent on the 'development', rather than the rural, economy.

And yet this history of retreat pre-dates the current wave of reforms. The withdrawal of state administration from the countryside can be observed in the writings of Suzette Heald, whose work on the Bugisu region from the 1960s noted the collapse of the authority of parish chiefs. Heald writes that 'the channels of communication between the local people' had been eroded and 'in a very real sense the state had withdrawn' (Heald 1989: 246–7). Joan Vincent, working in the Teso region at about the same time, observed 'the withdrawal of outside attention' from the local political field (Vincent 1968: 238). More recently Aidan Southall has reflected on the limited number of development episodes over the past century among the Alur population to the north-west, a region where state involvement should be regarded as uneven, and part of a longer story of marginalisation (Southall 1998: 258–60).

The withdrawal of the state has not been reversed by decentralisation. Paradoxical as it may seem, the type of donor dependency that made possible the government's commitment to decentralisation negated the many accountability mechanisms that are usually ascribed to the reform. Though decentralisation is meant to encourage the transfer of resources and power from the centre to the districts and from the districts to localities, this was not the way things worked in Teso. In having to rely on donor funds to finance the reform, the state has been taken further and further away from needing to have a relationship with the countryside. The rural economy no longer matters. For most of those working for the district government, their world has become limited to the district capital, where a world of

23 The language used in Himbara and Sultan's broadside has been criticised by Martin Doornbos, who, though agreeing with the point about the possible problems of donor dependency, points out that Bantustans were constructed around a racial ideology, making the comparison to the Ugandan situation somewhat tendentious (Doornbos 1996: 427; also Bazaara 1995).

careers, workshops, allowances and government funds has made it sensible to postpone any venture into the countryside. The local and national government bureaucracies have been turned upwards and outwards.

An interview with a member of the District Planning Committee demonstrated in more human terms how this sort of economy functions.[24] In 2001 there was an attempt, on the part of the district council, to move two of the three assistant central administrative officers (ACAOs) from the district capital, Kumi. They were to be stationed at the county headquarters in Ngora and Bukedea. In Ngora the county headquarters is located in the middle of a large tract of land which was also used as the site of the internment camp during the insurgency. By the time I arrived in Ngora the county headquarters was in a state of disrepair, though some of the outbuildings continued to be used as a prison. There was little to attract the county chief to the county headquarters. Or, as my interviewee recalled:

> When Mr Akileng went along to Ngora, he refused to stay in the house in the county grounds. Instead he went and stayed in the shops, but only for a short time. He started to complain, asking for compensation for being assigned there, and after a while simply returned.

What such a story reveals is not so much that civil society had disengaged from the state but rather that those working for the state no longer had any clear reason to engage with those living in the countryside (Azarya and Chazan 1987: 109). The flood of funding that had come into Uganda from the outside explained part of the reason why Mr Akileng stayed in Kumi. Aside from the fact that his salary was drawn in Kumi, what was more important was the fact that Kumi provided the best opportunities for civil servants to augment their monthly incomes through participating in workshops and arranging the assignment of district government contracts. That the story concludes with Mr Akileng's return to Kumi suggests both the lack of concern, on the part of district politicians, with enforcing those policies which might bring the state closer to the people, and the importance of the district capital as a place of opportunity.

There is a broader point to be made here about the weakness of state bureaucracies in many parts of rural Africa and the extraverted nature of the state. Falling tax revenues, the declining importance of the cash crop economy, the development of towns and trading centres, the increasing dependence of the salariat on central government support, and the influence of donor funding, all suggest ways in which the countryside had become ever more marginal to the concerns of district or central government officials. The problems of financing the local government system form a central concern of current scholarship on Uganda (cf. Steiner 2004; Francis and

24 Interview with a member of the Planning Committee for Kumi District, 23 January 2003.

James 2003). Livingstone and Charlton, for example, point to the irrelevance of graduated personal tax in the overall system of district government
budgeting (1998: 504–9). In Oledai sub-parish the parish chief – the salaried
representative of the civil bureaucracy – collected more in salary than in
taxes. At the same time, older mechanisms of government intervention,
which demanded labour rather than taxes, were no longer of relevance. The
work of the parish chief in terms of compelling people to clear by-ways, dig
pit latrines, and build granaries was no longer part of the job description.
The most recent District Development Report commented that the relatively low percentage of homes within the district with access to pit latrines
can be related to the 'reduction in the use of force on the population to
enforce compliance' (Uganda Government 2007: 8).

The Persistence of the Village Court

What remained of the government was that part most embedded in the
locality: the local court.[25] The council chairman judged cases, and brought
into being some notion of the state in the settlement of disputes. Unlike the
parish chief, the village council chairman was an integral part of life in the
village, and conflicts that arose were referred to him. He was a significant
player in the local political field.

To explain the significance of the village court, one needs to understand
that the work of the village council had less to do with the new structures set
in place by decentralisation, and more to do with the history of governance
in the village. Despite major shifts in official government policy, particularly in the years after independence – centralisation under Obote's first
government, militarisation under Amin, the *mayumba kumi*[26] of Obote's
second government, and decentralisation under Museveni – there has
always been a local court of some sort, presided over by someone regarded
as representative of the state, at the parish or sub-parish level. The chairman
of the village council was, like those who came before him, the 'eye' of the
government (*akonye nukapugan*). At the same time, it is important to note
that his work in the village, and a good part of his legitimacy, was tied to a
fairly complex landscape of institutions, obligations and relationships.

As far back as 1937 a village council was added to the list of institutional

---

25 As Burkey (1991) predicted, the political economy of 'district-isation' meant that
   problems found at the heart of government, particularly in terms of the sorts of
   extraverted relationships that came from dependence on foreign donors, were simply
   extended to local government structures (Burkey 1991: *passim*).
26 *Mayumba kumi* was a new tier of local government, where households were
   organised into groups of ten. This was meant to inspire cooperation, or *Ujamaa*,
   as it borrowed from the local government structures of Julius Nyerere's Tanzania
   (Milton Obote was a close friend of President Nyerere). Tidemand argued that
   mayumba kumi had little tangible impact on the way politics was organised in
   the countryside (Tidemand 1994: 23). *Mayumba kumi* is a corruption of the
   Swahili, *nyumba kumi*, ten houses.

arenas available to people living in the region (Vincent 1968: 54). In line
with the theories of government at the time, British administrators sought
to build on indigenous forms of political authority. Government policy in
the Protectorate of Uganda, as in other parts of Africa under British administration, was based on an attempt by the colonial authorities to borrow
as much as possible from existing political institutions (Mamdani 1996:
Chapter 3). In the case of Buganda this pattern of borrowing meant that
the levels of political organisation that existed in pre-colonial society (*ssaza*,
ggombolola, *miruka*) were co-opted by the British (Hanson 2003: 218).

The council system in Teso was similarly designed to build on the pattern
of 'traditional' authority. Established after the 1937 reform, the system of
councils was seen as building on the less hierarchical, more conciliar approach
to government that was understood to be the way of the egalitarian Iteso.
It was a way of diluting political power and circumscribing the authority
of the parish chief, in the hope that this would achieve a more peaceable
form of government than had been possible under the singular rule of the
chiefs. In its limited way, the reform introduced by District Commissioner
Kennedy formed part of a democratic vision, with elected councils meant
to serve as 'the true representative of the peasants, deriving their authority
from indigenous forms of social organisation of pre-administration days'
(Kennedy, cited in Vincent 1968: 56). In Kennedy's view at least, political
authority had to be given a popular face. (Unlike more recent reforms,
however, District Commissioner Kennedy expected to co-opt, rather than
replace, earlier governance structures.)

There is a certain irony in the Kennedy reform, as Beverly Gartrell
suggests: 'what was thought to be a restoration turned out to be, for many
parts of Teso at least, yet another innovation' (Gartrell 1983: 9).[27] Put
simply, village councils added to an evolving, and essentially new, landscape, rather than reviving pre-colonial forms of social organisation. The
councils that the reform institutionalised complemented a number of more
hierarchical structures which had developed around kinship and family
obligations as a way of dealing with the experience of colonial government
(offering some sort of brake on the violence of this radically new form of
administration). What Kennedy believed to be 'traditional' conciliar structures, organised around kin or territory, were actually new arrangements
that developed *in reaction* to a period of intense change. In the early decades
of the century those living in the region had had to transform themselves
from a population of pastoralists and shifting fallow cultivators to a society

27 Similar presumptions about the possibility of reviving pre-colonial forms of
   chiefly authority could be found in the line taken by colonial administrators
   in Lango (Tosh 1978), Bugisu (La Fontaine 1959), and West Nile (Middleton
   1960). The emphasis on 'traditional' authorities, as Beverly Gartrell suggests,
   tended to develop something like a chiefly class, even in those societies where
   chiefs were a colonial innovation (Gartrell 1983: 10).

of settled cash-croppers, tied to individual tracts of land and bound into administrative hierarchies. As a way of dealing with this transformation, a number of judicial spaces – public discussions, *ateker* courts, public moots – had developed as places to negotiate problems away from the gaze of the parish chief (Vincent 1968: 211–29).

This meant that the settlement of a land dispute depended not only on the actions of the parish chief, but also on the arguments put across in public moots, in churches, in schools, in drinking groups and in the decisions taken by *ateker* elders, 'big men', or government officials (Vincent 1968: Chapter 10; Henriques 2002: Chapter 8). Village councils succeeded in part because they *related to* or *borrowed from* evolving arenas of dispute settlement (see also Bierschenk and Olivier de Sardan 2003: 152).[28] The council mattered in the sense that it introduced an idea of governmental authority to the way villagers negotiated disputes. Within a process that would otherwise appear to be the complete subjugation of one society by another, there were limits to colonial transformation, and these limits were set by the evolution of such embedded institutional forms.

Neither Obote nor Amin managed to abolish the form of conciliar government developed out of the 1937 reform.[29] The master narrative of changing governments at the national level was somewhat out of step with the experience of change more locally. While Obote's recentralisation of powers away from the district councils appeared to close off certain opportunities, its effects were more evident in the district capitals than in the countryside. Similarly Amin's militarisation of the local government system, which was meant to increase the state's control over political society while rewarding supporters in the army with political appointments, should not disguise the fact that the central government was relatively haphazard in its administrative reach: authoritarian more than authoritative (see Southall 1980). Government-sponsored reforms, if they were taken up at all, did not necessarily erase what had gone before, at the local level at least. The *mayumba kumi* of Obote's second government (1980–5), a system of ten-household 'cells', was not entirely different from the village councils that had been maintained under earlier administrations (Tidemand 1995: 25).[30]

Away from the rhetoric of national reforms, there were practical continuities locally which made the differences from one government to the next

28 Here the idea of 'sedimentation', introduced in Chapter 2, is useful. The village court represented an accumulation of logics, structures and practices over time, rather than a direct translation of what was on the government's statute book.

29 As Tidemand observed, the basic work of the local government system, the collection of taxes for the payment of local government salaries, was maintained even during the closing years of the Amin administration (Tidemand 1995: 25).

30 In an echo of the capacity of new structures to take on old forms, Aidan Southall noted that the *mayumba kumi* system, when first introduced, was 'assimilated into the old *batongole* system, in which every landowner or local notable was held responsible for his neighbourhood' (Southall 1980: 647).

appear less remarkable to a villager with a land dispute, than to the historian of the Ugandan state. Or, as one older villager pointed out to me:

> I would say that the village council system of today is useful because the chairman is in charge of things. He knows his people and if there is a wrong man in the area, he can deal with the case. When there was the *mayumba kumi* under Obote II it was also something similar to this.[31]

Instead of attempting to calibrate the balance between continuity and change, and then using the tilt to gauge what has changed from one administration to another, outsiders have made very clear separations between different administrations. The neat division between Amin, Obote and Museveni works better when making sense of elite politics at the centre. There are problems further down in the system when this categorical approach is taken. Parochial or social considerations may have a more determinate impact on the changes in state institutions at the local level than the letter of government reforms. This is partly a comment on the way institutions change at the margins. It is also a comment on the relative unimportance of the state bureaucracy in the day-to-day running of the countryside. As Bayart comments, 'it is not necessary [for the political elite] to have control over the minor details of local political life in order to establish an inegalitarian system at the state level' (Bayart 1993: 219; 167).[32]

MPs, Party Politics and the Movement System

Although I am tempted to bypass this particular subheading, given the remoteness of the national political scene from the life of the village, some words should be said on the parliamentary system of representation and its relationship to the village. At the time of my stay in the area Oledai was served by two MPs: Francis Epetait, the MP for Ngora County, first elected in 2001; and Christine Amongin-Aporu, women's MP for Kumi District, returned to Parliament in the same year.[33] The role of either MP in the day-to-day life of the village was necessarily marginal; both served large constituencies and were expected to spend much of their time in Kampala. In line with the 'Movement' philosophy in place at the time, Epetait and Amongin had to stand for election as individuals, adjudged by the electorate on their personal merits and commitment to development, rather than as affiliates of a particular political party (Kabwegyere 2000: 42–3). The Movement system offered a quasi-democratic one-party system, one

31 Interview with Odongo Emmanuel, a retired primary school teacher living in Oledai sub-parish, 10 October 2002.
32 Indeed, if one takes Bayart's rhizome metaphor, one can think of the local level in rural Teso as having peeled off from the centre, with villagers somewhat disconnected to the trickle-down of resources that have kept those parts of the government system closer to the centre well-watered with donor funds.
33 http://www.parliament.go.ug/mpsdata/mps.hei (accessed 22 February 2005).

that claimed to work against the religious and ethnic divisions that had undermined Uganda's past attempts at economic and social development (Twaddle 1988: 315–16).

In recent years, this system of 'no party politics' has given way to pressure from both within and without. By the late 1990s, there was an obvious fragmentation of the military and political coalitions that maintained the one-party state. Divisions in the ruling elite surfaced, most obviously with the opposition candidacy of Dr Kizza Besigye in the 2001 and 2006 presidential elections. Dr Besigye was a former commander in the National Resistance Army and, with his wife, had been a member of President Museveni's inner circle. From without, the donor community has grown frustrated with certain aspects of Museveni's government. His half-hearted attempts at reinstating multi-party politics after the referendum of July 2005 were regarded by many of his opponents as a smokescreen behind which Museveni organised support for his desire to stand for a third term in office. Foreign governments and multilateral agencies have, in the past, been fairly forgiving of the government's military activities in the north of the country and the Democratic Republic of Congo, but have become more critical of Museveni in recent times (Tripp 2004). (That said, the close relationship between donor agencies and the Ugandan state throughout the 1990s means that they are not entirely blameless for the version of Uganda they now choose to criticise.)

Amidst the national drama involving Museveni, donor agencies, diplomats, the military and national 'civil society' leaders, the people who live in Teso have been marginal. The political class from the region has been assumed to be part of the opposition to Museveni, and few Itesots have risen to the top of civil-political administration or, more importantly, the army. Even during the years of the 'Movement' system it was well known that the core support for Museveni came from his home region of Ankole in the west, and this was reflected in the favoured position of Banyankole and Banyarwanda, particularly in the army. Teso, as a whole, was seen as an oppositional region, and more 'anti-Movement' candidates were returned to Parliament from the Teso region than from other parts of the country. Kumi District was one of the few regions that voted against Museveni in 1996 (a bitter pill for the electorate, as this meant voting for Ssemogerere, a politician from the Buganda region and an erstwhile leader of the Democratic Party, both attributes which would normally make him an anathema).[34] The region as a whole voted against Museveni in the 2001 elections and again in 2006.

---

34 That said, the consolidation of support around the UPC was partly related to the quirks of the first-past-the-post electoral system developed by the British. Though the UPC won all five Teso constituencies in both the 1961 and 1962 elections, there was more support in the countryside for the Democratic Party in Teso than is generally assumed. In the 1961 elections the DP won 40 per cent of the vote, while in 1962 the DP secured 43 per cent (Ocitti 2000: 114).

As far as I could tell, the Ngora County MP rarely visited his constituency, and there was little of substance to connect the political and economic concerns of the locality and the work of representatives in the national parliament. Epetait's predecessor, Fiona Egunyu-Asemo, was an elusive figure whose rare appearances and lengthy disappearances made her something of a joke with townspeople in Ngora.[35] The one politician from the Teso region who has achieved prominence under the National Resistance Movement – Mike Mukula, MP for Soroti Municipality – leads a life far removed from the social and political realities of Teso. An article in the lifestyle magazine *African Woman* described the layout of Mukula's Kampala home: there is 'the old house' and a new, 'more modern' wing with a 'pool area; there is a sauna, steam and massage room, gym, and a large lounge'. In the main, politicians from the region have not been particularly noted for their ability to bring home government projects. The few infrastructure improvements in the area related to donor-funded affairs such as the Northern Uganda Reconstruction Programme and occasional development schemes, including the renovation of Ngora hospital and the conversion of Bishop Kitching College, formerly a teacher training college, into a centre for vocational education.

THE WORK OF THE VILLAGE COUNCIL IN OLEDAI

If we take the authors of the decentralisation and democratisation reforms at their word, the village council should have been a democratic forum, part of a much more extensive system of local government. The sub-parish council was meant to be a ten-member committee representing a range of concerns – women, youth, the disabled, education, environment – as well as those covered by the managerial positions: chairman, vice-chairman, treasurer, secretary and defence secretary. It was meant to meet regularly as a committee, and to gather villagers together to discuss matters of public interest (Mutibwa 1992: 181). As the titles of the various office holders indicate, the committee's work was intended to be not only administrative but also developmental. In terms of 'grassroots democracy', the village council was meant to convene village meetings on a regular basis, so that concerns could be raised and policies formulated. Village council committee members are also responsible for 'sensitising' the local population on changes to government policy. Very little of this was going on. The village council mattered much more as a court, and the village council chairman was important as a judge, rather than as the head of a development committee.

Given his judicial role, the chairman appeared, on first impressions, to be

---

35 Despite, or perhaps because of, her absences, Fiona Egenyu-Asemo went on to become Senior Private Secretary on Political Affairs in the President's Office after the 2001 election (*Monitor*, 'Museveni names Kuka private secretary', 9 May 2005).

something of a singular figure in the village, and potentially authoritarian. He was the one person able to convey the 'idea' of the state in the settlement of cases. Of the nine other committee members, only the vice-chairman and defence secretary were of any importance, and their work was mostly to support his decisions. And yet, the authority of the chairman was also scrutinised and qualified by other institutions at the local level. Beyond the confines of the council, the provision of justice at the local level was shaped by other institutional spaces (see also Tidemand 1995: 35–7). The village court was often used as a way of reinforcing judgements made in *ateker* gatherings.

Alongside the idea of state-sanctioned justice authority embedded in the local courts there were other sorts of legitimacy – 'tradition', custom, religious belief. A case would be strengthened if it could refer to what was deemed acceptable and proper in church or in the various *ateker* institutions. These varied forms of institution and sources of legitimacy complicated the deliberations of the council chairman, meaning that his work was simultanesouly governmental and embedded in the institutional landscape of the village (see also Lund 1998; Berry 1993). For the chairman to be effective, he had to be capable of piecing together a broad consensus, and had to be careful not to offend younger men too much. A review of the notebooks kept by the sub-parish council chairman for the year 2002 lists a number of cases dealing with a variety of issues (Table 4.2).

There were fifteen civil cases and twenty-one cases of a criminal nature. These official numbers were far less than the actual caseload of the village council chairman, since he often helped to settle cases through participating in more informal social gatherings, and also tended to write down judgements only where written documentation was required (as in a land settlement, or when a villager promised to pay compensation at a later date).[36] Even when cases were referred on to a higher government authority, usually the sub-county court or the police post in Ngora, the details of the case would often rely on the oral testimony of the council chairman, rather than on written documentation.

In the twelve-month period from January 2002 to December 2002, eleven of the thirty-six cases listed above turned out to be concerned with the question of disciplining younger men. Of the more notable cases that reached the village council chairman there was the case of Aromait, who was considered to be the source of trouble in his home and was accused of thieving from his father (the case was settled in the father's favour on 21 March 2002). There was also the case of Opedun Paul, accused of being

---

36 Even when cases were referred to higher government authorities, such as the sub-county court or the police post in Ngora, the details of the case were not always logged in the chairman's books.

Table 4.2 Breakdown of court cases reported by the sub-parish council chairman, 2002[a]

Civil cases		Criminal cases[b]	
Loan repayment	1	Domestic violence	3
Marital dispute (non-violent)	3	Violence: men against women	3
Verbal abuse	3	Violence: men against men	1
Inheritance disputes	1	Murder accusation	1
Late payment of brideprice	1	Burglary	1
Land dispute (serious)	1	Defilement[c]	2
Land demarcation	3	Desertion of the father	3
Animals destroying crops	1	Theft	6
Late payment of dowry	1	Recovery of stolen items	1

Notes

[a] Where possible, I would sit in on the court judgements of the village council chairman. I also followed up court cases through interviews with villagers, as well as going through the case books with Akorikin John Vincent, to produce more complete versions of some of the more important cases he had been called on to adjudge.

[b] Though villagers were aware that criminal cases were for the police, and civil cases for the courts, the practical division was much less clear. The police tended to be one of a number of judicial actors involved in criminal cases, and also one of the possible actors involved in civil cases.

[c] 'Defilement' is defined as sexual contact outside of marriage involving girls younger than eighteen (regardless of whether or not the woman had consented to sexual relations, and regardless of the age of the man). This meant almost every marriage in the sub-parish was illegal. In practice, villagers brought charges of defilement in those cases where the female party was unmarried and young, and where the male party could convincingly be said to be older than eighteen.

disrespectful to his father-in-law, who had been visiting Opedun's home (the village council chairman decided against Opedun on 24 August 2002). A third case involved Otunga Justin: he was accused of insulting a village elder during a drinking session and judgement went against him on 4 April 2002. In some ways these cases were typical of inter-generational conflicts found in any community. At the same time, in the particular case of Oledai there was an added weight to any argument that portrayed young men as ill-disciplined and stubborn. In certain instances, cases that had very little to do with the role of younger men nonetheless ended up punishing a young man. The case involving Akol Stanislas, the first to be discussed below, offers an example of how a dispute, ostensibly about domestic violence, was turned into a debate on the manners of such a man.

In both of the following cases it is important to observe the way the council chairman was respected as the 'eye' of the government (*akonye nukapugan*). The Akol Stanislas case demonstrates the importance of the village council chairman in the village. Despite appearing to deal with something quite different, it revolves around the question of whether or not a younger man had been properly respectful to the council chairman. This case has a lot to do with the memory of the insurgency. The second concerns a wealthier villager who brings conflict to the village. The village court is shown to be part of a much broader network of judicial spaces (including higher courts in the local government system), which eventually manages to punish the actions of this man. In both cases the arguments and judgements put forward in the village court support our earlier discussion of the importance of the ideas of propriety and seniority that have gained in importance in the village in the years following the insurgency.

Case 1: Akol Stanislas vs the Village Council Chairman[37]

On 12 December 2002 the sister of Akol Stanislas, Atim Betty, was taken to hospital for medical treatment. She was bleeding from the stomach, which, according to Akol, was caused by a beating she had received from her husband, Obelan. Akol reported this accusation to the police, and paid them a fee to register the case. The brother-in-law was then arrested and charged. Two days after Obelan's arrest, his uncle visited the police post and secured his release. The charges were dropped. Obelan's uncle happened to be the village council chairman. Akol accused the chairman of bribing the officer-in-charge at the police post. After this accusation the case very quickly moved away from its concern with the alleged beating of Atim Betty; instead, Akol's lack of respect for the village council chairman was soon under the spotlight.

Two days after Obelan's release, Akol was summoned to appear before the man he had accused. The chairman then charged Akol on the technicality of not having asked his office for a letter before going to the police, though this procedure was not always followed. By way of punishment Akol was fined USh15,000 ($9) and a goat (the fine was later reduced to USh12,500 ($7) and he did not have to hand over a goat).[38] Akol was understandably unhappy about the case and what seemed to him the high-handed reaction of the village chairman, who was not only judge and jury, but also served as his own plaintiff. To me, as an outsider, the case against Akol appeared to be spurious and was an unhelpful diversion from the more important

---

37 Case evidence was pieced together through an interview with Akol Stanislas (14 January 2003) and through earlier reports on the problems with other villagers. Discussions were had with Apio Janet Loy (19 March 2002) and with the village council chairman (25 September 2002). Details of the case were also worked through in informal discussions with his friends among the bicycle taxi men (8 May 2002; 8 November 2002; 15 November 2002). The court records of the village council chairman were consulted, though it should be noted that the police post was unwilling to release any documentary evidence related to the case.

38 This practice of imposing heavy fines which are later reduced was common to the different courts in the area. This was, perhaps, because the later renegotiation of the fine was a way of bridging the division that the case brought between the judge and the guilty party.

question of how to deal with Akol's brother-in-law Obelan and the charge of wife-beating.

And yet, to the majority of those I consulted, the way the case turned out was not that remarkable, nor was the treatment of Akol seen to be particularly unfair. The background against which the case was understood was emphatically coloured by the violence of the recent past. Aside from the general convention in Teso society that young men should be respectful to old men, Akol's actions provoked memories of the Teso Insurgency. The charge that he had proved himself wilful, and had disregarded the authority of an established institution, meant that he was aligned with the sorts of disrespectful behaviour associated with the rebels. His actions confirmed a popular image of young men as difficult and stubborn, and, in this light, the decision of the village council chairman was not seen as particularly unjust or unfair. The decision to fine Akol was supported not only by other older men in the village, but also by Akol's younger friends. In the words of one of his peers, 'we know that he has been foolish and that he needs to learn how to behave'.

Many aspects of Akol's case are echoed in that of Okelai Samuel, discussed in Chapter 6. Okelai was also seen as an ambitious and independent-minded man, and the decision of the village court went against him in his case with his stepmother, Apulugeresia. Both cases suggest the desire to punish younger men who were felt to be wilful, and there were vested interests in seeing that the political and economic influence of such men was curtailed. That said, it is also important to note the care with which the village council chairman pieced together the decision against Akol. 'Big men' in the village were loath to provoke more hostility than was needed.

Case 2: Omagor Alfred vs the Village

In what follows it is possible to see the *relative* importance of the council chairman: by this I mean the extent to which the authority of the village court depended on the cooperation of other institutions, such as churches and *atekerin*. The case concerns an older man, Omagor Alfred, who was troublesome and wealthy. His wealth meant that Omagor could push the case up to the sub-county court, where he obtained a more favourable opinion than he got from the village court. Even so, the situation eventually turned against Omagor because the decision reached by the village court was regarded as more legitimate in Oledai. The point of the case is to show that the village court was powerful, in part, because it was embedded in the broader social landscape.

In May 2002, the sub-parish chairman appointed Omagor Alfred as secretary of the village council.[39] Omagor was also serving on the *ateker*

---

39 Much of the information for the story of Omagor Alfred comes from a discussion with Tukei Kosiya and Kokoi Magret (11 March 2002). There were also interviews

committee of Ogoria, and had recently retired from the job of police assistant for the neighbouring county of Serere. In many respects he was in a position to serve out his remaining years as a 'big man', with his prominence and wealth granting him considerable status. Yet he was a controversial figure, involved in a number of disputes, the most contentious of which was over land.

Omagor tried to claim title to four gardens (*amisirin*) which were also claimed by two younger men. These men had left the area in the late 1980s after the death of their father during the insurgency. Their mother had died in childbirth, and their father's sister, Akia Melissa, had come to the village to take them to be raised elsewhere. In recent times, however, she and her nephews had decided to return to the area to claim (on behalf of the young men) the land that had once belonged to Akia's brother. But Omagor had been farming the land in her absence, and Akia and her nephews found themselves in the middle of a conflict. Although both sides in the dispute agreed that Omagor had been acting as a caretaker, he suggested that in their long absence the nephews had given up any claim to the land.

The by-laws of the various *atekerin* in the area offered only suggestions as to who was right. More usually when a father died, the wife would be left to raise the children with the support of a levirate (a male member of the clan, appointed to be responsible for the wife and children after the death of the first husband). But in the case of Omagor and Akia there was no clear precedent; Akia was an aunt, not the mother, and her nephews had been living away from the land they hoped to inherit.

As the dispute developed public sentiment went against Omagor. Though he was aggrieved that these young men had returned to the village, many parishioners felt that the land belonged to the younger men and said so in church, drinking groups, and neighbourly conversations. One of the things that went against Omagor was the fact that he was a wealthy man, and his perceived greed offended the fairly strong belief in the idea that all men were entitled to some sort of inheritance.[40] There was also Omagor's own history as a troublesome man. He was an unpopular figure, and had already been drawn into a number of smaller conflicts, some of which involved accusations of witchcraft. His former career as a policeman did not endear him to villagers either. When the time came to settle the dispute, a number of elders of the *ateker* supported the claims of the nephews; they sent the agreement to the village council chairman to be stamped and from there

---

with Omagor Alfred (21 March 2002) and Akia Melissa (24 March 2002). The case came up in interviews with the village council chairman, Akorikin John Vincent (21 August 2002); the *ateker* elder Odongo Emmanuel (10 October 2002); Okalebo Lawrence (12 September 2002); Ibuchet Max (9 January 2003); Aguti Jennifer (27 August 2002); and the *ateker* leader Ichodio Stephen (30 August 2002). The records of the village council chairman were also consulted.

40 Omagor's household was ranked forty-seventh out of 126 in terms of asset wealth.

taken to the sub-county for the record – recognising that the case needed strengthening through the invocation of governmental authority.

But Omagor refused the decision of the *ateker*. The case then had to be referred to the village council, and was heard on 13 November 2001. The council chairman felt compelled to uphold the decision taken by the *ateker*. In this it is possible to see how the village court drew on its sympathetic relationship to other, non-governmental, forms of organisation. (Indeed the authority of the *ateker* court was such that Akorikin John Vincent decided against Omagor even though Omagor was his secretary on the village council.) Omagor refused Akorikin's judgement and asked that his case be sent up to the sub-county court, where money rather than precedent held sway. This time the judge favoured Omagor.

At this point in the case what can be said is that the sub-county had made it possible for Omagor to purchase a decision that could not be bought in the village. But, as Christian Lund demonstrates in his work on land disputes in West Africa, the fact that individuals are able to achieve formal settlements higher up the governmental system does not necessarily mean that these decisions correspond to what happens on the ground (Lund 1998: 12–14). Omagor's wilfulness, and his attack on what was deemed to be a more peaceable consensus reached in the village, made him an isolated figure. There was little chance of his now being able to put together favourable judgements. The fact that the sub-county court was *de jure* superior to the *ateker* or village court mattered less than the more mundane truth that Omagor had to live out his retirement, *de facto*, in the village.

Later in the year, an accusation of adultery was brought against Omagor. This was understood to be a further sign of his lack of respect (the charge was particularly offensive to the growing religious constituency in the village). Adultery cases had no place in the sub-county court, and the judge refused to hear the case, leaving Omagor to accept whatever decision was reached in the village. He was fined USh150,000 ($86) and, in reaction to his defeat, resigned from the village council.

From these two rather different cases it is possible to see that the village council mattered as an arena for dealing with disputes. The council's work was much more the image of the history of the village and a reflection of particular concerns than a version of recent government legislation. Despite the language of reform emanating from above, the village council was a conservative thing and continued to borrow from its earlier incarnation as a court. The council was not, as the literature tries to argue, significant for its role as part of a revitalised state bureaucracy (Wunsch and Otte-moeller 2004; Saito 2003), nor was it something that can be dismissed as the tail-end of the government system (Tukahebwa 1998). It is true that for people living in Oledai the village council mattered in ways that reflected a certain parochialism, and yet in this parochialism were ways of dealing with significant social and political concerns.

CONCLUSION

Earlier in the chapter, I observed the ways in which the state's coercive role during the colonial period – clearing by-ways, collecting taxes, forcing the cultivation of cotton, settling down the population – was, to some extent, mitigated by the institutionalisation of a village court. The court functioned as a relatively autonomous arena where disputes could be settled, away from the gaze of the parish chief. The autonomy of the village court, its dependence on the actions of villagers rather than government officials, suggests why it has persisted in recent years despite the withdrawal of other aspects of the local government system. Its survival is both a comment on the durability of local forms, and an indication of what might be maintained in places where the state has otherwise gone away.

Running through this essentially historical analysis there is also a broader thesis concerning the withdrawal of the state from the countryside. The increasing extraversion of the Ugandan government and the close relationship between Museveni's administration and the international community has turned government structures upwards and outwards. The livelihoods of civil servants, at all levels of the system, have come to depend more and more on funding from above, and less and less on the ability to extract taxes or labour from below. Civil servants and politicians in Kumi District have been drawn towards the uneven, and often erratic, patronage of the central government. The incomes generated from attending workshops, managing development schemes, or through simply maintaining a close relationship to those higher up, has far exceeded what could be gained from maintaining a close relationship with the countryside. The paradox, of course, is that the state has been extraverted at a time when – in formal terms, at least – power has been decentralised and democratised.

What persisted in Oledai, despite this pattern of government withdrawal, was the village court. The council chairman sat in judgement and listened to disputes, and did this by himself rather than as head of a ten-member committee. This council-as-court was not something brought in by the National Resistance Movement, nor was it best understood as a departure from what had been there in the past. Instead the court was better understood in terms of the history of local political institutions and past versions of the state in rural Teso.[41]

It may well be that state retreat is not at all an exceptional experience in rural Africa. As James Ferguson argues, Africa has seen its politics and economics narrow around a few resource-rich places in recent years (2006:

41 For a discussion of the tensions between different versions of the state in Africa, see Suzette Heald's work among the Kuria in Kenya (2006).

204). Since the late 1980s a number of enclaves have developed in Uganda – the wealthy expatriate suburbs of Kampala, a handful of international hotels, a number of development projects, and clinics where international pharmaceutical companies trial new drugs – that depend on external sources of funding. Investments do not 'flow' into Africa; rather, capital 'hops, neatly skipping over most of what lies in between'; and this absence of capital in the countryside also leads to the absence of aspects of the state bureaucracy (Ferguson 2005: 379). This is a very different way of imagining the continent than the 'state-society' approach favoured by most. The following chapter looks at a new form of Christianity, and takes us further towards understanding what developments may matter in a place where key elements of the state bureaucracy have withdrawn.

Plate 5 A shebeen on the outskirts of Oledai

The shebeen was situated near to the Pentecostal Assemblies of God (PAG) church. Later on in Chapter 5, I discuss how men drinking at the shebeen would laugh at Omadi John Francis, a born-again Christian, because his church made him sit outside the building as penance for adultery.

5

THE PENTECOSTAL CHURCH

In her 1968 study of village politics in Teso Joan Vincent did not dwell upon the role of churches.[1] *African Elite* discussed churches only in terms of party political loyalties. Christianity was best understood as an imported ideology, relevant for those who wanted a career in the higher reaches of the civil service, largely unimportant for those who remained in the village (Vincent 1968: 34). The Iteso, with their history of migration and pastoralism, were ill-suited to the formal hierarchies required by the Catholic and Anglican mission societies and this structural mismatch weakened the overall work of the churches. Louise Pirouet's study of the development of Christianity in early colonial Teso suggested that Christianity was shallow, dependent on the activities of missionaries, and much less successfully acculturated than in other parts of Uganda (Pirouet 1978: 169–89). Pirouet had the following to say on the state of the churches in Teso in 1978: their 'weakness is abundantly clear, and the widespread lack of devotion or even of interest in the church are the despair of the local clergy and the missions alike' (Pirouet 1978: 188).

By the time I visited Oledai things had changed. Churches were an integral part of village life, one of the main avenues through which people's ideological, social and economic concerns were expressed and organised. Though churches have been ignored in much contemporary writing on Teso society (cf. Henriques 2002; de Berry 2000; Zistel 2002) and have been sidelined in much of the burgeoning literature on Uganda's civil society (Karlström 1999, 2004; Tripp 2000) they were central to village life in Oledai. The physical geography of the village tells us of their significance.[2] Villagers congregated in churches, and these grass-thatched buildings were the only purposely designed public structures in the village (the village

---

1 It may be that Vincent's study was a reflection of a time when the regional economy was focused on the production of cotton, and the local political economy was more easily connected to changes in the national political economy, pushing churches to the background of village life.

2 One can see the desire to avoid discussing the significance of churches in Mikael Karlström's work on rural politics in Buganda. In his 2004 study, Karlström looked at the revivalist movements of the 1930s as less significant than renovations in customary rituals (Karlström 2004: 600–3), while his earlier essay on civil society in Buganda bypassed the role of churches (1999).

court met in the home of the council chairman). Church congregations met regularly, collected money, and offered places where political and religious concerns could be discussed.[3] All of the households claimed affiliation to one Christian denomination or other, even if they did not attend church on a regular basis.

Nowhere was the importance of Christianity more obviously demonstrated than in the growth of Pentecostal Christianity. By the time I arrived in Oledai eleven per cent of household heads confessed allegiance to the Pentecostal Assemblies of God (PAG), while the proportion of Sunday worshippers attending the PAG church – as a percentage of the total number of active worshippers in the village – was much higher.[4]

In the following chapter, I explain how the growth of Pentecostalism, a seemingly isolationist and oppositional form of Christianity, was central to broader developments in the sub-parish. Part of the significance of Pentecostalism came from the way it offered places for retreat and personal transformation. But another part of Pentecostalism's significance came from the way it allowed church members the means of engaging in village life in new ways. The church opened up new career paths to certain individuals, while others used the church as one more arena for settling disputes. Becoming a born-again Christian changed one's profile and this mattered not only within church, but also in the village. The church was part of a broader social landscape.

To explain the significance of the Pentecostal Assemblies of God, I discuss the nature of Pentecostalism, and the importance of Pentecostal revivalism in Africa. I then look at the particular context of rural Teso, where Pentecostalism took on significance during the insurgency years of the late 1980s and early 1990s. There follows a discussion of the way the church was incorporated into village life in the second half of the 1990s, with Pentecostalism adding to and complicating the way life was organised in Oledai. This point is illustrated through examples where church members use their religious identity in the course of everyday activities, such as developing a political career in the village, or settling a land dispute in church. But the chapter also recognises the ways in which Pentecostalism retained something of its isolationism, with women using the church as a distinct and separate space where they could bring about changes in the domestic sphere. In other words, Pentecostalism mattered not only in

---

3 By contrast Kevin Ward comments on the remarkable persistence of churches in the region despite the violence of the insurgency and the weakness of formal clerical structures (Ward 1995: 102).

4 The total number of household heads claiming affiliation with the PAG church was fourteen out of 126 (11 per cent). The number of Church of Uganda (Anglican) households was twenty-five (20 per cent), and the number of Catholic households eighty-seven (69 per cent). The actual attendance figures, in terms of numbers of households turning up to Sunday service were Pentecostal fourteen (22 per cent); Anglican twenty (31 per cent); Catholic thirty-one (48 per cent).

church, but also in public and at home, and the chapter shows how the church, as an institution and as a set of religious beliefs, created a range of new possibilities.

THE NATURE OF PENTECOSTALISM

Pentecostal churches have made enormous inroads into political life in Africa, and much of the developed and developing world, over the past two decades. The changing religious landscape of the continent represents, perhaps, the most significant ideological and political reformation of recent years (Gifford 1998: 21). As David Maxwell points out, Pentecostal congregations 'have mushroomed in a context of state-contraction, neo-liberal economics, poverty and growing political turmoil', and a link can be made between spiritual revival and the sense of crisis or insecurity that has enveloped that sphere of politics normally dominated by 'the state' (Maxwell 2006: 411). In urban areas, Pentecostal congregations have drawn in members of Africa's elite (and those who aspire to join the elite). A number of born-again churches have presented a doctrine of unfettered accumulation, a 'prosperity Gospel' in tune with the extreme economic possibilities of liberalism. This 'prosperity Gospel' has legitimised the growing gap between Africa's urban elite and the rest of the population (Hackett 1995).[5]

At the opposite end of the spectrum there are a number of more conservative Pentecostal churches, often mission-based, at their strongest in rural areas, where much greater commitment is shown to dealing with questions of physical security and bodily health: 'members of these churches are looking to their leaders for protection against angry spirits and witchcraft and provision of fertility, healing, work and stable marriages' (Maxwell 2006: 416). The Pentecostal Assemblies of God in Oledai can be placed within this second strand. The church focuses on spiritual gifts and acts of sociality rather than any sense of imminent wealth.[6] As a woman congregant commented:

> The Church has made people more peaceful. There is no fighting among us when you compare us to those who don't believe. The Bible teaches us that when you are beaten you should turn the other cheek, and that has made us have fewer conflicts, both at home and with our

---

5 In Nigeria the success of this 'prosperity Gospel' can be related to the experience of massive oil wealth at a time of political liberalisation (Ukah 2003). In other parts of Africa, the emphasis on sanctifying the accumulation of wealth has worked as a corollary to the economic inequalities that arise in places where international development agencies are active.
6 According to the World Christian Encyclopaedia, the Pentecostal Assemblies of God were first established in Uganda in 1935, an offshoot of the Pentecostal Assemblies of God in Kenya (Barrett et al. 2000: 765). The Encyclopaedia also records the membership of the PAG church in Uganda in 2002 as 40 per cent Iteso, a reflection of the strength of the church in the east of the country.

neighbours. When a neighbour falls sick we go to help them, bringing water.[7]

What made the PAG church in Oledai identifiably different from other churches in the area was the nature of Pentecostal worship. When compared to the rather formulaic Catholic Mass, or the Ancient and Modern sonorities of the Anglican Eucharist, Pentecostal worship was a more participatory and engaging sort of liturgy than could be found in the historic mission churches (see also Gifford 1998: 169). Though church services in the PAG church lacked the vitality and improvisation of some of Africa's more radical Pentecostal or African Independent churches, villagers regarded Pentecostalism as something quite different from what they could observe in the other Christian denominations. The Sunday service lasted longer, while the liturgy and singing were more obviously personalised and directed towards the concerns of church members. Throughout the week one could see the commitment of Pentecostal Christians in a roster of activities. On Tuesdays there were fasting prayers for all church members, the youth met on Wednesdays, the women on Fridays and students on Saturdays; the Sunday service was preceded by a meeting of 'prayer warriors' and followed by choir practice. In addition there were a number of 'cell' meetings held by a smaller number of Pentecostals who lived close to each other.[8] Not only were meetings at church much less likely to be postponed than similar gatherings in the Catholic or Anglican churches, but the level of commitment expressed within these meetings was of a different order.

What was most obviously striking to an outsider, such as myself, were the rules and observances that were meant to guide Pentecostal Christians. Pentecostal Christians were only allowed to marry someone who was 'saved' (or on the path to salvation). Women were not allowed to take an 'heir' (a second husband from the husband's clan, should the first husband die). The church also demanded that its members refrained from using traditional medicine.[9] The church asked that its members should test for HIV prior to marriage; and they had a rule that those free of the virus should not marry an infected person (this position was somewhat confused by the argument that intense prayer could reverse illnesses). In a less than subtle way they challenged many of the conventions or traditions of life in the area.

There were also prohibitions that marked out one Pentecostal denomi-

---

7 Interview with Akello Joyce Mary, 7 October 2002. Akello was a former women's leader of the PAG church, residing in Agolitom sub-parish.

8 Indeed, given the levels of participation required of born-again Christians, and their long history in the Teso region, it is surprising to find Suzanne Zistel remarking that: 'it is amazing to realise that in the most remote areas [in Teso] people know more about the Pentecostal church than about national politics' (Zistel 2000: 148).

9 The use of traditional medicine carried with it the obvious implication of having visited a witchdoctor.

nation from another. Ngora sub-county offered a home to a number of different Pentecostal churches. The Christ Disciples church, in nearby Agolitom, accepted that only 'prophets' of the church had the gift of speaking in tongues.[10] The Church Foundation Ministry congregation, in the parish of Tididiek, had a rule that women should not wear earrings and should not braid or style their hair. Rules and observances formed part of a well-regulated internal church culture:

> We have rules. For us in the PAG church our rules are well-known. Once you are saved you are not to behave like the non-believers, so you are not to drink *ajon* [locally brewed millet beer], you should not smoke cigarette, and so forth.[11]

As the above quote suggests, the most significant restriction Pentecostal Christians placed on themselves was the prohibition on drinking alcohol. Pentecostal Christians had no clearer way of separating themselves from the lives of other villagers, as beer drinking remained at the heart of life for many. The importance of beer extended across economic, social and political spheres (Henriques 2002: 182). For women, the brewing and sale of beer provided some sort of independent household income, even if their husbands tried to get hold of this money (de Berry 2000: 144; Orone and Pottier 1993). Across the board, beer offered an obvious avenue for social-ising and sharing and was proffered as a medium of celebration, commis-eration and negotiation (Henriques 2002: 168–72; Karp 1978: 97). While drunkenness was bound up with acts of violence, beer drinking also had its ceremonious aspects and could serve as the means for making peace. Beer was served after the settlement of a court case, and offered as a way of commiserating at funerals. For Ivan Karp, at least, '[T]he very definition of a neighbour [for the Iteso] … is associated with the sharing of beer' (Karp 1978: 89).

The above discussion would suggest that Pentecostalism was a more self-consciously radical form of Christianity than found in Anglicanism or Catholicism, and yet it is important, early on in the chapter, to realise that the PAG church had become a less remarkable presence in the sub-parish over time. Even though Pentecostal Christians had given up alcohol, did not smoke, typically married within the church, and avoided using tradi-tional medicine, the church was not separated from mainstream society to the extent observed by other ethnographers (Laurent 2001; van Dijk 1998). The clearest demonstration of the incorporation of Pentecostalism into village life, in the light of what has just been said, was the way fellow

---

10 The gift of 'speaking in tongues', one of the gifts of the Holy Spirit at Pentecost, gives Pentecostalism its name.

11 Akol Jane, a PAG church member, interviewed on 4 September 2002, Oledai sub-parish.

villagers offered tea alongside beer at burials and after court sessions. This was a fairly recent innovation. But there were also other examples, such as the inclusion of Pentecostals on *ateker* committees. With this story of gradual incorporation in mind, the following section traces the shifting role of Pentecostalism in the area, and observes the way a once isolated institution had become integrated into life in the village.

PENTECOSTALISM IN THE TESO REGION
A Marginal Presence

Only active in Oledai sub-parish since the late 1980s, Pentecostalism has nonetheless had a presence in eastern Uganda since at least the 1930s, led by missionaries from the Canadian Assemblies of God and the Volksmission of Germany (Barrett et al. 2000: 765). The Pentecostal Assemblies of God, the first church to evangelise in the area, had a presence in Kumi District as far back as the 1960s. As with many of Africa's Pentecostal churches, the Pentecostal Assemblies of God appear only to have made serious headway in more recent times. The Kumi area was only established as a 'seer' early in the 1970s (meaning that only by this date was the church capable of organising its own evangelical work).

To understand the special status accorded Pentecostalism in Teso it is important to appreciate the isolated position of born-again Christians during the years of the Amin government. Under Amin, the Ugandan state made an aggressive, if erratic, attempt at controlling public life (Southall 1980; Ward 1995: 81–3). However 'unsteady' the state appeared to be, Idi Amin's government was obsessed with controlling life in Uganda. Nelson Kasfir describes the politics of the period as 'departicipation' brought about by state restrictions on the extent to which individuals could choose to organise outside its structures (Kasfir 1976: 14). The concept of departicipation applies particularly well to the strained relationship between church and state. Amin prohibited all Christian denominations, except the Church of Uganda (Anglican), the Roman Catholic Church, and the small Orthodox congregation in Kampala, with the 1977 order banning such long-established groups as the Pentecostal Assemblies of God, the Seventh Day Adventists, the Salvation Army, and the Bahá'í (Southall 1980: 634; see also Gifford 1998: 116).[12]

At the local level the policy pronouncements of the government had certain tangible effects. Pentecostal congregations continued to meet in the villages, but their position could be exploited by those who were not 'saved'.

---

12 Amin's own biases added to this pattern of exclusion, with Islam being elevated to the same status as Christianity, and Friday becoming a day of prayer. A small number of Muslims benefited from certain policies such as the allocation of expropriated Asian businesses after 1972 (Pirouet 1980) – though most Muslims, like most other Ugandans, benefited little from Amin's time in office.

In the Teso region, where the Pentecostal Assemblies of God maintained some sort of presence in the countryside, those who worshipped in the born-again style were easily identified. In an interview with Akello Joyce Mary, an older woman from the village of Agolitom and an active member of a Pentecostal church, she spoke of the persecution. Her congregation was rounded up and taken off to the sub-county headquarters:

> We were in church. Some people were cooking porridge. But at the time when the porridge was ready, we were seized. We did not even finish the kitchen work.
>
> They tied us with ropes. All of us. When we reached the sub-county we were told to pick cotton, as the sub-county chief was not there. When he returned he told his men [security officers] to get sticks. He argued with us, and said that we were against the government. The soldiers beat us with the sticks until the sticks were made useless by the beatings.[13]

Villagers spoke of how Pentecostal Christianity was placed on the margins of village life, popular only with those who welcomed the isolation of the church. Women and youths made up the bulk of church membership in these years.[14] Of the women who joined the church, many saw the prohibition on alcohol as a possible means of dealing with violence within the home, while the Pentecostal opposition to the practice of leviration (the taking of a brother-in-law as a second husband, after the death of the husband) meant that widows joined the church as a way of escaping some of these customary obligations (see Christiansen (2008) for similar stories among PAG congregants in the Samia region to the south). Among younger people, Pentecostalism was popular with those who saw themselves as educated or more 'modern', those who claimed to be less attached to the traditions or conventions of village life. These various oppositional reasons for joining a Pentecostal church are part of what Birgit Meyer means when she writes of Pentecostalism's 'break with the past' (Meyer 1998: 318–19). Meyer's work links up with a number of other authors who have emphasised the way born-again Christianity allows church members to separate themselves from society (Laurent 2001; van Dijk 1998).

A significant observation made within the literature on Pentecostalism – one that will be taken up in the remaining chapters – concerns the ways in which born-again Christians challenge accepted notions of community, kinship and tradition. Becoming 'born again' means joining a new family, one bound together by faith. Within the community of the 'saved' there is

---

13 From an interview with Akello Joyce Mary, 7 October 2002.
14 The role of women in the early uptake of new Christian movements, and their subsequent demotion in the interests of men, is documented elsewhere (see, for example, Peel 2002).

often a strong opposition to past relationships, as these relationships are often seen as a vehicle for sin or a sense of personal misfortune. Meyer writes of Pentecostal discourse in the context of Ghana as fostering the idea that becoming born-again makes 'a complete break with the past' (Meyer 1998: 318–19). Church members are permitted to cut familial and kinship ties in the knowledge that they are leaving behind the worship of ancestors, gods or the use of traditional medicines. This leads to often radical social actions, precipitating some sort of retreat from wider society. This has been described, in notional terms, as an idea of 'rupture', and Meyer suggests that in the way it attacks the past, Pentecostalism also challenges and changes the way the past is understood, making it a morally suspect thing. The possibility of ill-health, of being susceptible to witchcraft or economic misfortune are taken as a sign of the past catching up with you; that you have not fully committed yourself to a life in Christ.[15] The distinctive identity of Pentecostalism, particularly the emphasis on leaving behind past relationships, achieved a particular significance during the years of insurgency.

Insurgency and Growth

It was only in the late 1980s that the Pentecostal Assemblies of God church came to have influence over large parts of rural Teso. The church was able to make inroads into village communities at a time of increasing violence and insecurity. Pentecostalism offered some sort of spiritual refuge. The idea of 'salvation', with its suggestions of a better life (and afterlife) proved to be a particularly powerful message given the perceived social and moral collapse evident in the violence of rebel groups. The insurgency produced a situation where Christian prayers and fellowship became valuable to those who wished to separate themselves from the violence around them.

At the same time these spiritual gifts were matched by instrumental advantages. Villagers recalled that those who joined the church were less likely to be conscripted into rebel groups, and less likely to be harassed by government soldiers. The different-ness of Pentecostalism, which had made life difficult for church members during the time of Amin, helped to place church members outside the social and political conflicts driving the rebellion in the late 1980s and early 1990s. Rebels were in the business of targeting local 'big men', none of whom were Pentecostal. Younger villagers who did not want to be conscripted into the fighting stood a better chance of being left alone if they presented themselves as committed, born-again Christians.

Conversion emerged as a reaction not only to the bush war, but also to the experience of the internment camps, which provided a setting where people could begin to consider a change in their religious life. The camps

---

15 As Harri Englund similarly suggests: 'the advances made by the Born-Again are often provisional' (Englund 2004: 302).

served as a useful space where a number of villagers could come to worship in the Pentecostal style.[16] Because a large number of people were concentrated in a small area, and because life was largely reduced to a pattern of sitting and waiting, evangelism was more straightforward. The PAG church prayed in the same building as the Catholic and Anglican congregations, and this meant that 'unsaved' villagers had the possibility of comparing Pentecostalism to other more established churches without having to take the bold step of setting foot in a different building. Another explanation that appeared to be particularly important in the context of Teso society was the shortage of foodstuffs in the camps, as this made the brewing of beer impossible. Though this may seem trivial, the impossibility of drinking beer made it easier for some to take up the life of a Pentecostal Christian. It was suggested to me that the later return of beer also resulted in a number villagers sliding back out of the church.

As well as the growing familiarity with Pentecostal forms of worship and the absence of beer, the social and psychological dynamics of living in the camps made the message of Pentecostal Christianity compelling. Pentecostals were skilled when it came to articulating a vision of the world that explained the devastation of the insurgency. The millennial elements in Pentecostal teachings, the belief that one should prepare for the life to come, and that the world itself might end, offered a vocabulary that made some sense of the particular situation in which villagers found themselves. At the same time, it can be argued that the advance of Pentecostalism in the late 1980s was not an isolated phenomenon and can be related back to earlier examples of religious revivalism in Uganda which appeared at moments of extreme violence or political dislocation (Vincent 1982: 244–7; Allen 1991; Behrend 1999). The PAG church offered a place of sociality that offered a way of understanding what had happened, and what was to come.

THE INCORPORATION OF PENTECOSTALISM

Since the end of the insurgency in 1993, the role of Pentecostal Christianity in the village has changed. The PAG church has become a more ordinary, more mundane part of village life. The church had, in many ways, become incorporated into the local landscape. Being born-again was less contentious than one would have expected, given the church's many prohibitions. The ordinariness of Pentecostalism was something that came across in interviews with villagers, and could also be observed in the way church members approached the politics involved in court cases or in building up

---

16 Kevin Ward has written of the 'stories of a revival of religious commitment in some of the camps' in the Teso region, but he is writing of the Church of Uganda, which would seem to have been more successful than the Pentecostal churches in the camp at Ngora (Ward 1995: 102).

Table 5.1 Committee positions of Pentecostal Christians in Oledai*

Church member	PAG Church committees	Other committees in the village	Wealth ranking (out of 126)
Oluka Lawrence	Leaders committee Youth committee	Elders committee, Ichaak *ateker*	107
Omadi John Francis	Youth committee Evangelists committee	Vice-chairman, sub-parish council	73
Omureje Charles	Youth committee Evangelists committee		40
Apolot Helen	Chorister	Women's committee, Ichaak burial society	73
Among Helen	Chorister		40
Amulen Jane	Chorister		107
Akello Joyce	Chorister	Women's secretary, Ikures *ateker* committee; husband treasurer of sub-parish council and of Ikures *ateker* committee	25
Auki William	Mobilisers committee	Married to women's secretary, sub-parish council	70

* The table is based on data gathered through the committee membership survey, the social networks survey and interviews with church members.

a political career. Though much of the literature on Pentecostal Christianity has focused on its exclusionary doctrine and taken this as the best indication of how born-again Christians approach political questions, the following examples show Pentecostals engaging in other institutions, including burial societies, the village court, and *ateker* committees.

One obvious explanation for the increasing un-remarkableness of the PAG church was the degree of familiarity non-church members had with the workings of Pentecostalism. By 2002, the grass-thatched church in which Pentecostals prayed had been part of the village for more than a decade, and Pentecostals had been in the village since at least the 1970s. Church-goers included some of the more prominent members of the village, including the vice-chairman of the village council. At the same time, the mainstream Catholic and Anglican congregations, which were at one time hostile to the PAG church – not least because the Pentecostal church poached some of their more diligent members – had made their own accommodation with Pentecostalism. Leaders in the historic mission churches appeared to welcome the spiritual revival brought about by the PAG church, while members of the Catholic and Anglican churches had instituted charismatic groups, appropriating many of the practices found in the PAG church (see Chapter 6).

Perhaps the most straightforward way of demonstrating the incorporation of the church into the broader political field is to look at those villagers who were prominent members of the PAG church in 2002, alongside their participation in other organisations (Table 5.1).

Table 5.1 tells us, in tabular form, that church members were able to sit on other committees in the village, customary as well as governmental. Auki William was married to the women's secretary of the village council, while Akello Joyce was married to a man who was treasurer of the village council and a prominent member of his *ateker*. In other words, being Pentecostal did not mean being precluded from a political career in the village: many of the more prominent members of the church occupied a number of other positions in the village, and Table 5.1 suggests the degree to which it was possible to be born-again while remaining (or even becoming) an active member of the wider community.[17] Omadi John Francis, who provides the subject of a later case study, was vice-chairman of the village council. It is also interesting to observe a wide spectrum wealth among church members. The view that emerges in the literature on Pentecostalism, that Pentecostal churches offer a bounded religious space, is contradicted somewhat by what people did in Oledai.

The following cases take up this point and show the ways in which Pente-costalism was increasingly incorporated into the local political landscape. The first discusses the way the church offered a place from which to become a 'big man' in the sub-parish. The second discusses how a father and son used the church as a place to settle a land dispute. In both cases the church could be said to offer a space that was complemented by the work of other organisations in the sub-parish, such as the village court or the *atekerin*. Both cases suggest the value of approaching church membership as an open-ended business related to life in the village more generally. It is an approach which moves away from simply accepting the view that Pente-costal Christians were only interested in their status as Christians within their church.

---

17 Englund makes a similar point on the possible avenues of incorporation, albeit on a more spiritual plane, when he argues that Pentecostal Christians living in Chinsapo township in peri-urban Lilongwe shared the preoccupation with the Devil that other residents had (Englund 2004: 301–2).

Omadi John Francis: a Pentecostal Christian Becomes a 'Big Man' in the Village[18]

Joan Vincent has written of leadership in the Teso region as the piecing together of a number of political roles across a range of institutions. Taking forward the work of W. Watson, Vincent has discussed the rise of 'big men' in the parish of Bugondo as the result of 'spiralist' practices. By spiralism Vincent means 'progressive ascent through a series of positions in one or more hierarchical structures' (1968: 283). In her analysis the possibilities of advancement depended on connections, and the manner in which an individual carried himself in the village. These personal attributes could be displayed in the different arenas such as the courts, public moots, or *ateker* meetings (Vincent, as we saw at the outset of this chapter, was not so interested in churches). In Oledai sub-parish churches have come to provide a further arena where an ascent could begin.

The following example concerns the way the Pentecostal church served as the starting point for a man's rise through the village hierarchy. The case involves a husband and wife who were able to draw on their membership in the PAG church as a way of becoming 'big men' in the village. They occupied a relatively modest position in terms of their wealth ranking in the village – eighty-eighth out of 126 – and one should regard Omadi John Francis's rise as having economic as well as political possibilities. After working actively in the church Omadi became the vice-chairman of the village council. He had also joined his clan committee, and his wife had become a committee member of the burial society of Ichaak. What was striking about the PAG church was that it was able to feed into a well-established pattern of spiralism with little difficulty.

The chronology behind Omadi's career is interesting in that the first institution in which he gained influence was the church. He had become assembly youth leader late in 1997. When compared with other forms of organisation the PAG church, it is worth noting, was relatively open to ambitious younger men such as Omadi.[19] There were a large number of roles and positions within the church, which encouraged the initiative of

---

18 The case material for Omadi's rise as a 'big man' was drawn from extended interviews with Omadi himself (23 January 2003) and with his wife Apolot Helen (28 January 2003). Omadi's example was also discussed in interviews with the village council chairman (21 August 2002; 30 September 2002), church members, and members of his burial society. Similar cases within the church could be found in the rise to prominence of Akello Joyce, who became women's secretary of the burial society of Ikures (interviewed 24 August 2002), and the career of Oluka Lawrence, who was both treasurer of the church and a member of the elders committee of his *ateker*.

19 This point is also made by Gifford (1998: 171).

its members and, all in all, was a place where the ambitious could gain a foothold on the spiralist ladder.[20]

In the particular context of Oledai the past played its part in Omadi's story. The experience of the insurgency gave a certain significance to his position of youth leader of his church. Omadi's work was to go out into the sub-parish and talk to young men on subjects such as personal salvation, respect for one's elders and the need to stand up to those offering violence. These values were not easy to sell to younger men in the village, as many remembered the insurgency – despite its violence – as a time of opportunity when they could challenge the status of older men. The assembly youth leader's attempts at mediating between older and younger generations thus made him a popular figure among those who feared the potential power of younger men. The fact that he appeared able to earn some measure of respect from younger men added to the esteem in which he was held by older men in the village.

A further reason why the PAG church provided a good entry point into village politics was the way in which Pentecostal Christians had developed a reputation for honesty over the years. The church relied on a rule-based culture, and this set church members apart from the norms or conventions that governed the actions of those who were not among the 'saved'.[21] The ban on drinking alcohol, the opposition to polygamy and the stance against witchcraft made Pentecostalism distinct not only as a faith in church but also as an identity that stood out in other places. Pentecostalism helped broaden the repertoire of political actions available to villagers; church members were able to develop a different sort of reputation in the village, one that emphasised rules and imposed norms.

An example of the rule-based culture of Pentecostalism, and its possible effects, came when Omadi John Francis was accused – by fellow church members – of the sin of adultery.[22] During one of the Sunday services the pastor announced that he wanted to know if it was true that a church

20 The way the PAG church fed into a pattern of spiralism can be contrasted with Pierre-Joseph Laurent's account of the Assemblies of God church in rural Burkina Faso. Where Laurent's example shows the church functioning as a self-sufficient community, opposing existing customary and political practices, and requiring parallel institutions for the management of familial and agricultural relationships (Laurent 1994, 2001: 270–1), the PAG church in Oledai shows Pentecostalism as one among a number of structures through which church members could do things.

21 The economics of Pentecostalism in eastern Uganda is quite distinct from the 'prosperity Gospel' found in urban congregations in Ghana and Nigeria (Hackett 1995; Ukah 2003). While the PAG church leadership collected slightly higher contributions from their members than their Catholic or Anglican counterparts, the money given was never enough to allow the pastor to consider living off church revenues (see Table 7.1 on page 139).

22 The adulterous act was committed with an 'unsaved' woman (church members were unclear as to whether this made his actions worse or not).

member had committed such a sin (rumours had been circulating in church for some time). Omadi confessed, and as penance was asked to stand outside the church for several Sundays, to demonstrate his isolation from God. This punishment was a public humiliation for the vice-chairman, a humiliation not eased by the fact that the church was situated next to a number of drinking huts. Several other 'big men' who had not joined the church would come and sit in these shebeens and mock Omadi (the proximity of the drinking huts to the church building is well illustrated in Plate 5 on page 90). Omadi's submission to church authorities was seen as faintly ridiculous, something of a joke.[23]

And yet, his act of submission demonstrated, in a rather simple way, the fact that Pentecostalism was different, that members of the church asked to be judged by different standards. A consequence of Omadi John Francis's public humiliation was that he was seen as a different sort of man, one with a reputation that was more honest than that of other 'big men' of the sub-parish. The culture of humility within the church marked an obvious departure from the more worldly ways of other politicians. Omadi was less open to accusations of corruption or self-interest and this had consequences not only for his personal standing but also for the institutions in which he held office. As vice-chairman of the village council, his reputation as a somewhat accountable man broadened the legitimacy of the council. Omadi was seen as more humble and more straightforward than some 'big men' of the old school; he was a man who embodied an idea of proper behaviour and respect for authority. Omadi's submission to his church in the adultery case offered an alternative view of how one could be a 'big man' in the sub-parish. His membership in the PAG church made for a reputation which extended across the village as a whole, rather than being confined to Omadi's church.

In its way Pentecostalism could be seen as adding to the life in the village. Prohibitions on alcohol, polygamy and marrying 'out' opened up a more extensive repertoire of possible behaviours. The rule-based culture of the church legitimated new sorts of actions, and offered a new place from which to start climbing the political ladder. The church opened up new ways of doing things.

---

23 Though the problem of adultery was not uncommon in the village, it was rare for the accused to face a public judgement, and unheard of for the accused to be publicly punished in this way.

A Father and Son Settling a Land Dispute in Church[24]

The PAG church in Oledai also offered a place where land disputes could be negotiated and resolved. During the course of the fieldwork, it emerged that some members used the church as a sort of staging ground where they could strengthen their case, building up public support, before going on to the village court. More surprisingly, Pentecostal Christians used the church as a court-like setting where land conflicts could be discussed during the service. The use of the church as a judicial space was a new development in the managing of land conflicts, and would seem to contradict the interests of the village council and the *ateker* courts, which also exercised authority in such disputes (in exchange for a fee). The reasons why the church was able to offer a court-like environment, and why this did not put the church leadership on a path towards conflict with *ateker* elders and the village council chairman, is taken up in this section. The following case also shows how the distinctive identity of Pentecostal Christianity helped establish the church as an effective arena for dispute settlement.

The particular case I discuss concerns the timing and scale of a son's inheritance. In the Teso region it is common for the father to allocate a portion of his assets, most importantly land and cattle, to his sons. The father is meant to do this during his own lifetime, as land and cattle make his son a better candidate for marriage, and also signal his graduation into manhood (Lawrance 1957: 143–4).[25] Despite this well-established convention, questions of inheritance are difficult to manage, and had become more difficult as land and livestock became increasingly scarce. The people living in Oledai sub-parish were still recovering from the insurgency and had to divide the available land between more and more men.

In this case, the son, Okello John, felt that his father, Omoding Justin, had delayed his handing over of land and cattle. Okello raised his grievances with the church pastor and several other prominent Christians. As the dispute involved two born-again Christians, the pastor asked that the case be heard in church, first through prayers of intercession and then through a relatively formal hearing. In this court-like space the father and son

24 The information for this case emerged out of an interview with Omureje Charles, who was not directly involved in the land dispute (interview 9 August 2002). The role of the church in settling conflicts became clearer after this interview, and I spent time visiting the church and engaging with the membership and the leadership. The particularities of the case were also discussed in interviews with the assembly leader, Anguria George William (27 August 2002) and with Omadi John Francis (23 January 2003).

25 Inheritance in Teso is typically patrilineal and patrilocal, with all of the sons inheriting part of the father's land within his own lifetime. The land that the father leaves on his death will then be inherited by the eldest son, who is also expected to take on the father's debts and obligations. If the sons have not reached adulthood by the time of their father's death, the widow is expected to take a levirate, or 'heir', normally the brother of the deceased, to manage the land until the sons come of age.

presented (and called on supporters to validate) their respective positions. This was done in a manner that consciously borrowed from how things were done in the village court. The pastor and church elders counselled the two parties to reach an amicable settlement, though they also suggested that Okello, as the son, had a legitimate case. This favouring of Okello carried considerable weight, in both moral and political terms. The father agreed to the consensus reached in church and signed a settlement that allocated land to his son.

This ability of the church to take on the role of a court was enhanced, no doubt, by the aura of moral probity that united Pentecostal Christians. There was an understanding among church members, including Okello and Omoding, that their faith made them less fractious than other villagers. Pentecostal Christians felt themselves to be in possession of certain gifts, such as an ability to step away from conflicts. As the incident of adultery-spotting showed, in the earlier example, the PAG church membership was also busy promoting a culture of vigilance. There was a keen interest in uncovering conflicts and bringing them to the attention of the church membership.

That the PAG congregation served as a court also draws us into a discussion of the increasing embeddedness of the church in the wider social landscape. I would suggest that the church drew some of its authority from the fact that church members were political actors elsewhere. Those who helped negotiate the above settlement included the vice-chairman of the village council and his wife. There were also two Parent–Teachers Association members who were active in the church, one of whom was treasurer of the village council. Another 'big man', for want of a better term, was the women's representative on the village council. In other words, the judgement reached in church carried the imprimatur of a number of other institutional spaces in the village; the ability of the congregation to put together a workable settlement related not only to the spiritual authority or the internal culture of the church but also to a decision reached in church by a number of villagers.

A pointer to the more general way in which the Pentecostal church had been incorporated into the life of the village came with the eventual inclusion of the village council chairman in the Okello–Omoding land dispute. Once Okello and Omoding had agreed terms, the settlement signed in church was sent on to the chairman, to be stamped and ratified. In the end he received his usual USh5,000 ($3) fee, and kept a record of the dispute and its reso-lution on his books. This meant that if Okello, as the father, chose to take the case to the village court he was likely to receive the decision that was given to him by the church. Aside from the fee, there were other reasons why the village council chairman and the *ateker* elders were not troubled by the role of the church in settling this dispute. First, the Pentecostal church was well-regarded and was afforded a good deal of autonomy. Second, land disputes were troublesome affairs, and the village council chairman was more than happy to see the conflict settled in church.

THE LIMITS TO INCORPORATION

But the above arguments concerning the incorporation of the PAG church should be qualified. Pentecostalism retained a measure of its distinctiveness and continued to be a somewhat difficult faith to follow. Not all church members had the 'big man' credentials of Omadi John Francis, nor were all of those who attended the church men with land disputes to settle. For many members of the church, particularly married women, the value of being born-again continued to relate to the separate and distinctive space provided by the church. In a number of interviews, older women suggested that they had joined the church, not as a means of engaging in the open-ended business of village politics, but rather as a way of effecting more personal transformations. First, there were the sorts of transformations that they felt came from accepting Jesus Christ as their personal saviour. Older women spoke of the help given by younger members of the church with farm work, or with the rethatching of roofs during the dry season:

> The Church organises for young people to come and help people like me build and maintain my house. Yes, they can come and help you with that... The house I am in was built by church members. I was suffering a lot before then, because the rain would come through the roof. I cried up to the day my house was built. My fellow Christians have helped me so much.[26]

Women members of the church also pointed to the way Pentecostalism worked as a basis for change within the home. For married women, the church offered the possibility of dealing with domestic violence by making certain distinctions possible that had been impossible in the past. Despite the fairly conservative doctrinal position of the Pentecostal Assemblies of God regarding the role of women in society, many of the women who joined argued that salvation helped them bring about profound changes.[27] In many salvation stories, Pentecostalism offered the wife the possibility of dealing

26 Taken from an interview with Akello Joyce Mary, a member of the PAG church in Okwii, in neighbouring Agolitom, 7 October 2002. The same point was made in interviews with Asige Martha (22 August 2002) and with Amuge Gabdesia, an older disabled woman, who had benefited from the help of PAG church members even though she had not yet joined the church (22 August 2002).

27 An observation also taken up in Maria Cattell's work among 'charismatic' Anglicans and Catholics among the Samia of western Kenya. In a 1992 article, Cattell shows how Samia women were able to refuse the practice of widow inheritance (leviration) because 'the ability of older women to bring about change in female roles and power is related to their positions in extended families and support from "saved" Christians' (Cattell 1992: 307).

with a husband who drank too much, or a husband who was violent at home. If a wife was 'saved' and was then able to get her husband to join the church, the prohibition on drinking would help to lessen the violence and impoverishment that came from drinking. Women argued that peace at home was visible proof of the presence of Jesus Christ in their lives, and they spoke of the value of the church as something set apart from the village. During a discussion with a group of women, not all of whom were Pentecostal, a man passed by and was given this brief biography:

> ... [t]hat man over there, he got saved. We did not expect such a man to get salvation. He was a drinker, who was poorly turned out, with dirty clothes. He would often fight with his wife and would cause trouble. But since his wife prayed for his salvation none of those things are there. He found Jesus on the very day his wife had fled the house after a beating, now he comes to church and has to follow the life of a proper Christian.[28]

If a woman succeeded in getting her husband 'saved' – though in this there was no guarantee – there was the possibility that the beatings would end.[29] This was due in part to the prohibition on drinking alcohol, and also to the mediation services offered (or imposed) by church leaders. As I have already noted, the Pentecostal Assemblies of God membership took a dim view of homes that appeared to be disorderly, and brought violent or argumentative church members to book. Just as there was a push for inheritance disputes or cases of adultery to be settled from within, so there was a desire to see marital disputes settled within the confines of the church.

Given the advantages that could come from becoming born-again, it is perhaps worth saying something as to the reasons why more women did not join the church. The majority of women in Oledai sub-parish remained loyal to the Catholic or Anglican churches, or did not attend church at all. Many of these women faced similar problems of impoverishment or violence at home. Many gave the reason that getting 'saved' proved to be a costly business. In terms of tackling domestic violence, an obvious problem came

28 This sort of Pentecostal transformation in the domestic sphere was also discussed in interviews with church members, even when they were asked to talk about other topics. Amulen Jane (interviewed 23 August 2002) spoke of the transformation within her own home as a result of her and her husband becoming saved, even though she was asked to discuss the costs and benefits of belonging to the *ateker* of Ichaak. In the neighbouring sub-parish of Agolitom, similar stories emerged in interviews with Atim Emmimah Loy (21 November 2002) and Akello Joyce Mary (7 October 2002).

29 'Unsaved' villagers usually dealt with domestic violence as part of a case brought by the wife's *ateker*, rather than the wife herself. Should the man be found guilty the fine was paid to the in-laws rather than to the wife. If a woman wanted to act independently of the *ateker*, the most common course of action was to walk out of the marital home. This was a difficult action to take, as the woman was expected to leave behind her children.

from the fact that the woman would get 'saved' before the husband. There was no guarantee that the husband would follow: a number of women who had at one time joined the church, in the hope that their husband would later join them, found that the husband refused. This often led to greater discord at home. If a wife refused to brew beer for her husband on the grounds that she was born-again, he could become more violent as a result. The loss of income that was another consequence of giving up brewing and selling beer also made the decision to join the Pentecostal church a difficult one. The benefits of joining had to be calibrated against possible costs.

CONCLUSION

The gradual expansion of Pentecostal churches, which started in Oledai in the mid-1970s, came to affect not only the spiritual and economic well-being of individual villagers but also the wider political landscape.[30] In the cases discussed towards the end of the chapter Pentecostalism did not demand an absolute separation of the life of the 'saved' from the ways of the world. In practical terms the division between Pentecostalism and the wider world was much less significant than is often imagined, and church members remained, or had even *become*, significant players in customary institutions, the court system, and the village council.[31] The PAG church dealt with prosaic, political activities – managing land conflicts, building reputations, becoming a 'big man' – that cut across the work of other institutions, and church members managed to involve these other institutions in the work of the church with little ceremony or fuss. In the fairly familiar environment of the village, the lives of church members were not confined to the church.

As it stood, Pentecostalism both complicated and developed the village; the church mattered more as an addition to the institutional landscape than as a place of opposition and retreat. Despite a doctrinal commitment to withdrawing from possible sites of corruption, church members engaged actively in local politics, and used the institutional space of the church, and the particular status of being 'born again', as a new way of approaching well-established questions over wealth, authority and meaning. What was striking about the church was the ordinariness of Pentecostalism. The tensions that existed between the church – as a certain sort of morally codified institution

---

30 A point developed more extensively in Harri Englund's work on Pentecostalism in Malawi (Englund 2004, 2002) and David Maxwell's work on the Pentecostal churches among the Hwesa of north-eastern Zimbabwe (Maxwell 1999: Chapter 7).

31 In this respect the argument of the chapter refers back to the most important study of religion and politics in rural Uganda, Middleton's *Lugbara Religion* (1960). Middleton went beyond the conventions of his day, and demonstrated that religion was, for the Lugbara, an arena where political competition and religious beliefs were elided, where people vied for access to and control over claims to religious authority (it was more than a system of belief that helped to stabilise the social order).

– and other forms of organisation were not particularly pronounced. The occasional conflicts that engaged the village pastor in a dispute with other local 'big men' were less common than those instances where the village council chairman came into conflict with *ateker* elders. In Oledai, as in much of eastern Uganda, Pentecostal Christians continue to participate in local courts, draw water from the well, and pay fees to burial societies. This was the practical world villagers inhabited, and born-again Christianity, the doctrine of personal salvation, the expressed belief in withdrawing from a world of sin, had to rub along with the economic, social and political necessities that governed life in Oledai.

There is a possible thesis here on the relationship between religious change and social and economic development. Norman Long's work on the 'spirit' of capitalism among Jehovah's Witnesses in rural Zambia in the 1960s, or Terence Ranger's arguments concerning symbolic resistance through religious protest, both capture instances where religious beliefs offer an opportunity to oppose the prevailing political orders (Long 1968; Ranger 1986). In Oledai, Pentecostalism introduced new ways of approaching political and economic questions. And yet, any trend or development should be thought of as contingent. I would argue that part of Pentecostalism's appeal comes through its ability to make sense of changing conditions.[32] The future depended on the broader social and political setting in which church was institutionalised, and this was difficult to predict. Should insecurity return, or should the youth grow frustrated with the church leadership, it is possible, even likely, that the Pentecostal Assemblies of God would emphasise isolation rather than cooperation.[33] Should security persist then the process of incorporation was likely to continue. What is important to observe is the way religious developments played into other transformations. We need to question those studies which manage, intentionally or otherwise, to treat Pentecostal churches as separate places, and religion as a marginal concern in the study of processes of development and change. One only had to look at what was going on in Oledai's Catholic and Anglican congregations to appreciate the influence of Pentecostalism.

32 Though Long placed his Jehovah's Witnesses in a Weberian thesis, suggesting that they would form a new sort of capitalist class, Seur shows that the 'big men' of the 1960s who were not Jehovah's Witnesses had proved themselves adept capitalists (Seur 1992: 133–5). Seur's more cautious view would be supported by Max Weber, who saw the doctrine of Calvinism not as something intrinsic to the future development of capitalism, but simply as the kickstart that got capitalism going (Weber 1985: 181–2). Capitalism was not a religion, in Weber's formulation, rather it had a spirit.

33 By the time I left, a new denomination, the Pentecostal Revival Ministries, had started evangelising in the neighbouring sub-parish, and the Christ Foundation Ministry and Christ Disciple's churches had already set up shop in other parts of Ngora sub-county.

6

THE ANGLICAN AND CATHOLIC CHURCHES

Over the past decade there had also been a period of renewal and reno-vation in the Catholic and Anglican congregations in the village of Oledai. The arrival of the Pentecostal Assemblies of God, discussed in the previous chapter, had been matched, to some extent, by the growth of charismatic forms of worship in the two historic mission churches. Church membership had become more important in defining one's social position, and church leaders had influence over parts of village life which had been off-limits to them in the past. Increasing importance was attached to rules and notions of proper behaviour among practising Christians. This transformation was described in the following terms:

> We have rules now. When a person crosses over to another church and then wishes to return to us ... that is not allowed. If there is some leniency then they will demand that you go to confirmation classes for six months before rejoining. It is only recently that they made those rules like that.[1]
>
> We have rules which are stronger. If a member of our church has committed sins like adultery, theft or heavy drinking then he cannot come and take Communion with us.[2]

At one level, changes to the religious life of the village can be under-stood as part of a wider renaissance in Christianity in Africa, an instance to match earlier moments of religious reformation (Welbourn 1961).[3] The changes that had taken hold in Oledai were also a local variant of the Pente-costal revival in Teso. Pentecostalism had come to affect what went on in the Catholic and Anglican congregations. There were charismatic groups which borrowed from the particular form Pentecostalism had taken in the region. There were also borrowings in terms of Pentecostal theology. The idea of having a more personal relationship with God, and using that rela-

1 Interview with Amulen Immaculate, a member of St Peter's Catholic Church, Agolitom, 11 October 2002.
2 Interview with Echai Charles, a member of Kaderun Anglican Church, Oledai sub-parish, 10 September 2002.
3 Eastern Uganda has been at the tail-end of earlier religious movements, notably the Malakite movement of the 1910s and 1920s and the reformist *Balokole* movement of the Church of Uganda (Vincent 1982; Ward 1989).

Plate 6 A village church from the neighbouring sub-parish of Agolitom

Church members were keen to replace grass-thatched churches, such as the one in the photograph, with more permanent burnt-brick and metal-roofed structures.

tionship to influence public and private conduct, were developments which cut across the different denominations in the village. This chapter seeks to establish the importance of the wider reach of Pentecostalism.

In what follows I also demonstrate the degree to which the renewal and renovation observed in the different churches related to developments elsewhere in the village. Pentecostalism was only one among a number of influences. Developments in more mundane, everyday forms of social interaction also explain why the two historic mission churches were more important in political and social terms than they had been in the past. The influence of the lay reader or the local catechist related directly to the growing importance of burials, and burials were primarily the responsibility of burial societies. Burial societies were new institutions, and are discussed in greater detail in Chapter 7. The point to make here is that burial societies were similarly concerned with questions of propriety and public displays of respectability. There was a complementary aspect to the work of different organisations in the village. Changes in church mirrored changes elsewhere.

In suggesting the equivalence of churches with other forms of organisation in the village the chapter develops an argument already made in the previous chapter on Pentecostalism. In looking at churches as part of a wider social field it is possible to move away from their usual treatment as separate places. The focus on Pentecostalism in the literature on African Christianity has, in recent years, encouraged a view of churches as singular, self-contained communities. As Birgit Meyer observes, in her overview of writings on Christianity in Africa, the literature is populated by studies of single movements or churches; there has been less interest in looking at how churches relate to other sorts of social organisation (Meyer 2004: 251).[4] In contrast to this somewhat limited focus, I look at churches as one element in a broader landscape, exploring the influence of Pentecostalism on the historic mission churches, and at the significance of customary and government institutions in shaping the work of all the different churches in Oledai.

I would like to make a final point by way of introduction. When reading the chapter it is important to remember the intimacy of the world within which change was taking place. Oledai sub-parish numbered 126 households as of 1 January 2002 and had a total population of 862.[5] The sub-parish was poor, even by the standards of Uganda. The majority of households were reliant on agriculture and the local government structures discussed in Chapter 3 were shown to have done little to develop the place in recent

4 This singular approach has been particularly well served by the advent of Pentecostalism. The presumption that Pentecostal theology, with its focus on separation or isolation, is best approached through looking only at Pentecostal churches has further encouraged introspection.

5 Data relating household numbers and church attendance figures are drawn from a survey carried out across all 126 heads of household between October 2001 and January 2002.

years. In contrast to the versions of Christianity that could be observed in urban centres, the theological commitment to joining a particular religious community did not necessarily translate into a separate social life. Within this poor, under-administered setting the three congregations of Anglican, Catholic and Pentecostal were relatively influential, and church members were central figures in village affairs. Active membership was divided between twenty households (Anglican), thirty-one households (Catholic) and fourteen households (Pentecostal).[6]

The chapter is organised as follows. First, a discussion of the history of Catholic and Anglican churches in the region emphasises the gap between the clerical bureaucracy and the lay church. A discussion of earlier moments of revival in the region is introduced to suggest the gradual acculturation of Christianity at the local level in Teso (despite the mismatch between mission structures and Iteso society). I then discuss the development of charismatic groups in the village, and the tightening of rules regarding church membership. As I have already suggested, these developments should be seen as a response to the success of Pentecostal Christianity and set against the experience of the insurgency. The chapter illustrates these general observations by looking at what these broad changes might mean for individuals. First, I give an account of the burial service of Edotun Jackson, during which the words of the Anglican lay reader helped to strengthen the position of Edotun's mother in a land dispute. Second, I offer a discussion of a year in the life of Okelai Samuel, a young man from the neighbouring sub-parish of Agolitom who used the competition between the different churches as a way of becoming a 'big man' in his community.

THE HISTORIC MISSION CHURCHES IN TESO

When religion is discussed in Uganda it is normally in relation to the confessional divide between Catholics and Anglicans that emerged at the beginning of the colonial period (Reid 2002: 5–7). There has been a particular interest in the legacy of this division for the post-colonial high politics of the Ugandan state. The wars that shook Buganda towards the end of the nineteenth century have offered an obvious point of departure for those interested in studying the links between religious competition and the development of state politics (Hansen 1984: 12–13; Low 1971: Chapter 1). The factions at the court of the Kabaka were divided between the *Bangareza* (English) and *Bafaransa* (French) groups, and this division provided the basic template for the way religious adherence was understood in relation to state power. The 'English' faction associated with the Church Missionary Society was able to overcome the 'French', associated with the Catholic missionaries of the *Société de Notre-Dame d'Afrique*, and

---

6 According to the 2002 national census the Iteso were divided: Catholic, 45 per cent; Anglican, 40 per cent; and Pentecostal 9 per cent.

the triumph of the *Bangareza* was credited mainly to the religious preferences of British colonial agents. Christianity was there at the founding of the Ugandan state, and for much of Ugandan history Catholicism has been identified with the politics of opposition, Anglicanism with the prejudices of those in power.

The fragmented nature of the Ugandan polity in the early 1960s, with very different societies and very different experiences of colonial government, made this simple division between Protestants and Catholics the main cleavage in determining party-political loyalties (Low 1971: 229–31). The Democratic Party (DP) had a strongly Catholic following, while the Uganda People's Congress (UPC) had an Anglican base. In Buganda, where the UPC lacked a strong following, a third party, the royalist Kabaka Yekka (literally, 'the Kabaka [king] above all else'), provided a political outlet for Anglicans. These divisions, as Paul Gifford reminds us, were entrenched by an education system which was only taken over by the national government in the 1950s (Gifford 1998: 113). The ingrained nature of this divide could be seen in the way that the abbreviation DP came to stand for *Dini ya Papa* (party of the Pope) while the UPC were the 'United Protestants of Canterbury' (Mittelman 1975: 65; Welbourn 1961: 1).[7]

In what follows I would like to turn away from national party politics and attend instead to the history of the historic mission churches in the Teso region. The first section details the experience of missions in the region in the early colonial period. It is, in a sense, the history of the attempt by mission societies to build up religious bureaucratic structures in the Teso region, a project that later came to be regarded as only partially successful. The second section looks at the history of revival movements in Uganda and reminds us of the significance of lay-led forms of Christianity. The third section conveys something of my impression of the condition of Anglican and Catholic church bureaucracies in the Teso region during my stay, with a focus on the 'NGO-isation' of church structures in the 1980s and 1990s. Running through the three sections is the story of an increasingly weak church administration, and a gradual acculturation of Christianity at the village level.

The Slow Pace of Christian Expansion

Available histories of both the historic mission churches in the Teso region have focused on the period of colonial rule in the first half of the twentieth century (see Pirouet 1978; Vincent 1982: 106–11, 134–40). Unlike Pentecostalism, which was always on the margins of the colonial enterprise, the

---

7 Twaddle has criticised the religious-historical literature on Uganda for drawing too easily the link between religious affiliation and political identities, and notes that in the 1980 elections the Democratic Party in Buganda was perceived not so much as the 'religion of the Pope' but as the party of Ganda interests against the northern-dominated UPC (Twaddle 1983).

history of the mission churches was tied up with the expansion of colonial rule. As described in Chapter 3, the introduction of cotton required the sedentarisation of the population, something achieved through a mixture of institutional innovation and blunt coercion. There was the invention of a chiefly class, part of a larger project to settle the population down so that they could grow cotton and pay taxes. A considerable amount of coercion was required to set up this system of government, as there were no indigenous hierarchies that could be co-opted. The introduction of colonial government therefore produced a tension between a relatively mobile society, reliant on contingent, small-scale social structures, and a new political economy focused on cotton (Gartrell 1983: 5–7). Missions were part of this transformation.

Mission churches provided a parallel set of hierarchical structures that made the transition to the cotton economy easier than it would otherwise have been. Without the churches there would have been considerable difficulty in educating a class of men that would administer the rural population. Mission schools offered the best hope for those wishing to achieve political and economic advancement.[8] From its entry into the region in 1908, the Church Missionary Society (CMS) focused on educating the sons of those favoured by the advent of colonial administration and Christianity (Lawrance 1957: 25). The first county chiefs appointed from the local population in 1920 were all 'old boys' of Ngora High School (Pirouet 1978: 184).[9] For those who aspired to join the salariat, the missions were the staging ground for entry into colonial government.

The Mill Hill Fathers of the Roman Catholic Church, who had also established a permanent base in Ngora in 1908, similarly emphasised education, though with a greater commitment to the industrial arts of brick making, bricklaying, carpentry, working in iron, road making and tailoring (Vincent 1982: 109). The Catholic Church also showed a greater concern with the religious instruction of the lay population. The more numerous Mill Hill Fathers, with more resources at their disposal, showed greater interest in the training of catechists and the promotion of religious education (Pirouet 1978: 185). (This emphasis on religious instruction may offer one explanation of the greater fidelity of lay Catholics to their church during the Pentecostal expansion of the 1980s and 1990s.)

The overall process of evangelisation was slow, with only 6 per cent reporting adherence to the mission churches in the 1921 census, and only

---

8 Prior to the mission being established, a catechumenate was established at Ngora by Father Kirk in April 1905. Father Kirk made little headway in terms of persuading Itesots to train as lay readers and had to be recalled (Gale 1959: 294).
9 That there was some bias towards administrative recruitment from the Anglican, rather than the Catholic, portion of the population may explain why, in the 1921 census, there were three times as many Anglicans as Catholics in the region (Vincent 1982: 140).

a modest improvement recorded in the 1931 census (Uganda Protectorate 1921, 1933). The comparable figure for Buganda in the 1921 census was 363,028 Christians (57 per cent) out of a total population of 639,417.[10]

The apparent failure of the people living in Teso to respond to the opportunities opened up by mission activity (particularly when compared to their Bantu neighbours to the south) has promoted a somewhat dismal view of Christianity in the literature. The mismatch between indigenous society and colonial hierarchy was obvious in the work of the churches as well as the state. Joan Vincent regarded churches as successful only in easing the rural population into a particular system of agricultural production (Vincent 1982: 134, 136). And in her 1968 study of the parish of Bugondo she treated Christianity as no more than an imposed ideology, with neither the Catholic nor Anglican churches seeming to matter in the social or political life of the community (Vincent 1968: 34–5). Louise Pirouet suggests that people living in the region were 'little interested in what the missions had to offer' other than opportunities for advancement in the colonial bureaucracy (Pirouet 1978: 188).

Examples of Religious Revival

The slow process of evangelisation nonetheless had an impact. District Commissioner J. C. D. Lawrance put the number of adult men baptised into the mission churches at 70 per cent by the mid-1950s (Lawrance 1957: 182). And for evangelisation to succeed, conversion had to be lay-led, as a Mill Hill Father later recalled:

> The lay involvement was very strong from the beginning. In Toroma we had about 15,000 Catholics. In Kidetok, where I was, we had 28,000. We were two of us [Europeans] at the best of times . . . that big development occurred through the laity, not through the clergy.[11]

It was the Catholic Church that achieved greatest success in the Teso region. With more money and more missionaries than their Anglican counterparts, the Mill Hill Fathers developed policies and programmes aimed at reaching out to rural communities. Attempts at reform were particularly pronounced in the 1960s and 1970s in response to the Second Vatican Council. The training of catechists – to ensure that there would be a level of religious education in the village – as well as the introduction of 'base communities' represented serious attempts at democratising the church.

And as villagers took on the roles of catechist and congregant, Christianity itself was subject to change. Church attendance was incorporated into prevailing notions of sociality and respectability, while Christian forms of worship and prayer offered a sense of community in the newly seden-

10 Uganda Protectorate 1921: 13, 45.
11 Interview with Father Bernard Phelan, 20 August 2001.

tarised society. Mission schools provided a place for education during the week and a building where the family as a whole prayed on Sundays. The gradual inculturation of Christianity is also suggested in the presence of reformist movements in the Teso region, such as the oppositional *Bamalaki* movement of the 1910s and the reformist *Balokole* movement which started in the 1930s. Christianity was part of an increasingly complex religious landscape (Vincent 1982: 247–9; Ward 1989). Although information on the significance of either movement is somewhat limited, their presence suggests the ways in which Christian structures and theology have provided a place for change and social commentary.

The Society of the One Almighty God (popularly known as the *Bamalaki*) sought to challenge prevailing orthodoxies of the historic mission churches (Twaddle 1993: 265–72).[12] Established in the region as early as 1915, and supported by an ageing Kakungulu, Malakites drew strength from a reading of the Bible which offered a response to the visible catastrophes of colonial conquest: famine, Spanish 'flu, plague, rinderpest and violent conflict.[13] Official records limit the Malakite movement to the towns in Teso. Even so, the *Bamalaki* signalled that there was room for the early fragmentation of mission theology in a newly administered population.[14] They used teachings from the Bible to draw the support of those who opposed colonialism. Mugema, the main proponent of Malakite religious beliefs, suggested Europeans were weaker Christians than their African counterparts, because their attitude to medicine and health had returned Europeans 'to the paganism of [their] forefathers' (Welbourn 1961: 41–2). In an echo of more recent versions of Pentecostal Christianity, Malakites saw their reading of the Bible as situating themselves at the forefront of change, far from any nativistic or authentic strands of 'African religion' (Vincent 1982: 244–7). Though of greater significance in other parts of the Protectorate, the *Bamalaki* presence in Teso shows how quickly Christianity could be used to criticise and challenge the colonial experience.

The more enduring reformist movement, one that lingers on in present-day Teso, is the *Balokole* (Saved Ones).[15] The *Balokole* movement, which

12 The Malakites were named after one of the movement's founders, Musajjakawa Malaki (Welbourn 1961: 36). Though successful in the early years, with an esti-mated 90,000 adherents, by the 1930s only a few followers were left (Lipschutz and Rasmussen 1986). Barrett sets the highest membership figure at 110,000 (Barrett 1968: 29).

13 Colonial expansion coincided with (and in some ways caused) a collapse in the relatively well-established trading systems of east Africa of the late nineteenth and early twentieth centuries. Competition over land when combined with the enforced sedentarisation of the population could be linked to the long famines of 1894–6, 1900, and 1917–19 (Vincent 1982: 114, 246).

14 By 1915 there were at least four congregations in Teso, including one in Ngora (Vincent 1982: 244).

15 The ascription *balokole* comes from the Luganda word *omulokole*, meaning 'saved' (Ward 1995: 74).

took root in the 1930s, sought to bring about the 'renewal and moral regeneration of the church' with support drawn from the lower clergy and committed members of the laity (Kassimir 1995: 130). In line with later born-again doctrines, the *Balokole* rejected 'any assimilation between the church and the world, and between Christianity and African custom', seeking to establish a culture of openness and accountability, set apart from the corruption of society (Gifford 1998: 152). The afterglow of this earlier encounter with revivalism was apparent when I interviewed the Anglican lay reader at Kaderun, Ongenge George Washington. Ongenge did not drink alcohol, and saw his work as a committed Christian as a continuation of his earlier decision to become a born-again Anglican in the 1970s.

Of relevance to arguments put forward later in the chapter is Ronald Kassimir's work on the Catholic Church in the Toro region, which suggests the parochial dynamics of religious change in western Uganda. While the *Bamalaki* or *Balokole* were movements that stretched across a large part of Uganda and are thus documented in the mission and colonial archives, the more normal course for religious innovation was less organised, smaller in scale, and usually more ephemeral and less successful (Kassimir 1995, 1998, 1999).

Kassimir analyses popular forms of Catholicism, juxtaposing weak clerical structures with strong religious movements supported by the laity. In his essay on 'Protestant revival and popular Catholicism', Kassimir describes a landscape of diverse religious practice:

> Catholic groups in Kampala and Toro in western Uganda devoted to the Uganda Martyrs have been holding exorcism sessions led by lay people. Similarly, in Toro and neighbouring Bunyoro, a former Catholic catechist and composer of hymns – Dosteo Bisaaka – established a popular independent movement based on exorcism and witchcraft eradication.[16]

In the specific case of Dosteo Bisaaka, here was a former catechist who had served in the Roman Catholic Church and then founded a religious movement based on a combination of Catholic theology and other beliefs. Bisaaka's Holy Quaternity Movement offered healing and exorcism through confession and the invocation of the spirit Obwosobozi. His work was regarded as blasphemous by the Catholic hierarchy in Toro diocese and was strongly opposed by church structures (Kassimir 1999: 262–5). The Holy Quaternity Movement was seen as syncretic, un-modern and a threat to the religious orthodoxy (the 'Quaternity' of the movement's title refers to the transformation of the Holy Trinity). Despite public opposition from the clergy and a large part of the lay leadership, many rank-and-file Catholics continued to support the work of Bisaaka. Kassimir's point is that the

16 Kassimir 1999: 250.

historic mission churches are not necessarily as powerful or authoritative as is often imagined or claimed, and that the history of Christianity in Uganda is one of parochial innovation alongside clerical administration.

Village Churches and the Clergy

In the particular case of Oledai the situation was one of a distracted clerical bureaucracy. The Catholic and Anglican congregations in the village had little interaction with the parish office in Ngora or the diocesan headquarters in Soroti or Kumi. In an echo of local experiences of the Ugandan state, a whole year could pass without the parish priest leaving his seat to visit the sub-parish, even though Oledai was only a few miles from the headquarters in the old Ngora mission station. Though there were examples of clergy, both Anglican and Catholic, who involved themselves with rural congregations, the general experience for village outstations was one of distance and detachment from the church hierarchy. This detachment showed up on the collection plate each Sunday; congregants contributed far more to those collections which they knew would be spent within the village. The fund for building maintenance always collected more than the standard offertory collection. From both sides there was a growing gap between the clergy-led structures in the towns and the lives of Christian congregations in the countryside. In an interview Father Bernard Phelan pointed to the gap that divided the clergy from the activities of village congregations:

> The ordained structure tends to be very clerical in mentality, proud of its status and often looking down on the lay people. It is only the national system of training priests that ensures the Iteso get their chance to enter the priesthood.[17]

An obvious explanation for the lack of interest on the part of the clergy was the extraversion of the churches in Uganda. As with the Ugandan government, the historic mission churches were increasingly turned upwards and outwards by sources of funding from abroad. The flow of funds increased substantially in the 1980s and 1990s as development agencies and Western charities sought to fight poverty and promote 'civil society'. It was in the particular context of the Teso Insurgency years that Western development organisations achieved a significant presence for the first time. The Red Cross and OXFAM worked with church organisations in the relief effort in the internment camps, while church buildings provided a base for a number of non-governmental organisations (NGOs) in the years after the end of the insurgency.

This 'NGO-isation' of the church is something that can be observed in many parts of the developing world (Gifford 1998: 147–8, 314–15). In the Teso region, the setting up of a number of church-based development

17 Interview with Father Bernard Phelan, 20 August 2001.

projects has created administrative structures entirely dependent on support from Western aid and charitable foundations, and entirely independent of the rural economy. At a time when the region's economy had all but collapsed these new sources of funding encouraged the creation of community-based organisations organised by church leaders. Paradoxically perhaps, the NGO-isation of church structures made it less likely that the clergy would involve themselves in what was going on in the countryside. Though speaking the language of 'grassroots development' or 'the empowerment of the rural poor' these local NGOs were at a considerable remove from the lives of those who attended church services in the village. Alongside SOCADIDO (a Roman Catholic non-governmental organisation serving Soroti diocese)[18] and the Kumi Diocese Planning Secretariat (the development arm of the Church of Uganda in the area) there were international religious charities, such as TEAR Fund (Australia), World Vision (USA), VECO-Vredeseilanden Coopibo (Belgium), Strømmestiftelsen (Norway) and Christian Engineers in Development (UK), ready to work with counterpart organisations at the local level. There were also non-governmental organisations with no particular religious mandate, such as ActionAid, who needed local partners to implement their development work. All of these Western agencies created a demand for 'civil society' and provided an avenue of opportunity and funding for the clerical and lay elite based in the towns.

Rather like their counterparts in the district bureaucracy, those serving in the higher reaches of the churches had to live with the paradox of being 'Africanised' in the years after independence, and of being 'NGO-ised' in the years after that. The gradual winding down of European involvement in terms of mission work in the 1970s and 1980s limited the pastoral focus of the church hierarchy. In place of the direct channel of funding available to missionaries, which could be focused primarily on the religious mission of the church, there came new sources of money focused largely on the economic and social concerns of Western governments and charitable agencies. In the diocesan headquarters of the Church of Uganda in Kumi, or in the home of the Roman Catholic bishop in Soroti, the houses, vehicles and salaries of the church leaders were dependent on these new sources of funding. In exchange church leaders could offer a degree of legitimacy to those development agencies keen to reach poorer people living in the countryside.

THE INFLUENCE OF PENTECOSTALISM

Despite a somewhat disengaged church bureaucracy, there were important changes taking place in rural Teso. There had been a gradual inculturation of Christianity, despite the uneven relationship between village congre-

18 An abbreviation of Soroti Catholic Diocese Integrated Development Organisation.

gations and church authorities. This is suggested by the persistence of churches in the years after independence and the readiness of many people to turn to Pentecostal or charismatic forms of worship in the 1980s and 1990s. Churches came to the fore during the insurgency, particularly during the months when the rural population was interned. As I described in the previous chapter, the camps, which were located on the outskirts of major towns, provided a place where people began to consider quite radical changes in their religious lives. Kevin Ward discusses 'stories of a revival of religious commitment in some of the camps' (Ward 1995: 102). Life for those interned was reduced to a pattern of sitting and waiting, and the relationships involved in conversion had time to evolve.

In the Ngora camp the Pentecostal Assemblies of God church prayed in the same building as the Catholic and Anglican congregations, and this meant that villagers had the possibility of comparing Pentecostalism to other more established churches in a familiar setting. Aguti Betty, a one-time member of the Pentecostal Assemblies of God (PAG) church, had the following to say about the importance of the camps to the growth of the PAG:

> It was the PAG that led so many people into salvation. They stayed in the camps, and their church was founded in the camps. They would pray and preach and the church grew big. I remember when we went to get the body of our deceased grandmother. I saw how they were in the camps, I found the Pentecostals preaching.[19]

The growth of Pentecostalism was also matched by a similar story in the Anglican and Catholic churches.[20]

Charismatics adopted a number of behaviours and practices which borrowed from Pentecostal Christianity. A charismatic Catholic or Anglican accepted prohibitions on alcohol and smoking, and took the same position on questions of personal morality. In a conversation with a young Pentecostal in the village of Oledai the similarity between charismatics and members of his own church was clear:

> Charismatics are the same [as us]. They have left behind many of the bad ways of others, they are like saved people. They reject the same things we do. They do not drink or have many wives. They do not see witchdoctors. Like us they have left behind those things that bring conflict and trouble to the lives of Christians. They now preach the Gospel in a true way, they say that 'Jesus Christ is their saviour', they say it aloud, not in a half-hearted way.[21]

19 Interviewed 4 October 2002.
20 Father Bernard Phelan, who was working in Bukedea for much of the insurgency, commented that 'daily we had a big congregation in the afternoon, something unheard of before or since'. Written communication, received 15 May 2007.
21 Interview with Akol James, a member of Agolitom sub-parish, 21 November 2002.

Charismatics stood slightly apart from others in the village. They met separately during the week to renew their faith, and held separate prayer meetings before the Sunday service. They also tended to sit together during the church service and this distinctive identity gave them a similar sort of profile to Pentecostal Christians. They had a reputation for being respectable and for self-discipline.

The distinctiveness of being charismatic went along with the intimacy of life in the village. Although a formal distinction was made between char-ismatics on the one hand, and ordinary church members on the other, this did not require an aggressive sort of separation. In contrast to joining the Pentecostal church the decision to become a member of a charismatic group did not require a forceful break with one's church. Those who were not charismatic, but who arrived early for the Sunday service, were welcome to join the assembled charismatics and share in their prayers. It was not uncommon to find a charismatic wife living with a husband who was only an occasional church-goer. And charismatics, like Pentecostals, saw no obvious contradiction between their personal faith and the desire to take on leadership roles in governmental or customary institutions.[22] Amongin Mary, a Catholic and a charismatic, was a committee member of the burial society for the Ichaak *ateker*; Agwang Angela, a similarly devout Anglican, was a committee member of the Parent–Teachers Association of the local primary school.[23]

Alongside the growing numbers of charismatics there were also more subtle changes concerning the meaning of church membership. When I asked what had changed, a common answer was that 'rules are more important now'. There was the understanding that those who had been absent from church for some time could no longer claim to be proper Christians, in contrast to the nominal sort of Christianity detailed in earlier accounts (cf. Pirouet 1978: Chapter 6). The redefinition around questions of what it meant to be a Christian was a reflection of the capacity of the historic mission churches to absorb something of the more committed, participatory faith envisioned by Pentecostalism. In other words, Pentecostalism had deepened and reformed understandings of what it meant to live a Christian life in the village.

Examples of this emphasis on rules came in the way offences such as adultery, theft, or excessive drinking were now regarded as questions that had to be addressed in church. Though these offences were more usually dealt with by the village council or the *ateker* courts, those Christians who

22 Interview with Ongenge George Washington, 22 October 2002.
23 As the names Amongin Mary and Agwang Angela suggest, charismatic groups depended on women more than men. J. D. Y. Peel makes a similar argument in his study on gender and religious change among the Yoruba. Peel describes how the new religious forms offered by Christian missions were seized upon by those social categories more marginal to the society in which missionaries sought to establish a presence (Peel 2002).

behaved in an un-Christian way could increasingly expect to be the object of scrutiny and punishment in their own church. In a mirror image of the way adultery cases were managed by the Pentecostal Assemblies of God, the Anglican church had instituted a rule whereby the adulterer was forced to stand outside the church, demonstrating his or her isolation from God (Jones 2005: 508–11).[24]

The setting up of charismatic groups or new rules on membership and personal conduct suggested the relatively open exchange between the different churches in the village. To a considerable extent this exchange took the form of a *bricolage*, a series of borrowings from one church by another. The most obvious borrowings came when the historic mission churches acquired something of the style and content of Pentecostal worship. That said, it was also the case that the Pentecostal Assemblies of God church had borrowed from the Anglican and Catholic churches. Not only had the PAG church borrowed from the organisational structures of these historic mission churches, but it had also become more bureaucratic and more obviously engaged in the 'normal' politics of the village.

There is a broader point to be made here. While a number of academics working on contemporary religious developments in Africa focus on the remarkable growth of Pentecostal Christianity in isolation, it is possible to look at Pentecostalism, or Christianity more broadly, in a more open-ended way. In Oledai the different churches borrowed from one another, meaning that an understanding of what went on in the PAG church only made sense when taking into account developments in the Anglican and Catholic churches. Churches also shared in changes that affected other, non-religious, forms of organisation. The increasing emphasis on respect was also reflected in the work of the village court, while a concern with propriety was shared with the work of burial societies. In other words, churches both influenced and were influenced by other institutions in the village. The following case demonstrates this by looking at the part played by the lay reader of the Anglican Church at a burial.

Case 1: The Burial of Edotun, Part 1: the Anglican Church

The death and burial of Edotun Jackson shows the increasing importance of the Anglican church in the life of the village.[25] Churches had been on

24 This sort of borrowing from one church to another should also be taken to exemplify the gradual incorporation of Pentecostalism into the life of the village.

25 Edotun was interviewed as part of the household survey and the social networks survey, and was known both to myself and to my research colleagues prior to his death. He participated in a group discussion on 31 May 2002 with three other bicycle taxi men, and his professional services were called upon on occasion to reach the far side of the sub-parish. The information used to piece together the case study is drawn from a series of interviews, observations, and written records. The subject of Edotun's death was discussed in detail in major interviews with Oberei Fastine (30 August 2002), Ibuchet Max (9 January 2003), Akol Florence (20 August 2002),

the margins of village life in the past, of little influence in conflicts over persons or property. The case also shows how the increasing influence of the Anglican church was complemented by the growth of burial societies. The public platform provided by Edotun's burial could be seen to combine with the new-found influence of the Anglican lay reader, and helped Edotun's mother strengthen her hold over the land she and her son had been farming (there was a risk that her son's death would leave her dispossessed). Both the influence of the church in the land dispute, and the outcome in favour of the young man's mother, were new things. Before going into the details of this dispute it is worth saying something about the events leading up to and surrounding Edotun's death.

In June 2002 Edotun had gone to the police to lay charges against two men from a neighbouring sub-parish. The charges concerned the theft of his radio, sponge mattress, and some USh13,000 ($7) that he had managed to save up and store in his compound. The day after the theft, one of Edotun's neighbours told him who the thieves probably were. Edotun went to the police and after he had paid the summary fee of USh5,000 ($3), the police recovered the stolen goods from the home of one of the two named suspects. The radio and sponge mattress were then returned to Edotun, and the thieves were obliged to pay double the money they had stolen from him by way of compensation. The USh13,000 stolen from Edotun was to be repaid as USh26,000 ($14). By the time of his death, however, the money had not been paid.

Two months after the theft, Edotun was shot dead. At the time of his death he was in a weak position within the village. Not only was he locked in a conflict with the two men who owed him the USh26,000, but he was also the only son of a poor widow, with no obvious allies in the village. Edotun lived alone. The grass-thatched hut in which he slept was not protected by the bustle of life that surrounded other homes. He worked long hours as a bicycle taxi man, and was criticised by members of the community for socialising in the trading centre of Ngora rather than spending time at home. Though he and his mother lived on his deceased father's land, Edotun's hold on this land was tenuous. At the time of Edotun's death the leader of his lineage, or *ateker*, was laying claim to some of the land apportioned to Edotun and his mother. [26]

Okaleke Peter (11 September 2002) and Tino Rose (23 August 2002). Aside from observing the progress of the case, and the burial, the most useful discussions of the chronology and politics behind Edotun's death emerged in a group discussion with younger men (12 December 2002). Atai Helen, the mother of Edotun, was also interviewed on 2 September 2002, though the proximity to the murder meant that she was happiest speaking instead on the history of the village council. A more in-depth interview was held on 27 January 2003. The notes taken by the village council chairman concerning the case were also used.

26 A lineage grouping, typically numbering between twenty and thirty households (pl. *atekerin*) (Vincent 1968: 48).

Given this already difficult situation, Edotun's death placed his mother, Atai Helen, in a precarious position. The burial itself was a costly business. In order to go ahead with the funeral, Atai Helen had to pay the police and the hospital a total of USh80,000 ($46) to have the body of her son released with the death certificate (required in murder cases).[27] Aside from the ensuing financial hardship, Atai was left with the problem of how to keep hold of the land she had been farming. Her son's death left Atai without a man from within her immediate family to guarantee the land apportioned to her. (It was commonly understood that land was only held in trust by a male member of the *ateker*, as land belonged to the lineage rather than the household.)[28] The death of Edotun threatened to impoverish Atai Helen yet further.

The vulnerable nature of Atai's situation would, in the past, have compelled her to take a levirate – a second husband from within the *ateker* – or else struggle on with a smaller piece of land. But the village had changed. Funerals, which had been rather small-scale affairs in the past, were much more public events by the time of Edotun's death. Churches had also come to have a greater say over what happened. Edotun's burial was consequently transformed into a very public affair, and was attended by most of the members of the sub-parish. The burial society helped organise and pay for the ceremony, with all of the registered members of the society meeting at his home prior to the day of burial.[29] The funeral itself was an elaborate and inclusive occasion; it contrasted sharply with the violence and isolation of the young man's death.

On the burial day, prayers were said by Ongenge George Washington, the lay reader of the Anglican church (Edotun had been baptised into the Church of Uganda). Ongenge was something of an independent voice in the village, a distance away from the conflicts and disputes that affected his parishioners. He drew his independence from his status as a 'saved' member of the Church of Uganda, as well as from his origins in a neighbouring sub-parish where he hoped later to return. Even though Edotun was not a regular churchgoer, Ongenge chose to give a sermon before he offered prayers for the family and the deceased. The sermon was delivered to a far larger audience than the lay reader could hope to attract at his Sunday service, and Ongenge took the opportunity to speak out against those who had done the killing. In fairly general terms he characterised the men of the area as violent and disruptive, as he later recalled:

27 The murder of Edotun was one of the few instances where poorer villagers contended directly with the local government bureaucracy.
28 It should be said that the principle that land was 'owned' by the *ateker*, rather than the household, was neither hard nor fast. Cultivating a piece of land for a period of time tended to promote a sense of ownership, and it was not unknown for land to be sold, even though this was notionally prohibited.
29 The committee met to plan the funeral while the society members had to come and pay their burial dues in advance.

I spoke strongly during the burial. I said so many things against the indiscipline of men. After the burial, some of those men came to my home and said that I had made a mistake; that I should not talk like that at a burial. But I replied that that was my duty as a Christian. I am doing God's work.[30]

At the heart of Ongenge's criticism was the belief that Edotun's death related back to the violence of the insurgency.

Ongenge's words publicised and strengthened Atai's position in the village. Atai's individual weakness – as a woman with no man to guarantee the land she was farming – was mitigated by the institutional influence of the church and the work of the burial society. The burial, as a public event, provided an arena where the lay reader's words could draw support. Atai also relied on the sympathy of her fellow congregants at Sunday service. Her precarious position was much discussed and debated, producing a new sort of publicity. In the weeks that followed a consensus emerged which meant that Atai could hold onto the land she and her son had been farming. The elders of her *ateker* reasoned that the land could be used to provide a livelihood for Atai's remaining daughters. This dissuaded the *ateker* chairman from taking the matter further.

When comparing Atai's land dispute with earlier accounts of violence and arbitration in the region, the radical nature of what had changed is more easily appreciated. Joan Vincent's study from 1968 gave no role for churches, while burials were not regarded as significant arenas for the settlement of land disputes. Rather disputes over persons and property were managed by the local courts or by a number of more informal arenas organised around the neighbourhood or the *ateker*. J. C. D. Lawrance, writing in the 1950s, regarded Christianity as having a marginal influence on the lives of those living in the region, and described burial rites as the responsibility of the family. Burials achieved prominence only on those occasions where a 'big man' – such as a government-appointed chief or an *ateker* leader – was laid to rest (Lawrance 1957: 100–1; see also Clark 1952, 1953). The death of a relatively poor man, such as Edotun, would be a more private, low-key event. Neither Lawrance nor Vincent mentions burial societies.

The situation surrounding the death and burial of Edotun Jackson marked a significant change in the landscape of the village. The influence of the lay reader at the burial was a relative novelty, and contrasted sharply with the marginal sort of Christianity described earlier.[31] The sermon and

30 Interview with Ongenge George Washington, 22 October 2002.
31 That said, the manner in which Atai's land dispute was resolved was not entirely different, in form at least, from what was observed in Joan Vincent's work from the 1960s. Vincent's work showed that disputes were negotiated through a number of arenas within a given locality (drinking groups, public moots, courts), which were presided over by a number of 'big men'. There was openness, in terms of institutions and persons, which could still be applied to the pattern of dispute settlement at the

burial prayers offered by Ongenge were innovations, and their influence was bound up with the work of burial societies. The sort of well-organised, well-attended funeral that followed on from the death of Edotun Jackson was a new thing and gave the Anglican church a public platform.

Okelai Samuel Becomes a Trainee Lay Reader, Despite Losing a Court Case[32]

The following case takes a slightly different tack, and looks at the way Okelai Samuel, a young man from the neighbouring sub-parish of Agolitom, with ambitions of his own, used the divisions that remained between different denominations in the area as a way of gaining influence in a local Anglican congregation. The case reminds us that political competition did not stop because there had been a shift in emphasis towards rules and respectability. Okelai was in many ways an exceptional young man, and his story shows how his innate abilities could translate into a leadership position because of the continuing rivalry between different churches.

It is important to hold onto the idea that there has been a degree of fragmentation in the religious landscape of the area. Many Anglicans and Catholics criticised the growth of Pentecostal Christianity, and such divisions continued to open up space for competition and negotiation. Leaders of the historic mission churches remained concerned about possible losses to Pentecostalism, and not all of the Anglicans or Catholics welcomed the incorporation of Pentecostalist practices into their way of working. In other words, there was a necessary tension between the increasing importance of churches, and the problems Catholics and Anglicans faced because of Pentecostalism's advance. In this example it is possible to see Okelai Samuel using this tension productively. He managed to cut a path through the different churches in a way that negotiated his appointment to a leadership position in the Anglican church at Kalengo. This he did despite a lengthy court case which damaged his reputation in his village. In what is written below, I describe how Okelai achieved the position of trainee lay reader in his Anglican church, despite being castigated as a 'stubborn' young man by those who presided over his case in the village court.

---

time of Edotun's death. What had changed was the configuration of those institutions through which disputes could be negotiated, with churches and burial societies achieving prominence.

32 Okelai Samuel was interviewed on the details of his case and career on 4 December 2002. Apulugeresia was interviewed nine days later, on 13 December 2002. I was not present when the dispute itself was raised, but Okelai's legal troubles were discussed in detail later on and were raised in conversation with Edoket James, chairman of Agolitom sub-parish (21 December 2002), and with the lay reader of the Anglican Church at Kalengo (4 October 2002). The case was also pieced together through referring to the court records of the village council chairman, and through observing Okelai's interaction with villagers, in church, in court, and in more informal discussions with Okelai and his fellow bicycle taxi (*boda boda*) men.

The court case occupies the first half of our story. Okelai had become embroiled in a lengthy and costly dispute with his stepmother. The dispute arose after Okelai had sent his children to eat at his stepmother's home, some fifty yards away. During the visit, the children behaved badly and Apulugeresia, Okelai's stepmother, disciplined the children, to the point where Okelai and his wife came over to complain. An argument ensued, after which Apulugeresia claimed she had been accused, by her stepson, of practising witchcraft. Apulugeresia said that she had been accused of cursing Okelai's wife (who was sick at the time). To punish Okelai for what she felt to be a false and hurtful accusation, Apulugeresia brought a case before the courts.

A multitude of court hearings followed, even though the case was, in and of itself, a somewhat small matter that could have been dealt with by the *ateker*. Okelai repeatedly refused the judgement of the *ateker* (who had decided in favour of Apulugeresia), and the case was passed on to a more senior clan authority (*emorimor*)[33] who also found Okelai to be in the wrong. But Okelai again refused the decision and went to the village council chairman. Over a number of months this pattern of judgement and refusal repeated itself, via the sub-county court, then back to the village court. At each stage in the proceedings Okelai and Apulugeresia paid their court fees and stated their case. In the end Okelai was forced to accept the judgement that he had been guilty of defamation and agreed to pay Apulugeresia USh150,000 shillings ($86) as compensation (the compensation was later negotiated down to a more manageable sum).

Okelai's case (like that of Akol Stanislas discussed on page 84 left him open to the accusation of being a stubborn and disrespectful young man. As I suggested earlier in the book, such a case can be thought of as part of a more general pattern where men were punished not just for their crimes and misdemeanours but for their youth. Stubbornness when combined with youth associated the actions of a younger man with the memory of the insurgency. In the years that followed there was a particularly powerful belief that younger men needed to be disciplined as they were a potentially malign force. What is interesting about Okelai's story, however, is that though the court case meant he was labelled a stubborn man, this did not end his political ambitions. Though the case went against him, and though he was disliked by many of the 'big men', the fragmented religious landscape threw up other opportunities. In the same year as his defeat in court, Okelai managed to secure the position of trainee lay reader in his Anglican church at Kalengo.

33 A number of contingent lineage groups (*atekerin*) could form part of a larger 'clan' if they wanted. These larger clans often shared a common name, with the particular *ateker* distinguished by a suffix, as was the case with Atekok Esasi (Esasi being the suffix of that part of the clan 'Atekok' found in Oledai). An *emorimor* had authority over a collection of *atekerin*.

In the space of a few months in 2002, Okelai went from the Church of Uganda (Anglican), to the Pentecostal Assemblies of God in Okwii, from there to the Pentecostal church in a neighbouring sub-parish of Kalengo, and from there, finally, back to his Anglican church.[34] On his return to the Anglican church he was given the position of trainee lay reader. His actions were viewed, by some, as another indication of his persistent wilfulness. Some felt his peripatetic approach to the question of religious affiliation was no more than a comment on the confusion Pentecostalism had brought to the village. Whatever the explanation, Okelai's rise in the church related to his sense of independence in dealing with the courts and his family. His initial move away from the church appeared to have been part of his falling out with Apulugeresia, who attended services in the Anglican church in Kalengo.

The rise to prominence of Okelai was somewhat different from that of many other would-be 'big men'. In place of the consensual 'spiralism' of Omadi John Francis (page 102), where success in the village came through piecing together roles in a range of institutions, Okelai's rise to prominence was more singular, as it was achieved only through the churches. In this way spaces of competition and conflict persisted, and had, in some ways, been opened up by the advent of Pentecostalism. Within the Anglican church Okelai's story becomes more that of a prodigal son who had returned to the church as a reformed man, after a period of aberrant and troubling behaviour. In a certain sense Okelai was a symbol of fortunes restored; his return to the Anglican fold was taken as a sign that his church was regaining strength.

CONCLUSION

Since the late 1980s churches had become increasingly influential at moments of political significance. Church leaders had more say at burials and in property disputes; there was a more general interest in getting involved in church; and outward signs of religiosity were more a part of village life than they had been in the past. These changes were related to the successes of Pentecostal Christianity in the area. Anglican and Catholic congregations, as much as the Pentecostal Assemblies of God, had witnessed a revival through the appropriation of new religious practices and beliefs. The setting up of charismatic groups, new rules concerning membership, and new codes dealing with personal morality and public conduct suggested a growing role for organised religion in Oledai.

The growing importance of churches in the village can also be under-stood in relation to developments outside church. The setting up of burial societies and the increasing emphasis on propriety in public life suggested

---

34 This is seen as one of the weaknesses of Pentecostalism within the village, that its membership lacks the fixed quality of established churches.

that churches were part of a broader story. The transformative experience of the Teso Insurgency, and the consequent desire for a sense of peace and security in its aftermath, had led to a number of developments at the local level, one of which was the increasingly public role of churches in the life of the village.

It is important to recognise that these changes came from the actions of villagers, rather than in response to a push for reform from above. Rather like Uganda's local government structures, the bureaucracies of the historic mission churches were turned upwards and outwards. The division between what went on in the towns and what went on in the countryside was deepening. Clerical structures, which had never had an easy relationship with rural congregations, had been distracted by the 'development economy'. The transformation of churches into 'civil society' organisations, and the 'NGO-isation' of church leaders, weakened the link between clergy and laity. At the same time, the decline of the rural economy meant that those living in the countryside had less and less influence on the centre.

From an analytical perspective these last two chapters can also be read against a literature which regards churches as a separate field of study. Perhaps, as Harri Englund argues, an emphasis on the religious aspect of churches, or on the peculiar quality of belief, encourages the separation of churches from the study of other ways of organising or thinking (Englund 2007: 479–83). There is something to be gained from looking at churches in relation to each other and alongside other institutions. While it is usual to look at churches from the inside out, examining the bonds between church members or the way congregations form part of broader religious networks, it is also possible to see churches as part of a broader landscape. I have looked at the relationship between churches, burial societies and the local court. In Oledai it is possible to see the influence of religious organisations on government and customary institutions *and* the influence of these non-religious institutions on what goes on in church.

Plate 7 Okello Constant, an instrument maker, working on the belly of a lute (*adungu*)

Okello went to Busoga during the insurgency and his knowledge of burial practices there features in the following chapter.

7

BURIAL SOCIETIES

The major innovation in Oledai's social arrangements was the introduction of burial societies. By the time I arrived in the area almost every villager was a member of such a society. They worked as insurance schemes, typically organised around a lineage group (*ateker*), and collected money on the death of a society member to help the home with the costs of burial. They provided labour and organisational support during the burial, and had somewhat eclipsed, or taken over, the customary arrangements that dealt with marriage negotiations or inheritance disputes. So profound had their impact been that interviews with villagers on the role of kinship networks invariably focused on discussions of burials, and the work of burial societies. The term *ateker*, which is typically used to refer to a lineage grouping in the literature on Teso society, was more commonly used by villagers as the term for a burial society. Joan Vincent, writing in the 1960s, found that *ateker* could embrace a number of meanings, including the lineage groups, an extended kinship network, or the Iteso as a people. That Vincent did not associate the term *ateker* with 'burial society' suggests the scale of the transformation.[1]

Burial societies represented a transformation in the local institutional landscape. They had allowed many poorer homes to achieve what had come to be regarded as a respectable burial, something measured in social as well as material terms. It was marked by high levels of community participation and involved the provision of food, burial cloth, coffin and cement for sealing the grave, all of which was to be paid for through the burial society. Paying burial dues and turning up to funerals were perhaps the strongest conventions governing public life in the village and the most important means of demonstrating one's membership in the community.[2]

---

1 For the sake of clarity, though, I shall use the term *ateker* to refer to the contingent lineage group (and will use 'burial society' to refer to a burial society).

2 One finds an echo of this in the literature on burial societies in Victorian England. As F. M. L. Thompson observes: 'having the means to avoid [a pauper burial] and to provide for a decent funeral that would preserve the family's standing in the community was the measure of basic respectability; around this minimum core could be built all the other defences against degradation ... Getting the means was a matter of resolve, regular habits, and social motivation, rather than any particular level of wages. It meant making a regular contribution, perhaps of no more than a

At the same time, burial societies offered an elaborate system of insurance and obligation. They were established without any obvious form of external assistance. From the perspective of the outside analyst, they offer a case study in institutional innovation, an example of the ways in which historical experiences, institutional borrowing, and improvisation coalesce to produce something new.

Despite the use of the term 'customary' when categorising burial societies, it should be clear that burial societies were not 'traditional' structures but were new (and had invented new traditions).[3] Burials had come to be managed through much more institutionally bound structures, with elected committees, codified by-laws, membership dues, and a list of punishments for those who failed to behave.[4] Prior to the 1990s burials were more usually organised by the household, with support from the community coming forward in a more *ad hoc* fashion (Lawrance 1957: 99–100). One of the older women in the village recalled the change between past and present, remembering how things were when she first married into the area:

> If a person died no one would do anything, you would just be relaxing in your home and they would be buried quietly. Now things have changed. We are more united, we are more organised. Burial societies have brought unity to us and have made it that people follow rules and regulations.[5]

Burial societies can only be understood fully against the backdrop of the insurgency. Burials organised in this way contrasted in absolute terms with the way deaths were managed during the bush war and in the internment camps. This contrasting image was intrinsic to the legitimacy of their work, and burial societies achieved a considerable degree of autonomy because they mattered in ideological terms. Unlike many of the donor-sponsored efforts at institutional innovation – micro-credit schemes, 'reporter' projects, women's groups – burial societies *meant* something. Their institutionalisation tells us something important about the significance of *meaning* in the maintenance of institutional structures. Though burial societies worked on one level as an insurance scheme, their strength at a more fundamental level came from the fact that they managed death and opposed the memory of the insurgency.

The chapter begins by discussing the present-day structure of burial

---

halfpenny or penny a week and perhaps at a sacrifice of food for a hungry family, to an insurance fund that paid out funeral money' (Thompson 1988: 200; but see also Best 1971; Harrison 1982; and Harris 1994).

3 See Whyte and Higenyi 1997; Whyte 2005; de Weerdt 2001.
4 The emphasis on rules came up in several interviews. Akol Florence commented that 'everybody's name is expected to be in the burial book, and it is the role of the committee to make sure that everything is done according to the rules' (interview, 20 August 2002).
5 Ibid.

societies. The second section focuses on the history of burials during the colonial period, and then in the time of the insurgency. Both of these experiences played a critical role. If the pattern of burials in pre-insurgency years shaped the work of burial societies, so too did the experience of violence and exile during the insurgency itself. A third section looks at borrowings – since burial societies owe much of their form and structure to other institutional forms in the sub-parish. I then discuss Edotun Jackson's funeral. Before concluding the chapter, there is a discussion of what burial societies *meant*, in which I suggest that much of their meaning was drawn from their opposition to the imagery of the insurgency.

THE WORK OF BURIAL SOCIETIES

In its simplest form a burial society is an insurance scheme that assists a household when a death occurs. Membership in one or other burial society was typically based on one's *atekerin*. Members are required to pay a joining fee, after which their names are added to the burial book. When someone dies all of the registered members of the society are summoned to a meeting in the home of the deceased to discuss how the burial is to be organised. Individuals are expected to pay burial dues to the treasurer, either at this meeting or on the burial day itself. The money paid is fixed by the burial society committee – typically USh300 for a man, USh200 for a woman and USh50 for a child – and recorded in the burial book.[6] The treasurer checks off the names of members when they pay their dues. It was usual for the burial book to be kept in a box in the house of the treasurer. Anyone failing to attend the pre-burial meeting would be visited by one or more young men known as *askaris*[7] whose job it was to make sure that everyone paid their money and attended the burial.

Once the money was collected, the treasurer would release specific sums for the purchase of the coffin, cement for the grave and the white cotton sheets that would shroud the corpse. Money would also be released to buy in extra food, particularly meat, which was needed to feed the guests. A small portion of the money would be used to pay an honorarium to the more important or more hard-working members of the society. According to the rulebook of Atekok Esasi burial society

---

6 The setting of burial dues appeared to depend mostly on the size of the burial society, with larger societies tending to have lower fees because of a larger tax base. Burial dues for 2002 were as follows: in Atekok Esasi, USh300 for a man, USh200 for a woman or youth, and USh50 for a child; in Ichaak, USh500 for a man, USh300 for a woman, and USh200 for a youth; in Ipagitok/Ogoria/Ikures, USh300 shillings for a man, USh200 for a woman or a youth, and USh100 for a child.

7 Across Uganda, the term *askari* refers to a soldier serving in the government army. 'Askari' was also used to refer to those men who used to be in the employ of the local government at the time when taxes were to be collected. Askaris were responsible for rounding up tax defaulters.

> Clan condolence collection shall be expected to meet the expenditure
> of the following items: coffin; cement; burial sheets; feeding mourners;
> visitors upkeep; grave diggers allowance; chairman secretary and
> warden allowances.[8]

As well as the payment of burial dues, households were expected
to contribute other things to burials. Women were delegated the task of
bringing food, water and firewood to the burial home. In the case of Atekok
Esasi the amount required was:

> 1 tin of cassava flour
> 1 tin of sweet potato flour
> 1 tin of sorghum
> 5 tubers of cassava or sweet potatoes
> 3 pieces of firewood
> 1 twenty-litre jerry can of water.

Along with the gathering of these items, women were responsible for the
bulk of work at the burial, including fetching water, sweeping the family
compound, preparing food before the burial and clearing up afterwards.
These responsibilities were divided in a relatively organised manner, and
it was typical for one woman to be in charge of a particular activity on a
regular basis. The woman responsible for cooking, perhaps the most labo-
rious task on the burial day, would expect to receive a small sum of money
in recognition of her work. Young men, typically *askaris*, would be asked to
build a grass-thatched shade at the burial site as well as digging the grave,
and these men could expect a meal of roast chicken as thanks for their
work.

The burial itself typically lasted two to three days. The first day was the
day of the burial proper, referred to both in the literature and by villagers
as the day of *aipud* (Lawrance 1957: 99). This was the day when the burial
society was most active. Many guests would gather, and the home would
be busy with women working in the kitchens, cooking food, preparing beer,
or serving and clearing up. The funeral would take place in the morning
or early afternoon: the time of day regarded as the most auspicious.[9] In
most cases prayers would be said by either the local catechist (Catholic), lay
reader (Anglican), or assembly leader (Pentecostal), depending on the religious preferences of the family. Afterwards the elders of the burial society

8 See Atekok Esasi Burial Society, n.d. In the case of Atekok Esasi these allowances
   were set at the following levels: USh1,000 to the committee members (chairman;
   vice-chairman; treasurer; secretary; auditor; and the warden sergeant); USh700 to
   the warden corporal; and USh500 to the other wardens. Once these expenses were
   met, the remaining balance was given to the home of the deceased.
9 The late afternoon was reserved for the burial of criminals or other undesirables.
   Later on in the chapter I show that the way rebels deliberately buried 'big men' at
   the wrong time of day was part of the politics of the insurgency.

would speak about the deceased.[10] At the point of actual interment the coffin would be lowered into place and an iron sheet would be laid on top of it (to stop the earth from pressing on the corpse, a way of ensuring that the spirit of the deceased was not oppressed).[11] Signs of protest and noise would accompany the lowering of the coffin into the grave. Considerable importance attached to burying the person in the right position, and facing the right direction. This was to ensure that the spirit of the deceased would not trouble the living.[12] When the burial was over the treasurer would report the income and expenditures of the burial as well as the remaining balance, which was handed over to the family of the deceased.[13]

At this point in the proceedings people were given food to eat, and beer would be served. This was regarded as the high point of the day. The guests were fed first; only then would the burial society members be allowed to eat. Men took precedence over children, while women were the last to be fed. In discussion with villagers it was clear that the way in which food was served, and money handled, were subjects that were widely discussed, offering obvious indicators of the health of the burial society.[14] To be well-organised and respectful towards guests, making sure they were fed first, and then to offer a proper accounting of the funds was a way of demonstrating competent leadership and diligent membership. After the festivities of the first day had passed, the *ateker* would assemble again a day or two later to seal the grave with cement and decide on how to organise the inheritance (and debts) of the deceased.

What has so far been described is an ideal version of what was observed, and it should be noted that burials varied in form and content. Gender, age, the economic condition of the household, the reputation of the deceased and the religious preferences of the family all played a part in determining the shape of a particular burial. And yet what was striking about burials in

10 Despite the opposition of many other Pentecostal denominations towards traditional burial rites or funerary customs, Pentecostal Christians in Oledai were active members of burial societies.

11 The use of a wooden coffin was a recent innovation according to Amuge Gabdesia, interviewed 22 August 2002.

12 Written communication from Father Bernard Phelan, received 15 May 2007.

13 The pattern of burials differs slightly from those recounted by Henriques, who refers to the practice of 'last rites', a 'big event, which takes place a year from the actual burial' and would have marked the sealing of the grave (Henriques 2002: 179). Like others before him, Henriques appears to be referring to the burial of a 'big man'.

14 In interviews, villagers made comparisons between burial societies. Okaleke Peter noted that 'our friends in the Atekok Esasi clan lost a child and they collected money such that there was some left over after the burial. The balance was announced, but there was some difficulty in handing over the money to the parents of the child. That is why I say that our clan is doing well, because we do not have incidents like that. All the money will be counted and handed over to you' (11 September 2002). A similar argument was put forward by Aguti Jennifer (27 August 2002). Odongo Emmanuel suggested that the burial society of Ipagitok/Ogoria/Ikures, not his own, had the better-organised *askaris* (clan soldiers) (22 August 2002).

Oledai was the general commitment, both in discourse and in practice, to achieving something close to equality in death. In this the Iteso differ from their neighbours, a reflection of their acephalous and essentially egalitarian inheritance (Beattie 1961; Whyte and Higenyi 1997; Whyte 2005). There was a strong belief that all members of the society should receive a similar burial, and if the wife failed to receive the same sort of burial as her husband then the burial society would come in for criticism. An older woman stated the belief that 'the poor person has to be buried in the same way as a rich person, the woman the same as a man'.[15]

Moreover, if we think back to the long list of things required from each household – food, firewood, water, labour – burial societies marshalled considerable resources. The money collected represented by far the highest form of 'taxation' in the sub-parish. Burial societies proved much more capable of raising funds than either the parish chief or the village churches.

Table 7.1 shows the relative strength of burial societies in the sub-parish. They raised more in taxes than the local government or the churches. The 123 households contributed USh2,390,000 ($1,366) in 2002.[16] This was more than four times the amount paid to the local government in tax, and was drawn from a tax base half the size (Oledai was one of two sub-parishes within the parish of Nyamongo). And if this level of difference was not stark enough, what should be remembered when looking at Table 7.1 is that burial societies (and churches) required contributions in kind as well as money. Gifts of food, labour and time were an important part of a household's contribution to their burial society.[17]

If we turn away from the question of money and towards the question of membership, what also stands out is the way all but three of the households in the sub-parish were members of burial societies. Burial societies were understood to be open institutions.[18] Though there was an obvious bias towards organising burial societies along kinship lines, those villagers who belonged to none of the established *atekerin* could choose to join the burial society of another *ateker* without losing their primary affiliation. In the burial society that went by the name of Ogoria – because it was founded

15   Interview with Aguti Jennifer on the work of the Irarak Ikures clan and burial society, 27 August 2002.
16   Three households on the outskirts of the sub-parish worked in the sub-county head-quarters and were only resident some of the time; they were not members of burial societies.
17   Table 7.1 can also be related back to earlier chapters on churches in the sub-parish, with the relative strength of the Pentecostal church showing up in the high financial contributions of individual church members, suggesting that Pentecostalism required a greater personal commitment.
18   This point was made in interviews with Amuge Gabdesia (22 August 2002), Asige Martha (22 August 2002), Okaleke Peter (11 September 2002), Omuron John Simple (17 September 2002) and Oonyu Joseph (27 August 2002).

Table 7.1 The 'tax rates' of different organisations in the village in 2002

Type of organisation	Name	Amount collected per event	Number of collections in 2002	Number of 'taxable' households	Approx. total revenues in 2002	Approx. contribution per household
Burial society[a]	Atekok Esasi	USh90,000 per burial	11	52	USh990,000 $566	USh19,038 $11
	Ogoria	USh80,000 per burial	10	43	USh800,000 $457	USh18,604 $11
	Ichaak	USh75,000 per burial	8	28	USh600,000 $343	USh21,429 $12
Church[b]	Pentecostal	USh2,800 per week	52	14[c]	USh145,600 $83	USh10,400 $6
	Anglican	USh3,600 per week	52	20[c]	USh187,200 $107	USh9,360 $5
	Catholic	USh3,900 per week	52	31[c]	USh202,800 $116	USh6,542 $4
Government[d]	Head tax	USh525,000 per annum	1	256[e]	USh525,000 $300	USh2,051 $1

Notes

[a] An approximation of what could be gleaned from the burial books of Atekok Esasi, Ogoria and Ichaak.

[b] These figures were derived from the church survey. Several homes were interviewed for each church, over the course of eight weeks (the interview was either on the Sunday of the service or the Monday immediately after). The congregants estimated the number of those attending the service, including children. The collection figure was taken from what was stated at the church service: the catechist, lay reader or pastor typically announced the week's collection at the Sunday service.

[c] Average number of households *attending* church (rather than the total number of households claiming affiliation).

[d] Source: Uganda Government 2003.

[e] Number of households listed on the books of the parish chief (the parish was made up of the sub-parishes of Oledai and Nyamongo).

by members of the Ogoria *ateker* – a majority of the members actually came from the *atekerin* of Ipagitok and Ikures. In interviews members of the different burial societies not only emphasised the degree to which burial societies were inclusive, but also took pride in the belief that this openness made them appear more progressive and modern. The only part of the burial organised by the *ateker* was that part which dealt with questions of inheritance (and even this has been affected by the establishment of burial societies).

THE GENEALOGY OF BURIAL SOCIETIES
Burials in the Pre-colonial and Colonial Periods

By the 1950s there were two parts to the burial: the *aipud* and the *asuban*.[19] The colonial administrator and part-time ethnographer J. C. D. Lawrance suggested that the *aipud*, the ceremony of interment, and the memorial rite of *asuban* were long-established 'traditions', going as far back as the pre-colonial past. It should be said that Lawrance's work on the Teso region was infused with a desire to uncover the customs of the people, and his 1957 study is determined to find the pre-colonial 'tradition' of the Iteso. Anything that leans towards ceremony or an institutionalised practice is regarded as having a precedent in nineteenth-century Iteso society. Yet there are also historical accounts which indicate that it was commonplace for the Iteso to leave the corpse of the deceased exposed to the elements, meaning that there was no burial at all (Clark 1953). In all likelihood the *aipud* and *asuban* ceremonies that Lawrance recorded in the 1950s were a hybrid achievement, a combination of the burial practices of earlier periods and a particular response, on the part of villagers, to the structuring effects of colonial government.

Whatever their origins, *aipud* and *asuban* were established practices in central and southern parts of the Teso region by the 1950s. Lawrance records *aipud* (literally 'to trample down') as that part of the burial where mourners threw earth on the corpse before filling the grave. The grave was then watched over to 'guard against ghouls or animals' (Lawrance 1957: 100). On the second day of the burial, the *ateker* gathered to count the property of the deceased, and to call for debts to be paid. On the third day beer was contributed by mourners and shared. Some time after the burial, a second ceremony, *asuban*, was convened where the members of the *ateker* would gather to throw ashes from the fire that had been lit to attend the grave (Lawrance 1957: 101).

In other words, something of the ceremonies of the past persisted in the work of burial societies. The basic form of *aipud* (the funerary rite) existed prior to the 1990s, and the ideal of a three-day burial was something that connected past to present. Similarly the particulars of what happened after a villager died borrowed from the basic architecture of burial cere-monies from earlier decades. The most obvious difference was the decline of *asuban*, the memorial rite, which lived on only in those wealthier homes where memorial services were used as a way of bringing together distant

---

19 According to Nobuhiro Nagashima the term *aipud*, or *aipuduno*, refers also to the ritual of taking out the wife and baby from the hut three or four days after giving birth (Nagashima 1976: 50). This difference may be a reflection of local variations or changes in meaning over time. A similar difference can be found in the way J. C. D. Lawrance refers to *asuban* as a memorial ceremony while Nagashima suggests that the term applies to any ritual (Lawrance 1957: 100; Nagashima 1976: 59).

relatives to commemorate the death of a 'big man', typically around the time of public holidays such as Christmas or Easter. These larger funeral rites can be very elaborate affairs, and are meant to bring a formal end to the grieving.

Aside from the practical continuities, what emerges strongly from the available material on the late colonial and early post-colonial periods is the symbolic and emotional importance of death as a rite of passage. Fr Bernard Phelan recalled in an interview with me the following experience of dealing with village burials in the 1970s:

> If anyone died in the village, then people would drop everything they were doing and would attend the burial. The fear was that if you did not attend you might be accused of being responsible for the death ... Once the person was dead, he or she would be ritually washed, and those doing the washing would speak to the spirit of the dead person saying *sirikiyanga iso erono* (do not take us ill) ...
>
> Once the time of burial was ready, all the wailing would cease, and the body tied securely in a sheet ... Putting the body in the grave would be accompanied by a lot of shouting to ensure that the body was facing the right way, and usually on its side ... all of this was to make sure that there was a good relationship between the dead person and the living.[20]

Doris Clark, writing in the *Uganda Journal* in the 1950s, describes the mourning of a community in the Usuk region along the Karamoja–Teso border. In her account, responses to a death in a community could produce considerable trauma: 'very often women will attempt suicide, and it is a common practice for them to keep a special cord in their grain baskets for the purpose' (Clark 1953: 75–6; see also Gulliver 1952). She speaks of the expressive manner of the burial, the sense of loss and the significance of death, and her observations point to the importance of death as something connected to ideas of crisis and exposure.

More generally, a point needs to be made about the relationship between the living and the recently departed. A large part of the legitimacy of burial societies came with the understanding that they helped pacify potentially destructive influences. Problems of sickness or conflict within a household were often explained in terms of the influence of a recently departed member of the family. A poorly organised burial ceremony was to be avoided, as it would otherwise give the deceased justifiable cause to trouble the living. Fr Phelan recalled the following story about a family attempting to make amends for an improper burial:

20 Fr Phelan started his mission work in Teso as a Mill Hill Father in 1968. At different points in his career he has served in Toroma, Serere and Bukedea (written communication received 13 July 2005).

> I remember a Secondary School student coming to me to purchase a bag of cement so that they could cement the grave of their grandfather. I asked him why. The *emuron* (traditional healer) had told them that the sickness affecting their mother was the result of the unhappiness of the Grandfather not having his grave cemented.[21]

In such a story there is the understanding that the spirits of the recently deceased have a relationship with those who are living, and that a disrespectful burial is likely to bring sickness and misfortune to the family (Thomas and Scott 1935: 97). Ivan Karp writes something similar in his study of the Iteso of western Kenya, where 'failure to participate in funeral rituals is sanctioned through adverse public opinion, and it is believed that *ipara*, spirits of the dead, will malevolently attack those who fail in their funeral duties' (Karp 1978: 71).

The Experience of Death and Burial during the Insurgency

Yet the belief that death mattered because it affected the lives of those left behind did not mean that the management of death had to be institutionalised in the form of a collectively managed insurance scheme. What appears to have promoted the development of burial societies was the particular context of the Teso Insurgency. In making funerals more orderly, organised and respectful, burial societies opposed, in a fairly direct way, recent experiences of violence.

The insurgency saw the collapse of the economic means through which villagers had been able to manage burials in the past. The depletion of cattle stocks, as well as the looting of granaries, meant that richer homes could no longer afford to pay for what they considered a decent burial, while poorer people found it harder to meet what was regarded as the bare minimum. Acts of commensality could no longer be paid for and the disappearance of burials as ceremonious occasions encapsulated the sense of isolation and decline. At a mundane level, everyday forms of sociality and sharing, whether in drinking beer or holding a conversation with a neighbour, became rare events. The insurgency was spoken of as a time when life retreated inwards, first to the household, and then to the individual:

> It was impossible for us to keep the burials going in the way we wanted. Everyone was at risk and people were poor. For us, everyone had to keep to themselves and their own family, and there would be no proper burials for the dead. We had problems with food, and burials could not go ahead under such conditions.[22]

The insurgency thus represented a breaking down of the usual pattern of village life. Established mechanisms for dealing with disputes were set to

---

21 Written communication from Fr Bernard Phelan, received 15 May 2007.
22 Interview with Odongo Emmanuel, Oledai sub-parish, 22 August 2002.

one side, and conflicts which had been managed in the past were resolved through violence. Instead of having to negotiate with someone there was the possibility of silencing the opposing voice. One of the remembered ways of doing this was to report someone either to the government soldiers or to the rebels, charging them with being a collaborator – with the expectation that the accused party would be threatened or killed.

Most striking of all was the way rebels – typically younger men – chose to kill 'big men'. Rebels went out of their way to attack the idea that a 'big man', such as a village chief or *ateker* head, should be buried in a respectful way, and rebel groups made a point of denying the rite of *aipud* to the family of a big man. The most remembered way of killing a big man was referred to as 'digging potatoes' (*aibok acok*). 'To dig potatoes' meant to be taken from home, by a group of rebels, to a field where a hole would be dug to serve as a grave.[23] In certain other cases, killings resulted in the body being dumped in the swamp, a sacrilegious act since swamps were regarded as dangerous places where punishment for transgressions such as incest and adultery were meted out (Henriques 2002: 177; Okalany 1973: 140). Big men were purposely buried in the late afternoon, the time of day typically reserved for the interment of thieves or other undesirables. The local catechist recalled in an interview that 'You could get a man killed like a goat, his dead body would be strewn along the road; the rebels could kill a man and tell his people not to mourn.'[24]

Added to these rather graphic memories of death and dying was the experience of the internment camps.[25] The internment process, which lasted for nine months in 1990, made death a much more immediate concern for those who had escaped the politics of the bush war. Unlike killings of big men, which were targeted and somewhat predictable affairs, death in the camps was the result of poor sanitation, poor food and lack of medicine

23 As late as 2003, the phrase could still be used in the national media. An article from the *Monitor* newspaper was titled: 'Has Kony come to tie Teso dogs or dig potatoes' (15 July 2003). The meaning of this rather cryptic headline concerns the possible dilemmas facing the population of the region should it fall under the influence of Joseph Kony's Lord's Resistance Army (as has been the case for northern parts of the country for many years). The headline speaks of two possible scenarios, one where the LRA would be able to 'tie Teso dogs' which would mean that the LRA had secured enough fear or loyalty from the rural population to stop villagers from 'barking' [releasing information] to the government soldiers. The second scenario involves the LRA coming to 'dig potatoes', which would mean that the rural population had sided with the government. In all likelihood villagers would be forced to try to combine strategies of resistance and collaboration.

24 Interview with Ikara Patrick, catechist serving the Roman Catholic Church, 4 December 2002.

25 An Amnesty International report stated that the numbers of those who died in the camps far outweighed those who died in the bush war, putting the overall figure at 10,000 (Amnesty International 1992: 7; see also Zistel 2002: 214–15). If these figures are to be believed, then, in the space of nine months, one out of every twelve internees died in the camps.

(Amnesty International 1999: 21).[26] Social rather than political categories were punished, with the oldest and the youngest dying in greater numbers.

The National Resistance Army's response to the crisis of so many deaths, in so confined a space, was to require that the dead be buried in communal pits.[27] One of the older men in the sub-parish recalled: 'In the camps a person would be buried without respect. The burial would be done in a bad way. You would be thrown into a pit without sheets or prayers.'[28] These pit burials, away from one's home and without the proper rite of *aipud*, caused considerable distress, and villagers tried to avoid pit burials if they could. Some paid money to camp guards in order to leave for a day, so that they could take the body home for burial. (This option carried considerable risks, as rebels were often hostile to those who returned to the village.[29]) Those who could not afford to pay soldiers, or who felt it too risky to return home, could leave a mark on the body as a way of allowing for the retrieval of the corpse once the camps were disbanded.[30] The retrieved remains could later be laid to rest at home.

The development of burial societies took place in the shadow of the Teso Insurgency. Their work, like the work of the local courts or the village churches, related to the violence of the recent past. In their emphasis on orderly behaviour and collective action burial societies confronted the past with a counter-image. A decent burial contrasted sharply with the experience of the bush war and the sorts of dying that took place in the internment camps. A point to be discussed later on in the chapter is the way in which burial societies were institutionalised because they provided a way of dealing with the remembered past. They mattered not only because they offered a form of insurance but also because they *meant* something in relation to the history of the place. A good chunk of their legitimacy came from the way burial societies marked a purposeful separation from the nature of death and dying in the recent past.

Much of the work of burial societies in Oledai was to ensure a sense of

26 The deaths that occurred in the camps were, to all intents and purposes, 'planned' by the government. The internment process was not a hastily assembled response to a sudden humanitarian crisis; rather, it was part of a thought-through military strategy. Despite the opportunity for advance planning, the camps recorded death rates as high as 15 per 10,000 people per day. This apparently places the camps well above the normal CMR (crude morality rate) of 0.5 per 10,000 for such places, and also far ahead of the 2–3 deaths per 10,000 that is used by relief agencies to categorise a 'dire situation' (Teso Relief Committee 1990; de Berry 2000: 110).

27 Pit burials were discussed in several interviews, with the most detail coming from Amuge Gabdesia (interviewed 22 August 2002) and Okaleke Peter (11 September 2002).

28 Oonyu Joseph (27 August 2002).

29 Interview with Oluka Charles, from the neighbouring sub-parish of Agolitom, 24 September 2002.

30 The point was made in an interview with Amuge Gabdesia, a member of Atekok Esasi, on 22 August 2002.

respect and properness at the time of death, and this may be understood, in part, as a response to changes in the way people were dying. It is likely that the growing importance of burial societies also had something to do with the impact of HIV/AIDS in the region. Though the connection was never made in conversation, it is possible that HIV/AIDS may have produced increases in the numbers of 'wrong' sorts of dying – deaths of the young, the healthy and the better-off – and that this promoted the work of burial societies. Susan Reynolds Whyte makes a similar point in her work among the Banyole to the south of Teso: 'the frequency with which adult women are dying in circumstances of doubt about where they should be buried' had increased because of HIV/AIDS (Whyte 2005: 155).

The Role of Returnees in Building up Burial Societies

What also appears to have aided the setting up of burial societies in the 1990s was the exodus (and later return) of a number of young men during the insurgency years. Burial societies were an amalgam of different experiences and represented a response not only to the violence of the insurgency and the degradation of the internment camps but also to the influence of exile. Ibuchet Max, leader of the Ikures *ateker*, and a member of Ogoria burial society, observed that 'The idea of having a burial society came from Pallisa (neighbouring region). That is where we learnt about it. We copied what they did, and put it into action here.'[31] Other interviews with those who left the area confirm that the experience of exile involved a good deal of learning about the practices and institutions of neighbouring areas. A number of young men moved away from the sub-parish, mostly to the Pallisa and Busoga regions to the south. Many of the men who migrated as the insurgency reached its peak lacked the sorts of political connections or the money that aided the flight of earlier refugees.[32] Usually with less formal education and more dependent on the kindness of others, they had to make sense of life in a place very different from their own.

A particularly striking example of the experience of exile and the way it informed later developments in the village came in an interview with Olupot Constant. Olupot was a young man who decided to leave the sub-parish some time in the late 1980s. He was eventually 'adopted' by an older man living near to the town of Jinja in the Busoga region. During his time of exile Olupot learned to speak Lusoga and was apprenticed by his adoptive father in instrument making, a skill that continued to offer him a living

31 Interview with Ibuchet Max, 9 January 2003.
32 It is impossible to offer a complete accounting of the numbers of younger men who left during the insurgency. Alongside Olupot Constant and Ibuchet Max, I was able to identify three other men who told a similar story. These were Echai Stephen (who later became a committee member of the Ogoria *ateker*); Ochodio Andrew (a member of Ipagitok *ateker*); and Oluka Lawrence (chief *askari* for the Ichaak burial society).

through the sale of orchestral drums (*imidirin*), lutes (*adungui*) and finger pianos (*akogoi*) to churches and village schools (he is pictured at work on some *adungui* on page 132).[33] Olupot had also been apprenticed in Soga life, and during his exile had become a member of the burial society of his 'father'.

The type of learning that Olupot found in exile, which was based on practical forms of sociality, influenced his own role in setting up a burial society. His experiences from Busoga found expression in the rules and procedures that had been introduced to his burial society.[34] Olupot had an understanding of how burial societies were best organised, what the potential problems were, and how best to deal with them when they arose. This sort of past learning forms part of the explanation of why burial societies were institutionalised with such speed and economy of thought. It is a point that Frances Cleaver puts across in her work on *bricolage*, where knowledge is already embedded in existing individual experiences and institutional arrangements (Cleaver 2002: 15–17).

Whyte and Higenyi trace a similar pattern of learning among the Banyole to the south-east, where local practices were found to have conscientiously borrowed from neighbouring societies (1997). In a mirror-image of the form and function of burial societies in Oledai, Banyole met the costs of funerals, both in cash and kind. The people with whom Whyte and Higenyi spoke also discussed the importance of the strict set of rules that governed their burial society: 'the payment of a contribution does not free one from the obligation to be physically present at some point – a society member may not simply pay the secretary'. This pattern of borrowing can be understood as a form of *bricolage*, where burial societies resemble the fragments of other experiences.

And if we go back into the historical literature, an essentially similar point is made in a study of marriage patterns among the southern Iteso of western Kenya. Nobuhiro Nagashima's study argues that new social practices around marriage were the product of interactions with neighbouring societies and the experience of young men returning from military service. Changes in the social institution of bridewealth payment are traced to the years immediately following the Second World War, a time of rapid change. The shift from a 'lump sum' payment to a series of incremental payments is explained in the following way:

> [T]he reasons given by Iteso elders were twofold. First, soldiers who returned from the service introduced the piecemeal payment together with cash as a part of bridewealth. Second, the radical change was the

33 Interview with Olupot Constant, 23 December 2002.
34 Unfortunately D. W. Cohen's work on the Basoga from the 1960s does not discuss changing Basoga burial rites; the only account I could find of burial practices in the region was J. H. M. Beattie's discussion of Nyoro mortuary practices in the 1950s.

result of adopting the idea of piecemeal payment from neighbouring peoples. (Nagashima 1982: 14–15)

In other words, social institutions develop and change because of the influence of neighbouring societies and the experiences of living in other places.

BURIAL SOCIETIES AND LOCAL BORROWINGS

Burial societies were also made by piecing together social 'bric-a-brac' with a more local source in the area. They drew on logics, structures and practices which could be found in other institutional arrangements in the sub-parish. Something as basic as the burial society committee, which had a certain look to it and its own way of dealing with shirkers, drew from the range of practices that had a more particular history in the village. The leadership was elected in a familiar way, and key positions were dominated by men of a certain age with a certain reputation for toughness. Committee members brought along a range of skills that they had developed from working on other committees. The chairman of the Atekok Esasi was also on the elders' committee of his *ateker* (responsible for dealing with land disputes and conflicts between clan members), and was vice-chairman of the church committee of the Catholic congregation at Nyamongo.[35] This man knew how a committee should be structured; what minutes were; how to keep an account book; and what a well-run organisation looked like.

There were also more particular borrowings. The most striking example came in the way in which those who did not pay their burial dues were punished. By the time I went to the area the *askaris*, or 'soldiers' of the burial society, had a policy of tying a rope around those who had failed to pay their fees, before bringing them before the burial society committee for punishment (usually a fine, though beatings were not unknown). This rope-tying referred back to a time when a hut-tax defaulter would have a cord placed around his waist before being carted off to the sub-county headquarters. In other words, the burial society borrowed from the authoritative way of doing things found in earlier versions of the local government system. A similarly specific borrowing could be seen in the way leaders were elected, with villagers lining up behind their preferred candidate.[36] This was explained to me as something that copied the way local elections used to be carried out in the years before the introduction of the secret ballot (see

35 Other burial society leaders had similar institutional profiles: Odongo Emmanuel (vice-chairman Ogoria/Ipagitok/Ikures) was also the LC committee member for education; Okitoi Gabriel was the senior church elder for Nyamongo's Catholic congregation and a former member of the village council.

36 The point on the public election of leaders was made in several interviews, including those with Amuge Gabdesia, a member of Atekok Esasi burial society (22 August 2002); Okaleke Peter (11 September 2002); and Okalebo Lawrence, a member of Ipagitok *ateker* (12 September 2002).

also, for a description of council elections in the late 1960s, Vincent 1968: 55).[37]

Another borrowing, so to speak, concerned the public reporting of accounts. Here the borrowing came, partly, from earlier experiences of administration in the region, most obviously the management structures developed around the cooperative societies responsible for the collection and sale of cotton (Vincent 1968: 242, 245). At the same time, the public reporting of accounts was also understood in relation to the rather high-minded 'anti-corruption' discourse promoted by the Ugandan state and its partners in the international development community throughout the 1990s. In the case of Oledai, a place otherwise unburdened by the work of development agencies, the particular language of accountability and transparency had a certain residual power and was used to legitimise innovations at the local level.[38] The most self-conscious borrowing was the establishment of 'auditors' who were elected to the burial society committee (the word 'auditor' was used in Ateso as well as English). Auditors were typically older men, who were asked to scrutinise the work of the treasurer (usually responsible for handing out money) and the secretary (responsible for purchasing goods); this practice was particularly important as a way of fighting corruption.

> We do not have corruption, because we have an auditor to check the books of the treasurer. The auditor will first announce the name of the bereaved household. He will then tell you the total contributions raised for the burial, the amount of money spent on that burial and then the balance, which he then gives to the bereaved household.[39]

At a certain level, auditors could be seen as yet another example of the unintended consequences of development work. A number of studies have found similar examples of the 'side-effects' of projects and programmes (Bierschenk et al. 2000). Stacy Leigh Pigg, for example, shows how the desire of development agencies to fund 'traditional' institutions in Nepal pushes certain individuals to take on a 'traditional' role in the hope of getting a few cents from the development dollar (Pigg 1997). Pigg, like many others, was working in a project community.

---

37 A reflection, perhaps, of the way votes held in public continued to carry greater popular legitimacy than the idea of the secret ballot (Southall 1998: 260). The 1992 Report of the Uganda Constitutional Commission found that at the level of the sub-parish, 73.3 per cent of those interviewed saw 'lining up' as preferable to the secret ballot (which scored 20.4 per cent).

38 This trickle-down came mostly through the radio, though there had also been the occasional government project, or church-run workshop. Sixty-seven out of the 126 households in the sub-parish owned a radio, and those who did not have a radio at home would go around to a neighbour and listen from there.

39 Interview with Asige Martha, a member of Ichaak *ateker*, interviewed on 22 August 2002.

What is interesting to note in the context of Oledai is the way the language of 'development' mattered in a place that was somewhat removed from the loops of development work. 'Auditors' and the 'fight against corruption' were innovations even though there were no direct benefits to be had from co-opting the language of development. The language of 'corruption' had affected the work of burial societies, and it is possible that the liberal discourse of rights and responsibilities made burial societies more open than other more established institutions in the village. This openness could be observed in the way the burial book had to be open for society members to see; or in the way, at the end of the first day, the treasurer of the committee would report the accounts to the society and expect to be audited. He or she would have to account for what money had been collected, how much had been spent and what balance remained.[40] The discourse of fighting corruption or promoting accountability also resonated with the local variant of Pentecostalism. Pentecostalism in Teso placed a similar emphasis on individual responsibility and demonstrated a comparable belief that corruption and venality were endemic to public life.

What was also striking was the connection drawn between changes seemingly modest when measured in material terms, and the understanding that these small improvements meant that there had been meaningful development in the village:

> In our burial societies we have four saucepans, two hundred plates and cups, a water drum and many jerry cans. Our goal is to have twenty-five jerry cans so that women can fetch water more easily, not having to wait for one of the few jerry cans to become available. As you see our burial society has made great improvements; without it we would be stuck in the past.[41]

In emphasising the significance of a few pots and pans, Omuron John Simple reminds us of the hard-won nature of the gains made.

The Burial of Edotun, Part 2: the Burial Society

As with the land conflicts they so often bring to the fore, burials offer a rich terrain for the investigation of social, economic and political change. The study of burials as places where changes in a society can be observed has produced one of the better bibliographies on East Africa (see Beattie 1961; Cohen and Atieno Odhiambo 1992; Ojwang and Mugambi 1989; Whyte 2005). The death of Edotun Jackson, introduced in Chapter 6, showed the influence of the Anglican church at the burial. In what follows I would like

---

40 'The treasurer will tell you the total collection, the amount of money spent on the burial and the balance that will be given to the family of the deceased. It is all clear and above board.' From an interview with Asige Martha, 22 August 2002.
41 Interview with Omuron John Simple, 17 September 2002.

to focus on the burial society. The burial society was a new form of social insurance which had helped families meet the costs of funerals. In the case of Edotun's funeral it was also able to influence and affect the outcome of a land dispute involving his mother, Atai Helen, and the *ateker*. In understanding the influence of the burial society, it is possible to reflect on the evolving landscape of the village.

In revisiting the bare bones of the case it should be remembered that Edotun was believed to have been killed by two young men. Back in June these two men had stolen some belongings and money from his house and were subsequently charged and convicted of the theft. They were also prime suspects in the murder of Edotun some months later. But as the case progressed the police dropped the charges against the men, either because there was a lack of evidence, or because the families of the young men had paid more money to the police than the family of Edotun. The dropping of the case did not, however, absolve Edotun's mother of the bills she had to pay. As well as the funeral costs money had to be paid at the hospital and the police post. There was also the matter of dealing with her late husband's *ateker*, which, in principle, owned the land she and her son had been farming. In the past, a woman in Atai's position would have had to accept the protection of a levirate (a second husband from the *ateker*). Otherwise she would have had to face her own impoverishment.

And yet, despite this difficult situation, Atai was able to meet the various costs involved in her son's death, and was also able to establish something close to a consensus that allowed her to continue farming the *ateker* land allocated to her son. Chapter 6 spoke of the influence of the Anglican church in this regard (the lay reader spoke during the burial and this won Atai some sympathy). The burial society played a similar role: as well as paying for most of Atai's funeral costs, it also made the funeral a much more open affair, creating a new sort of publicity around Atai's land dispute.

On the economic front, Edotun's death proved to be costly. Opening the murder case against the two accused young men was something in which Atai had little choice, though it meant that she had to pay money both to the hospital and to the police. The hospital demanded USh50,000 ($29) while the police required USh30,000 ($17). (The murder of Edotun served as one of the few instances where poorer villagers contended directly with the otherwise latent coercive power of the state bureaucracy.) Since the combined total of USh80,000 was far in excess of the value of Atai's saleable property, she was in a particularly vulnerable position.[42] In the past the most likely outcome would have involved Atai having to accept a second husband from the *ateker* to take the debts on her behalf. This would also have meant giving up any claim over the land she and her son had been farming.

---

42 Atai's household was ranked 118 in the village in terms of wealth (out of a total of 126).

The greater part of the sum required was raised by the burial society (some money was also contributed by Edotun's fellow bicycle taxi men); the burial society also paid for the funeral. Without the burial society it would have been impossible for Atai to raise that sort of money, leaving her future in the hands of the *ateker* authorities. The burial society was thus instrumental in helping Atai survive her son's death without becoming ruined financially. While burial societies have often been open to the accusation that they push their members towards making burials more elaborate, and more expensive, it should be understood that these expenses were paid incrementally in the form of burial dues. Rather than facing a one-off cost at the moment when a family member died, a household would pay burial dues only on the death of a member of the burial society from another household. Without the money collected from other members of the burial society, it is also difficult to see how someone in Atai's position would have been able to pay either the hospital or the police.

Burials, it should be remembered, were a more regular part of life in the village than any other formal gathering, as the following table shows:

Table 7.2 Average attendance at different sorts of meetings, 2002[a]

Type of meeting	Number of times attended in 2002
Burials[b]	15.3[c]
Village court	1.3
Ateker council meeting	3.3
Church marriage	1.5

Notes

[a] Meeting attendance was based on an averaging of the responses given to the question: 'How many times over the last year have you attended [said institution]', part of the social networks survey.

[b] While the high number of burials attended may be an indication of the impact of malaria, HIV/AIDS or hepatitis, it should be pointed out that villagers themselves did not suggest that there had been more deaths in the place in the present compared with the past. This is in contrast to Whyte's work among the Banyole (2005). Embedded within the burial figures was also a comment on the tendency for villagers to attend as many funerals as possible (often in neighbouring sub-parishes). This was partly to pay one's respects, partly to have an opportunity to socialise, and partly to get a square meal.

[c] This table includes attendance at burials outside the particular burial society of the respondent. In most cases the respondent was the household head.

Burial societies also conferred a new sort of publicity on the occasion of a funeral. Edotun's burial was better-attended and better-organised than was likely to have been the case in the past. In effect, burial societies helped make funerals more of a public ceremony, in which a much larger proportion of the village had a stake and could express political or social concerns more readily. This could be seen in the way Edotun's burial afforded a new sort of public role to the lay reader of the Anglican church in the village. More generally, burials achieved a certain sort of public-ness. In Atai's case this changed the terms of the debate concerning the land dispute that followed on from the death of Edotun. The publicity surrounding the burial cast Atai Helen's situation in a more sympathetic light.

THE PAST IN THE PRESENT

In thinking about Atai's case, it is useful to reflect on the ways in which burial societies drew a certain moral authority from the way they related the present to the recent past. Writing on Bunyole society, Susan Reynolds Whyte observes, simply, that 'home is where you are buried', and goes on to discuss the ways in which burials, graves, and rituals of remembrance mark the attachment of an individual or a family to a home or a place (Whyte 1997: 87). Whyte also makes the point that burials demonstrate how a society has changed over time. In burying the dead a community demonstrates its relationship with its own past; in the particular case of Teso, burial societies were understood in relation to memories of the Teso Insurgency.

In their commensality and sociality burials such as Edotun's marked a sharp contrast with the experience of death during the insurgency. Something of their legitimacy was drawn from this opposition, and it is important to understand the extent to which burial societies made sense in ideological terms. Like other new forms of organisation which manage to endure, they are understood not only in terms of rules and incentives but also in terms of ideas and meanings. Burial societies were bound up with the *idea* that a 'proper' funeral marked out a decent life. The work of burial societies made the death of Edotun an orderly affair in what remained a potentially violent world. Villagers explained how ceremonious burials, with high levels of community participation, and sizeable contributions from the burial society, offered an antithesis to the sorts of dying that took place during the insurgency. They offered visible proof that life in the village had changed, that villagers had moved away from a time when rebels refused respectful burials to those they killed, and when the internment camps forced many villagers to bury the dead in communal pits.

It was against the experience of the bush war and the camps that burial societies achieved much of their legitimacy. In their orderliness and proper behaviour they served as a response to the insurgency and the internment camps:

> Our people got the idea of the burial society from their experience in the camps. At that time we were struggling under a culture where you would refuse to help your neighbour in his hour of need. No one would help anyone. It is better now, when people started to move

forward in setting up these groups a few years ago others saw that they were a good thing.[43]

As I argued in Chapter 2, notions of propriety were central to the story of what had changed in Oledai. Villagers attached increasing importance to a certain sort of morally codified or religiously inflected way of doing things. This was demonstrated through public displays such as having a decent burial, attending church, or showing due consideration in court. Such behaviour not only worked to strengthen one's standing in the village, but, in a more general way, forged a separation between an orderly present and the disorder of the past. Proper behaviour, based on agreed rules and conventions, could be said to draw a line between the shock of the insurgency and the relative order of the present, re-establishing an idea of predictability to life in the village.

One way of thinking about the increasing importance of propriety is to borrow from notions of rupture developed elsewhere. Birgit Meyer, for example, writes of Pentecostal discourse and practice in Ghana as something that offers the individual Christian a chance to 'break with the past' (Meyer 1998: 317; see also Engelke 2004; van Dijk 1998). Prohibitions on alcohol, traditional medicine and polygamy serve as outward signs of this inward rupture. In a not dissimilar way, life in Oledai had been organised around the desire to draw a line between the recent past and the present, though this was achieved in a much more open-ended way than allowed for in Meyer's study of Pentecostalism. In Oledai 'rupture' also applied to the work of burial societies or the local courts. The sorts of orderly funerals that were organised by burial societies made for a purposeful separation from the sorts of burials that took place during the bush war or in the internment camps, while the writing down of names in the burial book by the treasurer, or the purchasing of the burial sheet and coffin, signified a world where small details mattered because they underscored how much had changed in the village.

What can be drawn from Meyer's study of Pentecostalism is the observation that, in breaking with the past, the past gets institutionalised in certain ways in the present (Meyer 2004: 457).[44] For Meyer, Pentecostal Christians who become ill, get poorer, or suffer some other misfortune are a reminder that salvation is never guaranteed; rather, it is something that continuously has to be remade. In a not dissimilar way, the memory of the insurgency in Oledai was remade in the work of various institutions. Villagers presumed young men to be capable of extreme violence, and the work of the village court was adjusted because of this presumption. The memory of the insur-

---

43 Interview with Odongo Emmanuel, Oledai sub-parish, 22 August 2002.
44 Meyer suggests that 'Pentecostal-charismatic practice ultimately affirms the impossibility for born-again Christians to escape from forces grounded in and emanating from the local' (2004: 457).

gency was also apparent in the work of burial societies and at the funeral of Edotun Jackson. There was the understanding that his elaborate funeral was different from the ways of death and dying during the insurgency. There was also the knowledge that the way in which he had been killed was a continuation of the violence of that time.

This memory of violence explains why certain sorts of behaviour, and certain ways of organising, had become institutionalised: why churches had been able to tighten up rules in the 1990s and also why cases in court went the way they did. Most obviously the insurgency was one of the reasons why villagers had sought to transform the ways in which their dead were buried. Living a respectable life – whether attested by attending church, or by making younger men show due deference in court – suggested a fairly insistent drive towards making public actions different from the past. When an *askari* tied a rope around someone who had failed to pay his burial dues, before bringing him before the burial society committee, there was an understanding that this signified order and respect for rules and authority.

While I do not want to become too reductive in explaining why life in the village had changed in the way it did (the setting up of burial societies or the influence of Pentecostalism were not unique to Teso), it is fair to say that many developments were understood in part, and made real in part, because of the particular experience of the place.

CONCLUSION

New institutions refer to old ones, and while burial societies should be seen as relatively autonomous structures, unlikely to be co-opted or subsumed into the work of other institutional arrangements, the scaffolding that surrounded them borrowed from elsewhere. Earlier on in the chapter, I argued that the manner in which fees were collected, the structure of the committee, the way the book-keeping was conducted, and the sorts of rites that surrounded death could be related to what was found in neighbouring areas. These new practices also related to the work of churches or clan committees, and to the history of burials in the Teso region.

But new institutions also refer to old experiences, and towards the end of the chapter I have argued that the burial societies drew symbolic importance from what it meant to die in the years after the insurgency. As with all of the institutions discussed in the book, burial societies were more than management structures organised around ideas of efficiency or self-interest. They had become embedded because of the way their orderliness, prosperity and commensality forged a break with the past. Decent burials, well-organised, well-attended, and well-funded, opposed the experience of the insurgency. Though new institutions borrow from other institutions, and other experiences, it is important to recognise that new institutions are also understood in ideological terms. Just as the various churches in the sub-parish drew on the spiritual domain of Christian beliefs, or the village court drew upon a certain idea of what the government did in the past, so burial societies drew upon what it meant to die, what this said about the life of the individual, and what a decent funeral meant in relation to the memory of the Teso Insurgency.

Burial societies changed the social landscape of the sub-parish, and opened new possibilities for individuals. This was apparent in what happened to Atai Helen after the death of her son. The burial society provided her with a basic form of insurance, meaning that the death of her son did not lead to her own impoverishment. At the same time the institutional aspects of the burial society offered a sort of defined public space that opened up new sorts of opportunities for debate and discussion. Indeed, they also changed the terms of debate. The publicity that surrounded Edotun's burial was informed by the sense that burials (and burial societies) had to protect the interests of the family of the deceased. In Atai's case, this meant that the claim to her son's land came to be publicised at the burial, making it harder for men in the *ateker* to dispossess her. That Atai's case involved the church and the *atekerin*, and that each institution was affected by the others in the days surrounding the burial of Edotun, suggests that burial societies were one element in a broader landscape of change.

Plate 8 A woman draws water from the village swamp

The thorns and brambles were to keep livestock away from the open well.

8

CONCLUSION

That Uganda has been considered a 'success story' for the past twenty years would come as something of a surprise to the people I spent time with in Oledai. In particular, the idea that the few material improvements in the lives of villagers relate, first and foremost, to the policies and programmes of the government agencies or development organisations would be difficult to comprehend. The avenues through which the state was supposed to have mattered were closed off. Decentralisation and democratisation did not play a particularly important role. The government was more interested in the funds coming in from foreign donors than in economic or social possibilities in the countryside. The more significant developments in the sub-parish – the growth of Pentecostalism, the establishment of burial societies – related to the world of government or 'development' only in the most marginal ways. The parish chief was a rare visitor, and taxes were not collected in any serious sense. Earlier attempts at collectively enforced public works, such as the digging of pit latrines or the clearing of by-ways, had faded.

When villagers spoke of the state, it was more usually in the remembered past than in the lived present. One young man, Alemu James, had the following to say about a cattle restocking scheme, funded by foreign donors, which aimed at restoring the rural economy in the wake of the insurgency:

> I did not register my name with those government people from the town, because I knew that cattle would not be brought back. And I knew that it would make no difference to me, whether I registered or not. The only way I would get cattle back would be through my own money, my own efforts. Some people paid five hundred to register in that scheme but that money was just eaten, it achieved nothing.
>
> Since that time people have slowly forgotten about such things. They have not seen anything for so long. Instead they are trying to find a way of earning a living by themselves. If the raiding does not start up again, I think that people will slowly increase what they have.[1]

There are two things to say about the above commentary. First, Alemu James remarks on the failure of the scheme to make much of a difference,

---

1 Interview with Alemu James, 19 November 2002.

and instead suggests that development will come in more incremental ways, as a result of more personal efforts. Second, throughout the above commentary Alemu does not need to talk about 'the state' to describe the failings of the cattle restocking scheme. Instead, he refers simply to 'those government people'. Alemu, like everyone else in Oledai, did not talk of 'the state' when speaking in English and used the word *apugan* in Ateso, a word whose meaning is much closer to 'government'. This captures the then considerable gap between how people in Oledai conceptualised the fairly erratic workings of the government bureaucracy, and how government bureaucracies tend to be represented and theorised in academic work.

In many ways life in Oledai stood at a distance from the idea that the state existed as some sort of coherent entity whose influence could be seen at work in the village. The local government bureaucracy was instead detached and uninvolved. This lack of interest was expressed in many ways, most obviously through the absence of the parish chief. There was also the absence of any sort of meaningful relationship between the village council and the wider local government bureaucracy. Instead the village council had reverted to its older role as a sort of local court, where cases were presented on a weekly basis. It was a version of the state in the village that depended more on the actions of villagers and on the state's earlier history as an agent of authority.

The core of the explanation I have offered for the rather distracted government system in the present is that the Uganda government is 'extra-verted'. Uganda's political system is governed by a ruling elite which depends for its economic survival on its ability to mobilise resources from its relationship to the outside world. Each layer of the political and civil administration is turned upwards and outwards, depending on the next level up in the system rather than the level below. This trail of dependence flows one way: from the parish chief to the district government; from the district government to the central government; and from the central government to foreign donors. Although this logic of extraversion predated the dependencies of Yoweri Museveni's administration, the rate of 'turning upwards' under Museveni has been of a different order. Locally raised taxes paid for less than 2 per cent of government expenditures in Kumi District. In this figure is an indication of the non-presence of tax collectors in the countryside; of the unimportance of the rural economy in the maintenance of the local government system; and of the extraverted nature of Uganda's political system as a whole.[2]

In this final chapter, I would like to flesh out some of the points raised in the book in more general terms. In other words, I would like to join earlier sections together in ways that might be of use when thinking about processes of development and change in other places. I look again at churches

2 Uganda Government 2007: 21.

and their part in the life of the village, as well as at burial societies and the significance of people's ideological concerns. What follows restates my concern to approach development and change in an open-ended way, treating the role of government with greater scepticism, and considering the possible relationships between very different forms of organisation and different sorts of meanings. What my own work says about much of the available research on development in Uganda in recent years is touched upon again in the final paragraphs.

CHURCHES AND THE MEANING OF CHANGE

While earlier studies of the Teso region saw nothing remarkable or significant about churches, their importance in the life of Oledai was central to any understanding of what had changed in recent years. Churches, unlike other forms of organisation, had their own buildings in the village, and were, in a very physical sense, part of the landscape of the Teso region. Within these buildings congregations continued to meet even though there was a difficult relationship with the higher clerical bureaucracy.

The advent of Pentecostalism was the most obvious development in the religious landscape of the village of Oledai. Pentecostalism was a new and fairly radical version of Christianity, and required a high level of personal commitment. Joining the Pentecostal church meant accepting a number of prohibitions including bans on drinking of alcohol, smoking and using traditional medicine, all of which suggested the ways in which joining the church was something different. Married women suggested that becoming a member of the church had helped them deal with problems of drunkenness and violence within the home, while older villagers pointed to everyday ways in which the church was more useful than other forms of organisation. Being a church member meant that it was easier to get help at harvest time, or when a roof needed to be thatched.

Born-again Christians achieved prominence in the village, and took up important positions on the village court or the committees of the various burial societies that had been established in recent years. Those who converted continued their new lives once they left the church door. Omadi John Francis, a committed Pentecostal Christian, had also been asked to join the village council, taking up the position of vice-chairman. In Omadi's case the church had become a stepping-stone to something new as the church offered him a place to demonstrate his leadership credentials. At the same time the involvement of men and women such as Omadi in the life of the village altered the meaning and shape of non-religious institutions. The reputation of the village court shifted because of Omadi's involvement with it, while the participation of Ongenge George Washington, the Anglican lay reader, at burial ceremonies generated new sorts of publicity around the work of burial societies. In a sense, this is simply another way of taking into consideration the fact that church membership had to sit alongside other relationships, affiliations and obligations, and that these relationships, affiliations and obligations were affected by the new ideas and practices introduced by Pentecostal Christianity.

This leads on to a point concerning method. In looking at the relationship between Pentecostal Christianity and the public life of the village I have tried to move away from regarding churches as very separate places. While a number of researchers have focused on the internal workings of Pentecostal congregations, taking the exclusionary doctrine of born-again Christianity as also indicative of how Pentecostal Christians live their lives, it is also important to understand that religious identities are necessarily played out in wider social circuits.[3] The view of churches as singular and somewhat self-contained places, removed from the workings of more prosaic social organisations, is, in my view, unhelpful. Church membership in Oledai was understood in relation to other things. When Omadi stood outside the church door, after an accusation of having committed the sin of adultery, it was something not only witnessed by church members, but also commented on by others in the village. The embeddedness of Pentecostalism in the wider landscape of the village suggests that there is much to be gained from taking a more open-ended view of the significance of religious developments in the study of social change.

A more open-ended view makes it easier to see why Pentecostalism affected not only the lives of those who attended the Assemblies of God church but also the lives of Catholics and Anglicans. These historic mission churches had, after a number of years, experienced a period of renewal and revival. This renovation and renewal was partly a response to the growth of Pentecostal Christianity. Catholics and Anglicans had taken on many of the rules and regulations of Pentecostalism and adopted a number of practices from the new church. New rules on burial prayers, or on the understanding that membership signalled attendance rather than baptism, reflected the ways in which born-again Christianity informed developments in these older churches. There was an appropriation and institutionalisation of some of the signs and values of Pentecostalism.

One of the points I have wanted to make in this book is the extent to which developments in one sort of institution can be understood in relation to developments elsewhere. Pentecostalism's influence can be best understood when looking at developments in the historic mission churches and the village court alongside what went on in the local Pentecostal congregation. In more general terms, I have suggested that churches – as a broad institutional category – relate to changes observed elsewhere. There were certain equivalences that link together developments across what are otherwise very different sorts of organisation. The way in which churches

3 See Meyer 2004.

introduce rules on burial prayers, or the way church leaders are able to take a more public position at burials, were part of a more pervasive story where different aspects of village life had coalesced around ideas of propriety and commensality. Churches, of whatever denomination, are only one among a number of spaces where social, economic, political or religious concerns find their expression.

BURIALS, IDEAS AND INSTITUTIONAL CHANGE

The Teso Insurgency shadowed developments in Oledai. As a time when the social and economic fabric of the village unravelled, the insurgency was remembered, above all, for the localised, politicised nature of the violence perpetrated by rebels against others in society. Most obviously there was the killing of local 'big men', which was done in an intentionally sacrilegious way. No one had forgotten *aibok acok* ('digging potatoes'), a form of murder where the victim was taken from his house to a neighbour's field, to dig the hole that would later serve as his grave. 'Digging potatoes' made it impossible for the dead man and his family to rest in peace; the burial was without ceremony and took place away from home. Along with the more general sense of violence and degradation, these killings were remembered as a particularly powerful attack on ideas of respect and social order.

The work of churches in the wake of the insurgency was bound into concerns over notions of propriety and sociality. These concerns found expression in a growing interest in certain sorts of religiously inflected behaviour. Discussions on the role of village institutions were often framed by the question of what it meant to lead a good life; or what it was that constituted a decent burial. There was a fairly insistent concern with the need to show how institutional developments signified that life had moved on from the time of the insurgency. And it was also possible to see in the practice of village affairs how life in Oledai had come to be framed by a desire to break with the violence of the past. Orderly funerals, or the enforcement of new codes of personal behaviour, shared in similar sets of images, and there was, embedded in their work, a purposeful contrast to the memory of the insurgency.

Far removed from concerns about decentralisation, or the impact of government reforms, the subject that most exercised people's minds was the question of what constituted a proper burial. While topics such as decentralisation or democratisation were difficult to get going as a topic of conversation, burials and the work of burial societies were something which people were very ready to discuss, and the consensus that emerged from these discussions suggested that proper burials were marked out by the participation of a large proportion of the village, and by the pulling together of a fairly elaborate system of rituals and requirements. Each individual member of the burial society had to pay money on the death of a fellow society member, and the burial society as a whole was responsible for financing and organising the logistical aspects of the burial day. That burials were now managed by burial societies rather than the individual household also meant that a new sort of public space had opened in the village, where a range of political and social concerns could be addressed. More money was paid to burial societies than to either the village churches or the local government.

If the insurgency represented a breakdown in the social order, then a decent burial signified restoration and the possibility of civility. The work of burial societies was more than that of a simple insurance scheme. They mattered because they *meant* something. Intrinsic to their work was the idea that they marked a break with the violence of the recent past, and an absolute contrast to the sacrilegious burials experienced during the insurgency. That burial societies were able to invoke a number of sanctions and punishments was tied into the understanding that a decent funeral meant something in the particular context of the village. To put it another way, burial societies acquired an ideological as well as an instrumental logic. They were more than simple insurance schemes.

In their institutionalisation burial societies also tell us something of the reasons why certain types of organisation persist while others do not. Institutional analysis has been dominated by liberal or economistic explanations which rarely give weight to ideological concerns. Individuals are characterised as rational actors who respond to economic incentives and structure their choices accordingly. Development projects are based on the presumption that people are best described by their economic condition – beneficiaries are 'poor' or are 'living in poverty' – and so must be interested principally in economic development. This emphasis on the importance of incomes or the benefits to be had from participating in 'development' schemes detaches the question of development from ideological considerations and downplays the significance of religious, customary or social identities. I would argue that one of the reasons why externally funded community projects had a short lifespan in the Teso region was that they failed to link into people's political or ideological projects.

While material concerns were pressing in Oledai, the social arrangements that people invested in – burial societies and churches – mattered because they linked into larger frameworks of meaning. Burial societies or churches tied political organisation or social insurance to questions of religious belief and the experience of the Teso Insurgency. Something with an obvious instrumental function – the insurance aspects of a burial society, for example – achieved legitimacy because it evoked a telling contrast with the violence of the recent past. In Oledai, at least, those forms of organising which kept going did so because they made claims that went beyond people's immediate economic concerns.

In a not dissimilar way, Mary Douglas points to the ways in which institutional arrangements have to 'borrow' from outside themselves if they are to seem legitimate and natural. Institutions need to acquire some sort of meaning because it is meaning that gives naturalness to invented social arrangement. Douglas explains this point in the following terms:

> There needs to be an analogy by which the formal structure of a crucial set of social relations is found in the physical world, or the supernatural world, or eternity, anywhere so long as it is not seen as a *socially contrived* arrangement. When the idea is applied back and forth from one set of social relations to another and from these back to nature, its recurring formal structure becomes easily recognisable and endowed with self-validating truth [my italics].[4]

Douglas's conception of 'analogies' is useful. It explains why externally driven attempts at building local institutions dissolve and decay. Without a connection to something 'outside themselves' institutional innovations such as micro-credit initiatives, women's groups or development projects appear socially contrived. This makes it difficult for people to invest time and energy in them and explains why so many development initiatives fail in the longer term.

BEYOND THE STATE

In the introduction to this book I described how I came to challenge the proposed object of my research. Instead of attempting to explain local transformations through the lens of the state, I have chosen to explore a broader terrain of institutions and influences. Churches and burial societies, religious beliefs and a history of violence form the changing landscape of social and political life in rural Teso. Development is an open-ended business, best explored through a range of activities and ideas.

Though it may seem obvious that churches and customary institutions are likely to provide an arena for politics, it is surprising how little attention has been paid to institutions outside the state in recent work on local politics in Uganda. The earlier body of work to which Southall, Middleton and Vincent all made important contributions, and which suggested an open approach to the study of development, has given way to a more narrow and refined research agenda. In the literature which I have found myself writing against, developments in the Ugandan countryside have come to be regarded as reactions to government policies or development programmes. The study of decentralisation, for example, dominates the literature on social change in rural Uganda, though it offers only a partial view of developments at the local level. The desire to place the state at the heart of things

4 Douglas 1987: 48.

makes it difficult to see what people are doing when they are not reacting to a piece of legislation or government reform.

James Scott coined the term 'seeing like a state' to convey the utopian or totalising visions that governments sometimes try to impose on populations (Scott 1999).[5] It would appear that the incentives that lie behind much academic thinking on Uganda, rather like the incentives that guide its state bureaucracy, are extraverted, turned outwards towards the concerns of the donor community.[6] Instead of research being framed in a way that takes into account actual changes that have occurred in Uganda, such as the religious transformations taking hold in the towns and the countryside, research reflects the rather partial logics of a policy-oriented bureaucracy. The narrowness of the terrain is seen not only in the cursory treatment of religious institutions, but also in the view that government policies have brought 'success' to the countryside, and in the avoidance of any discussion of coercive or militaristic aspects of the Ugandan state in accounts of political administration. Though it would appear that the agenda for research has shifted in recent years, away from a favourable view of the Museveni government towards a more critical position, this is a shift in emphasis rather than orientation.

Research needs a more sceptical view of what constitutes development. This means viewing the countryside as a place where people do something more than respond to the incursions of the government or the ministrations of development agencies. Although I have not argued that bureaucracies are without importance, or that donor interventions do not matter (in many ways my arguments on extraversion suggest the opposite), it is instructive to take a more open-ended approach. Where change does occur, it need not be related, first and foremost, to the work of government officials, district politicians or development workers. It may well be that it is in its *absences* that the state matters most. In Oledai the weakness of the state bureaucracy denied villagers access to the sorts of services that might have brought improvements to their lives, yet also led them to venture beyond the coercive relationships that had marked earlier experiences of the state bureaucracy in the countryside.

A more workable proposition would be to suggest that the state is mostly

---

5 The examples Scott draws on in his African cases are Haile Mariam Mengistu's Ethiopia and Nyerere's Tanzania – both rather exceptional.

6 Indeed, if we think about the ways in which researchers enter Uganda, which is to say through NGO-sponsored work, development projects, World Bank background reports, collaborative research efforts, or as private consultants, then they first encounter 'Uganda' through the state. This is a biased entry point, and translates into a view of Uganda that overstates the importance of the state in academic thinking and writing. On a very mundane level, dealing with the Uganda National Council of Science and Technology, with the immigration office, or with line ministries and university departments may make the state much more a part of Ugandan life in the minds of researchers than it actually is.

uninterested in rural Uganda. Rather like the academics who study it, the state has been turned upwards and outwards towards the incentives that pervade an economy of international 'development'. A few showcase development sites – 'project villages', district capitals, Kampala, the clinics where international pharmaceutical companies trial new drugs – are islands in a sea of neglect. Villagers operate in a constrained environment, one of limited opportunities where there is little overlap between what is written about development in rural Uganda and the actual experience of what it is to live in the countryside. Instead, many significant changes belong to logics, structures and practices that have a different provenance. Customary and religious institutions define the parameters for social action. In Oledai, as in much of the world, life is organised around a more disparate set of spaces that nonetheless continue to promise the possibility of change.

Plate 9 A villager sells millet grain

The venue is the fortnightly market on the outskirts of Ngora. Farmers attended the market from across the sub-county.

APPENDIX A:
RESEARCH METHODS

To borrow from J. Clyde Mitchell (1983), this book is essentially an extended case study, an heuristic device, which allows the researcher the freedom to investigate and put together a number of observations, which may be construed as one manifestation of a more general problem. Drawing on the work of van Velsen (1967), Mitchell suggests that the concern of rather narrow studies such as this is not so much to offer a total view of a 'culture' or 'society', but rather to understand the social processes which might be abstracted from a particular course of events or micro-history. In Mitchell's view such an analysis may tell us something of the means through which continuity or change is achieved, linking the local to the conceptual rather than making generalisations about what is going on in society.[1] It should be clear, though, that I am less perfect in my approach than Mitchell, as I have tried to suggest ways in which some of what was observed in Oledai may be useful to those undertaking similar work elsewhere. Mitchell's is a rather idealised version of what a case study usually sets out to do, and in this book I have attempted not only to reach towards the conceptual but also to link my work into other studies. While I would accept the need to delimit the claims made in any piece of ethnography, it is also possible to open out the analysis through the use of historical data and comparable sorts of research from other authors (on this point see Sally Falk Moore 1986: Chapter 1).

In terms of the way I went about doing fieldwork, what is written below is written in retrospect; and it is a tidier version of the methods than what was lived on the ground. As indicated on the first page of the book, my research had to shift from a concern with investigating the impact of democratic decentralisation towards a more standard piece of ethnography. And in shifting away from an impact study the research methods made a similar move. This was most obviously apparent in the move away from the rather voguish methodology of Participatory Rural Appraisal.[2]

1 In defending the value of case study analysis J. Clyde Mitchell criticises those who do statistical analysis for their tendency to conflate results with the production of causal inference. Mitchell reminds us that even the statistician must go beyond observing the correlation to find some theoretical explanation linking the two variables together: any inference must be based on the plausibility or logicality of the nexus between the two characteristics (Mitchell 1983: 198). In case study analysis, by contrast, Mitchell points out that any material inference can only be causal, not statistical. In either case, though, the extent to which generalisations can be made (whether from a population sample or a case) must depend upon the reasoned logic of the underlying argument.
2 Participatory Rural Appraisal is part of a family of methods which includes a number of participatory learning approaches. The emphasis is on the idea that participatory

So perhaps, before going into a longer discussion of the methods eventually taken up, it might be useful for the reader if I said something of my own experiences, and problems, with Participatory Rural Appraisal.

Participatory Rural Appraisal has gained currency in recent years, both for development agencies working in poorer countries and for academics conducting research around questions of interest to development agencies. It would seem to offer a short-cut to the sorts of qualitative information gathered through more established, long-term ethnographic approaches (Olivier de Sardan 2005: 9). In its desire to consult people living in the countryside it sits well with the language of much development assistance (empowerment, ownership, voice, exchange, grassroots governance) (Chambers 1999). A number of illustrative tools – ranking, mappings, classifications – are used to help draw out the views of the assembled individuals in a time-efficient and replicable way. Such methods are said to open up the possibility of more obviously comparative work than has otherwise been possible.[3]

My attempts at Participatory Rural Appraisal were frustrating. Even though I made a conscious effort to keep my own version fairly open-ended, the various 'exercises' made 'participants' reluctant to share certain sorts of information. Group discussions seemed to shear off the political or ideological arguments that mattered in less structured interactions.[4] Debates concerning the significance of religious belief, the politics of the insurgency years, or the role of conflict between fathers and sons were not discussed.[5] It is, perhaps, too much to argue that participation and participatory techniques are a new 'tyranny' in development practice (Cooke and Kothari 2002); development work is too occasional and uneven to sustain such a charge. The more important point is that participatory research techniques produce a situation where people feel the need to downplay the importance of politics, ideas and beliefs.

The research moved towards a more conventional ethnographic approach. I was fortunate to have a copy of Joan Vincent's *African Elite* with me during my stay, as Vincent's study of a rural parish provides a number of clues on how to go about

---

methods take into account the views of people on the ground and open up new possibilities in the design of development projects.

3 A number of applied anthropologists regard Participatory Rural Appraisal more reflexively, as part of an ongoing conversation with a target population. This is a dialogical device where the facilitator is obliged to listen to the views and opinions of the various groups, going back and forth over the life course of the project (see, for example, Mosse 2005).

4 This is something that can also be found in the nation-wide Participatory Poverty Assessment funded by the World Bank and the Government of Uganda (Uganda Government 2000a; Uganda Government 2000b). The material collected for the Participatory Poverty Assessment in Kumi District was unable to capture quite basic observations about life in the region. The politicised nature of the violence during the insurgency, the popular hostility towards the Museveni government, the significance of religious institutions, the importance of burial societies – all these were remarkably absent from the final report (unsurprisingly, perhaps, development work and government reforms were discussed in detail).

5 There was no easy answer to the question posed by Jean-Pierre Olivier de Sardan: 'how can a handful of enquirers, aided only by oversimplified methodological tools and insufficient anthropological competence ... possibly unearth relevant political, economic and cultural information?' (2005: 210).

producing sustained and detailed descriptive analysis. Vincent's study suggested how best to broaden out the case study approach so as to gather the sorts of data that could explain how political actions were pieced together at the local level. My time in the area was gradually reorganised around a number of less imaginative methods which focused on gathering information on the different sorts of organisations within the sub-parish.

With the help of four colleagues, two surveys were conducted: a household survey and a survey of villagers' memberships in organisations and networks.[6] The household survey was particularly useful in establishing a wealth ranking of households, based on the value of livestock and material goods such as mattresses, radios and bicycles.[7] The questionnaire also included a systematic inquiry on household structure, assets and household expenditures (on milk, cooking oil, kerosene, salt, soap and school costs) and in its formulation borrowed from the National Household Survey 1999/2000 of the Uganda Bureau of Statistics (changes had to be made to some of the questions to make the survey comprehensible). The second survey collated data on people's participation in institutions and social networks. Both surveys were conducted at the level of the household head, which necessarily produces certain biases (where the household head was unavailable for interview another adult member of the household was interviewed). In a fairly useful way the two surveys required introductions and conversations with all of the households in the sub-parish, obviating some of the problems of relying on the rather partial introductions that are offered by local 'big men'.

After pulling away from Participatory Rural Appraisal, I continued to use discussions with groups of a few people, though without the paraphernalia of rankings and listings. These more free-form discussions were particularly useful as a way of corroborating or contradicting other accounts. Groups tended to be somehow self-assembled, and discussants often found it easier than I did when it came to opposing or challenging what others were saying. Of particular value were the bicycle taxi men, who were happy to joke with each other and found it easy to speak critically of each other and of the village (they regarded themselves as more sophisticated and worldly).[8] A total of forty group discussions were held during the fieldwork, and I tried to make the discussion as relaxed as possible, even though my preparations were considerable.

Alongside survey work and group discussions there were a good number of interviews (see appendix B).[9] Interviews were conducted with the leaders of the

6 Research assistance was provided by Aguti Stella, Akello Suzan, Osakan Christopher and Enou Andrew Benjamin. Stella, Suzan, Christopher and Benjamin were aged in their twenties, and lived in the trading centre of Ngora.

7 The wealth measure used for ranking households was livestock assets measured by market prices for January 2002. If we were to use the value of household assets, including durable goods (mattresses, watches, sewing machines, etcetera) as well as livestock, the welfare ranking would remain similar (see Hu and Jones 2004: 14).

8 Bicycle taxi men were also interesting informants because they saw themselves as more urbane and more modern, and so tended to cast a critical eye over village life.

9 Despite my earlier characterisation of Oledai as a backwater, a number of villagers spoke English. English remained the language of the higher courts, of the education system, and the *lingua franca* of negotiations with traders from outside the region.

various *atekerin*, churches and the village council, as well as at least two other council members. Wherever possible both women and men were interviewed, and I tried to get as many villagers, from as many different economic categories as possible, to comment on their experiences (see Appendix B for the ranking by wealth, education level, age and gender status of the various respondents). Certain people were interviewed repeatedly, and if a particular crisis or point of contention appeared to dominate the workings of a particular institution, more material was gathered as a way of building up more detailed case studies (Bauer and Aarts 2000: 31–6; Mitchell 1983). A total of 92 interviews, each typically lasting two to three hours, were conducted in Oledai during my stay, and 74 interviews were undertaken in the neighbouring sub-parish of Agolitom. A further 15 interviews were conducted with officials, politicians or observers from outside the sub-parish.[10]

Recent writings on the Teso region have discussed the difficulty of talking with people about the insurgency. Joanna de Berry, in her work on post-war recovery in eastern Teso in the late 1990s, wrote of the problems she faced when trying to investigate the lived experience of the insurgency (2000: Chapter 1). The politics of the insurgency, in particular, appeared to be too sensitive a subject for de Berry to explore and this resulted in an analysis which did not take into account the level of conflict and violence experienced at the local level. Peter Henriques, who lived in the region in 1994 and 1995, provides a largely social account of life in the Teso region because of the apparent difficulty in gaining information on the political dimensions of the insurgency (Henriques 2002: 33–4).[11]

By contrast, villagers in Oledai were relatively comfortable discussing what took place during the insurgency, and their account of that time fills in some of the gaps of earlier ethnographies. Conversations and discussions brought forward some of the debates on the micro-politics of the insurgency. It was possible for villagers to connect the way the violence of the period linked into later social and economic developments, such as the growth of Pentecostalism or the building up of burial societies. The main reason for their openness came from the fact that more time had elapsed since the end of the insurgency. Even though a few older men were uncomfortable when it came to discussing the history of their own home during that time, the greater number spoke with candour. It was perhaps easier for women to relate their experiences of the insurgency, as they were not directly implicated in the violence of the rebellion; few women served as rebels and most of the women in the sub-parish had married into the area (meaning that they were one stage removed from the family conflicts that drove much of the rebellion). Discussions of the insur-

---

Half of all households in the sub-parish had at least one family member who spoke English, and interviews with *ateker* leaders, church leaders and the village council chairman were conducted in a mixture of English and Ateso. English was also the language of primary education. In those instances where interviewing was conducted in Ateso, a research assistant did most of the questioning, as my limited Ateso meant I could only offer help and guidance. (The language in which the interview was conducted is also indicated in Appendix B.)

10   This parallel research effort has given me greater confidence in the way I have understood developments throughout the Teso region.

11   This explains why Henriques, like de Berry, also presents the insurgency as if it was a disaster that befell his informants. There is little discussion of the insurgency as a political conflict.

gency were also helped by the advent of new forms of Christianity. Those who joined new religious groups, whether Pentecostal, Catholic or Anglican, explained how their new lives were distanced from the violence of the recent past.

In terms of gathering written information, my experience was less straightforward. The insurgency engendered a general antipathy towards handing over written information to anyone who appeared to be 'official'. Outsiders like me were associated with a government that villagers had little reason to trust. Texts concerning land claims, burial lists, tax receipts, records of educational attainment, or voting cards were handed over only with a certain reluctance and many simply refused to help. In the end the village council chairman was prepared to hand over some of his case books and was available to discuss some of the more contentious cases (many of which were written in a cursory fashion, comprehensible to the council chairman only, or were not written down at all). Three burial society chairmen released documents regarding the rules of the society, and the books in which burial dues were paid. A number of more educated villagers were able to offer up documents they had kept over the years, including pieces of government information, education certificates and photographs. School teachers and church leaders were also happy to release what information they had in their personal archives – though much of this material had been destroyed during the insurgency. Photocopies of all of these documents were made in Ngora and the originals returned to the household. Documents were also gathered from the sub-county and district offices (even here my 'official' status seemed to inspire a certain hesitance).[12] I was, perhaps, fortunate that my efforts at collecting written information were undertaken towards the end of my time in the area, rather than at the beginning.

Cutting across these various approaches were a number of more targeted attempts at piecing together reasonable accounts of significant events that occurred during my stay in the area. The murder and burial of Edotun Jackson and the tribulations that beset his mother, Atai Helen, were documented in as much detail as possible. So were a number of other cases, including the career history of Omadi John Francis, a member of the Pentecostal Assemblies of God church; Ogwapit Joseph, who had a number of court cases on the go; and the troubles of Okelai Samuel and Akol Stanislas, both younger men who were punished as much for their stubbornness as for any actual crime or misdemeanour. Such cases were part of the normal flow of conversation in the village and information from a number of villagers meant that they could stand up as extended case studies from which fairly elaborate activities could be analysed and interpreted. The collection of data for these cases was as exhaustive as possible, and included not only repeated interviewing with participants, but also seeing how the case was broached.

A final point on methodology. While it is usual to assume that there are clear and categorical distinctions that divide religious, governmental and customary forms of organisations from one another, the approach in this study has been to try to link

12   Information was also gathered on the political and social infrastructure of Ngora subcounty and Kumi District (which forms the southern half of the old Teso region). This entailed going over the somewhat thin archival records at the sub-county headquarters, the tax books for the sub-county, and material released by the office of the District Planner. Case material from the sub-county court was also gathered, though, in an indication of the complex politics of my own presence in the area, the police post in Ngora refused to share their case books.

together developments across different sorts of organisation. Village courts, churches and burial societies shared in similar sorts of changes, all of which related to each other. The perspective developed through the book turns away from studying one category of organisation towards understanding the particular landscape of a place. This more open-ended perspective where institutions are understood in relation to each other better explains how individuals develop those reputations or social relationships that matter in economic or political terms.

APPENDIX B:
INTERVIEWS AND GROUP DISCUSSIONS

Leaders

The first set of interviews groups those occupying leadership positions in Oledai. The template is as follows: [name], [position], [organisation], [date of interview], [age], [gender], [ateker], [household wealth ranking out of 126], [language of interview]. 'n/a' means that the information was unavailable. Interviews are organised by date.

Esukau Pius, head catechist, St Aloysius Catholic church, 20.08.02, n/a, male, n/a, n/a, English

Akorikin John Vincent, village chairman, Oledai sub-parish, 21.08.02, 30.09.02, age 46, male, Ogoria, 9, English

Anguria George W., pastor, Nyamongo Pentecostal church, 27.08.02, age 45, male, n/a, n/a, English

Okitoi Gabriel, *ateker* chairman, Ogoria, 28.08.02, age 65, male, Ogoria, 24, English

Okiria Fastine, *ateker* chairman, Ichaak, 29.08.02, age 45, male, Ichaak, n/a, Ateso

Ichodio Stephen, *ateker* chairman, Ipagitok, 30.08.02, age 70, male, Ipagitok, n/a, English

Oberei Fastine, *ateker* chairman, Atekok, 30.08.02, age 55, male, Atekok, 94, Ateso

Ongenge George Washington, lay reader, Kaderun Anglican church, 22.10.02, n/a, male, n/a, n/a, English

Otoi Anthony, ex-village council chairman, Oledai, 02.12.02, age 70, male, Atekok, 1, English

Ikara Patrick, catechist, Nyamongo Catholic church, 04.12.02, age 58, male, n/a, n/a, English

Members of Local Institutions

The second set concerns those interviewed with a focus on particular local institutions. The template is as follows: [name], [institutional focus], [date of interview], [age], [gender], [ateker], [household wealth ranking out of 126], [language of interview]. 'n/a' means that the information was unavailable. Interviews are organised by institution and date.

Akol Florence, *ateker*, 20.08.02, age 35, female, Atekok, 85, Ateso

Omong Cyprian, *ateker*, 20.08.02, age 75, male, Atekok, 98, Ateso

Amuge Gabdesia, *ateker*, 22.08.02, age 60, female, Atekok, 68, Ateso

Auma Agripa, *ateker*, 21.08.02, age 50, female, Inyila, 27, English

Papa Ogwapit, *ateker*, 21.08.02, age 75, male, Ogoria, 6, Ateso

Asige Martha, *ateker*, 22.08.02, age 55, female, Ichaak, 51, English

Odongo Emmanuel, *ateker*, 22.08.02, age 59, male, Ipagitok, 46, English

Amulen Jane, *ateker*, 23.08.02, age 23, female, Ichaak, 57, Ateso

Okurut Gereson Nairobi, *ateker*, 23.08.02, age 85, male, Ogoria, 3, Ateso

Tino Rose, *ateker*, 23.08.02, age 60, female, Ichaak, 100, Ateso

Akello Joyce, *ateker*, 24.08.02, age 24, female, Ipagitok, 29, Ateso

Aguti Jennifer, *ateker*, 27.08.02, age 50, female, Ikures, 40, Ateso

Oonyu Joseph, *ateker*, 27.08.02, age 62, male, Ogoria, 2, Ateso

Olaro Merabu, *ateker*, 28.08.02, age 70, female, Atekok, 11, Ateso

Okaleke Peter, *ateker*, 11.09.02, age 31, male, Ichaak, n/a, Ateso

Okalebo Lawrence, *ateker*, 12.09.02, age 40, male, Ipagitok, 76, English

Omuron John Simple, *ateker*, 17.09.02, age 35, male, Ikures, 48, Ateso

Olupot Constant, *ateker*, 23.12.02, age 45, male, Ikaribwok, n/a, Ateso

Atai Helen, Kaderun Anglican church, 02.09.02, age 57, female, Ogoria, 119, Ateso

Echai Charles, Kaderun Anglican church, 10.09.02, age 28, male, Irarak, 41, Ateso

Kokoi Magret, Kaderun Anglican church, 10.09.02, age 56, female, Atekok, 55, Ateso

Ojilong John Cocas, Kaderun Anglican church, 14.10.02, age 48, male, Ogoria, 21, English

Amujal Joyce, Kaderun Anglican church, 24.10.02, age 60, female, Ogoria, 22, Ateso

Ejobi Felix, Nyamongo Pentecostal Assemblies of God church, 04.08.02, age 26, male, Ichaak, 101, Ateso

Omureje Charles, Nyamongo Pentecostal Assemblies of God church, 09.08.02, age 28, male, Atekok, 84, Ateso

Akol Jane, Nyamongo Pentecostal Assemblies of God church, 04.09.02, age 25, female, n/a, n/a, Ateso

Aujo Joyce M., Nyamongo Pentecostal Assemblies of God church, 31.10.02, age n/a, female, n/a, n/a, Ateso

Omadi John Francis, Nyamongo Pentecostal Assemblies of God church, 23.01.03, age 30, male, Ichaak, 88, English

Apolot Helen, Nyamongo Pentecostal Assemblies of God church, 28.01.03, age 24, female, Ichaak, 88, Ateso

Adelo Vincent, Nyamongo Catholic church, 05.09.02, age 31, male, Ikures, 28, Ateso

Ejobi Ben, Nyamongo Catholic church, 10.09.02, age 43, male, n/a, 82, Ateso

Akello Joyce, Nyamongo Catholic church, 11.09.02, age 38, female, Ikures, 29, Ateso

Amulen Immaculate, Nyamongo Catholic church, 11.10.02, age 55, female, n/a, n/a, Ateso

Aguti Betty, Christ Foundation Ministry church (Agolitom), 04.10.02, age 62, female, n/a, n/a, Ateso

Akello Joyce Mary, Pentecostal Assemblies of God church, 07.10.02, age 53, female, Isaalin, n/a, Ateso

Atim Emmimah Loy, Christ Disciples Pentecostal church (Agolitom), 27.11.02, age 62, Igolitoma, n/a, Ateso

Atikiro Silver, Township Primary School, 16.09.02, age 46, male, Atekok, 63, English

Amongin Rose, Township Primary School, 17.09.02, age 30, female, n/a, n/a, Ateso

Opolot William, Nyamongo Primary School, 18.09.02, age 71, male, Ichaak, 66, Ateso

Agelun Gilbert, Onyede Primary School, 19.09.02, age 40, male, Irarak, 35, Ateso

Otai Gerefansio, Nyamongo Primary School, 19.09.02, age 56, male, n/a, n/a, Ateso

Apio Janet Loy, local government system, 25.09.02, age 28, female, Ikures, 98, Ateso

Apinyi Bena Lucy, local government system, 10.10.02, age n/a, female, n/a, n/a, Ateso

Odongo Emmanuel, local government system, 10.10.02, age 59, male, Ipagitok, 46, English

Malinga John, local government system, 12.10.02, age 25, male, Atekok, 80, Ateso

Amuge Immaculate, local government system, 14.10.02, age 50, female, Ogoria, 16, Ateso

Emukwajo Gilbert, local government system, 18.10.02, age 40, male, Ogoria, 4, English

Alemu James, local government system, 19.11.02, age n/a, male, n/a, n/a, English

Case Study Interviews

The third set concerns case study interviews. The template is as follows: [name], [date of interview], [age], [gender], [language of interview]. 'n/a' means that the information was unavailable. Interviews are organised by date.

Omagor Alfred, 21.03.02, age 61, female, English
Akia Melissa, 24.03.02, age n/a, female, Ateso
Oluka Charles, 24.09.02, age n/a, male, Ateso
Akol James, 21.11.02, age 22, male, English
Okelai Samuel, 04.12.02, age 28, male, English
Oonyu Tom, 04.12.02, age n/a, male, English
Apulugeresia, 13.12.02, age 61, female, Ateso
Edoket James, 21.12.02, age 46, male, English
Akol Stanislas, 14.01.03, age 28, male, English
Atai Helen, 27.01.03, age 57, female, Ateso
Ibuchet Max, 09.01.03, age 45, male, English
Tukei Kosiya and Kokoi Magret, 11.03.02, age 57, age 55, male, female, Ateso

'Outsiders'

The fourth set lists interviews with 'outsiders'. The template is as follows: [name], [position], [date], [gender], [language of interview]. 'n/a' means that the information was unavailable. Interviews are organised by date.

Fr Bernard Phelan, St. Joseph's Missionary Society, 20.08.01, 18.06.02, male, English

Peter Auruku, district schools inspector (Kumi District), 21.01.03, male, English

Daniel Agellan-Akwap, sub-county council chairman (Ngora sub-county), 21.01.03, male, English
Lambert Ojala, sub-county chief (Ngora sub-county), 22.01.03, male, English
Benjamin Ilak, district education officer (Kumi District), 22.01.03, male, English
Richard Ojilong, district planner (Kumi District), 23.01.03, male, English
Sam Aogon, water engineer (Vision Terudo NGO), 25.01.03, male, English
Ismail Orot, district council chairman (Kumi District), 28.01.03, male, English
Okello Omoding, co-ordinator (Ireland Aid, Kumi District), 29.01.03, male, English

PARTICIPANTS IN GROUP DISCUSSIONS IN OLEDAI

Topic	Social category	Date	Name of participant
Bush war	Young men	12.12.02	Alito Fastine
			Ekadait Francis
			Ekongo John Charles
			Oluka Lawrence
			Etonu Simon
			Adelei George Patrick
			Adelo George Michael
	Old women	10.12.02	Akia Kevina
			Atai Helen
			Akol Florence
			Amuge Gabdesia
	Old men	11.12.02	Odongo Emmanuel
			Ogii Adolf
			Okiror Pascal
			Omong Cyprian
			Okaleke William
			Agama Pascal
			Ichodio Stephen
			Okiror Agustino
Period of internment	Young men	20.12.02	Alito Fastine
			Ekongo Charles
			Ekedait Francis
			Adelo George
	Old women	18.12.02	Atim Claudia
			Atai Helen
			Akia Kevina
			Agonyo Jesca Norah
			Akol Florence
			Amuge Gabdesia
	Old men	13.12.02	Odongo Emmanuel
			Ichodio Stephen

Okiror Agustino
Agama Pascal
Opedun Paulo
Oonyu Joseph
Angiro Silver
Tukei Gerald
Omong Cyprian

Present-day institutions	Bicycle taxi men	31.05.02	Amuja John Max

Ipua
Omuwen Joseph
Edotun Jackson

	Young women	23.05.02	Alupo Suzan

Agwang Jane Florence
Akadet Christine Elizabeth
Akol Helen Magret
Amongin Florence
Akola Salome Rose
Angida Godlive
Akol Florence
Apiede Jesca Mary
Asio Emmimah Loyce
Amulen Jane
Ikiring Betty
Apolot Hellen Betty

	Old women (mainly widows)	17.05.02	Aturo Magret

Atim Claudia
Asige Martha
Imalingat Gabdesia
Olinga Justine
Amuge Gabdesia
Akello Gorety
Akol Engarai
Agonyo Jesca Norah
Isukau Norah
Acham Angela Rose

	Old men	16.05.02	Ogii Adolf

Omong Cyprian
Okiror Pascal
Okaleke William
Opolot William
Okiror Samuel
Opolot Joseph
Okiror Agustino
Alito Jacob

Unstructured	Old women	04.06.02	Isukau Norah
			Imalingat Gabdesia
			Asige Martha
			Kia Kevina
			Akol Florence

PARTICIPANTS IN GROUP DISCUSSIONS IN AGOLITOM (CONDUCTED IN ATESO)

Topic	Social category	Date	Name of participant
Present-day institutions	Old women	06.05.02	Adongo Helen
			Asio Ketty Loyce
			Akol Christine
			Musenero Emmimah Loy
			Anyago Helen Magret
			Aluka Maureen
			Adongo Angela
			Atim Debra
			Kokole Esther Catherine
	Old men	07.05.02	Ogwang Yapesi
			Okedi John
			Olupot Eugenio
			Akol John
			Opolot Joseph Pistler
			Malinga Pius
			Iriere Benifers
	Bicycle taxi (boda boda) men	08.05.02	'Mau Mau'
			Ojakol
			Otim
			Osingada
			Okuda John
Bush war	Old men	06.11.02	Okedi Justin
			Olupot Eugenio
			Akol John
			Malinga Pius
			Ongole Israel
			Obokoya Joseph
			Opetor John Michael
			Okolimong Agustino
			Okedi John
	Bicycle taxi (boda boda) men	08.11.02	Ojakol Samuel
			Otim Edward
			Osingada

			'Mau Mau' Okuda John
	Old women	10.11.02	Angejet Jennifer Loy Agwang Jane Akiteng Rose Debra Akurut Domitila Akello Joyce Mary Katoko Lemeteria Amuchu Magret Agwang Janet Mary Akokole Esther Apii Joyce Mary
Period of internment	Bicycle taxi (*boda boda*) men	15.11.02	Ojakol Samuel Otim Edward Osingada 'Mau Mau' Okuda John
	Old women	19.11.02	Katoko Lemeteria Angejet Jennifer Loy Agwang Janet Adongo Christine Apii Joyce Mary Atim Hellen
	Old men	20.11.02	Ongole Israel Erigu William Apetor John Michael Olupot Eugenio Okedi Justin Okolimong Agustino Erimu John Obokoya John Peter Akol John Egune Emmanuel

BIBLIOGRAPHY

This book is based on several years of research and fieldwork. It could not have been written without the work of scholars and key texts which have shaped my thinking over time. The following bibliography refers both to texts cited in the book (in that sense it is in part a set of references) and to this broader literature.

Abrams, P. 1988. 'Notes on the difficulty of studying the state', *Journal of Historical Sociology* 1, 58–89.

Allen, T. 1991. 'Understanding Alice: Uganda's Holy Spirit Movement in context', *Africa* 61 (3), 370–99.

Amnesty International. 1992. *Uganda: the failure to safeguard human rights*, London: Amnesty International Publications.

—— 1999. *Breaking the Circle: protecting human rights in the northern war zone*, London: Amnesty International Publications.

Appleton, S. and S. Ssewanyana. 2003. *Poverty Estimates from the Ugandan National Household Survey II 2002/03*, Nottingham: School of Economics, University of Nottingham.

Apter, D. E. 1961. *The Political Kingdom in Uganda: a study in bureaucratic nationalism*, Princeton, NJ: Princeton University Press.

Atekok Esasi Burial Society. n.d. 'Atekok Esasi Rulebook', unpublished document.

Azarya, V. and N. Chazan. 1987. 'Disengagement from the state in Africa: reflections on the experience of Ghana and Guinea', *Comparative Studies in Society and History* 29 (1), 106–31.

Barker, J. 1982. 'Thinking about the peasantry', *Canadian Journal of African Studies* 16 (3), 601–5.

Barrett, D. B. 1968. *Schism and Renewal in Africa: an analysis of six thousand contemporary religious movements*, Nairobi: Oxford University Press.

Barrett, D. B., G. T. Kurian and T. M. Johnson (eds). 2000. *World Christian Encyclopedia: a comparative survey of churches and religions, AD 30–AD 2000*, New York: Oxford University Press.

Bates, R. H. 1984. *Markets and States in Tropical Africa: the political basis of agricultural policies*, Berkeley, CA: University of California Press.

Bauer, M. W. and B. Aarts. 2000. 'Corpus construction: a principle for qualitative data collection' in M. W. Bauer and G. Gaskell (eds), *Qualitative Researching with Text, Image and Sound*, London: Sage, pp. 19–37.

Bayart, J-F. 1993. *The State in Africa: the politics of the belly*, New York: Longman.

—— 2000. 'Africa in the world: a history of extraversion', *African Affairs* 99 (395), 217–67.

Bazaara, N. 1995. 'Making sense of the character of change in the Ugandan society debate', *Review of African Political Economy* 66, 559–61.

Beattie, J. H. M. 1961. 'Nyoro mortuary rites', *Uganda Journal* 25, 171–83.

Behrend, H. 1999. *Alice Lakwena and The Holy Spirits: war in northern Uganda, 1985–97*, Oxford: James Currey.

Bender, L. M. 2000. 'Nilo-Saharan' in B. Heine and D. Nurse (eds), *African Languages: an introduction*, Cambridge: Cambridge University Press, pp. 43–73.

Bernstein, H. 1981. 'Notes on state and peasantry: the Tanzanian case', *Review of African Political Economy* 21, 44–62.

Berry, S. 1993. *No Condition is Permanent: the social dynamics of agrarian change in sub-Saharan Africa*, Madison, WI: University of Wisconsin Press.

Best, G. A. 1971. *Mid-Victorian Britain, 1851–1875*, London: Weidenfeld and Nicolson.

Bierschenk, T., J-P. Chauveau and J-P. Olivier de Sardan (eds). 2000. *Courtiers en Développement: les villages Africains en quête de projets*, Paris: Karthala.

Bierschenk, T. and J-P. Olivier de Sardan. 1997. 'Local powers and a distant state in rural Central African Republic', *Journal of Modern African Studies* 35 (3), 441–68.

—— 2003. 'Powers in the village: rural Benin between democratisation and decentralisation', *Africa* 73 (2), 145–73.

Birungi, H., B. Kwagala, N. Muwanga, T. Onweng and E. J. Trondsen. 2000. '"What makes markets tick?": local governance and service delivery in Uganda', *Asian Review of Public Administration* 12, 26–49.

Boone, C. 2003. *Political Topographies of the African State: territorial authority and institutional choice*, Cambridge: Cambridge University Press.

Bourdieu, P. and L. J. D. Wacquant. 1992. *An Invitation to Reflexive Sociology*, Chicago: University of Chicago Press.

Brett, E. A. 1973. *Colonialism and Underdevelopment in East Africa: the politics of economic change 1919–1939*, London: Heinemann.

—— 1992. *Providing for the Rural Poor: institutional decay and transformation in Uganda*, Kampala: Fountain Publishers.

—— 1995. 'Neutralising the role of force in Uganda: the role of the military in politics', *Journal of Modern African Studies* 33 (1), 129–52.

—— 1998. 'Responding to poverty in Uganda: structures, policies and prospects', *Journal of International Affairs* 52 (1), 313–27.

Bunker, S. G. 1987. *Peasants Against the State: the politics of market control in Bugisu, Uganda, 1900–1983*, Urbana, IL: University of Illinois Press.

Burke, F. G. 1964. *Local Government and Politics in Uganda*, Syracuse, NY: Syracuse University Press.

Burkey, I. 1991. 'People's power in theory and practice: the Resistance Council system in Uganda', Masters dissertation, Yale University.

Cattell, M. G. 1992. 'Praise the Lord and say no to men: older women empowering themselves in Samia, Kenya', *Journal of Cross-Cultural Gerontology* 7 (4), 307–30.

Chambers, R. 1999. 'Relaxed and participatory appraisal: notes on practical approaches and methods' in *Notes for Participants in a PRA Familiarisation Workshop*, Sussex: Institute of Development Studies.

Christiansen, C. (2008). 'The new wives of Christ: paradoxes and potentials in the remaking of widows lives in Uganda' in W. Geissler and F. Becker (eds), *Searching for Pathways in a Landscape of Death: religion and AIDS in sub-Saharan Africa*, Leiden: Brill.

Clapham, C. 1994. 'Review article: the longue durée of the African state', *African Affairs* 93 (372), 433–9.

Clark, D. 1952. 'Memorial service for an ox', *Uganda Journal* 16, 69–71.

—— 1953. 'Death and burial ceremonies among the Karamojong', *Uganda Journal* 17, 75–6.

Cleaver, F. 2002. 'Reinventing institutions: bricolage and the social embeddedness of natural resource management', *European Journal of Development Research* 14 (2), 11–30.

Cohen, D. W. and E. S. Atieno Odhiambo. 1992. *Burying SM: the politics of knowledge and the sociology of power in Africa*, London: James Currey.

Colson, E. 1969. 'African society at the time of the Scramble' in L. H. Gann and P. Duignan (eds), *Colonialism in Africa, 1870–1960*, Cambridge: Cambridge University Press, pp. 27–65.

Cooke, W. and U. Kothari. 2002. *Participation: the new tyranny?* London: Zed Books.

Crush, J. 1995. *Power of Development*, London: Routledge.

Davies, M. n.d. *Iteso Voices: oral testimonies from northern Uganda*, London: Teso Development Trust.

de Berry, J. 2000. 'Life after loss: an anthropological study of post-war recovery, Teso, east Uganda, with special reference to young people', PhD thesis, Department of Anthropology, London School of Economics and Political Science.

de Weerdt, J. 2001. *Community Organisations in Rural Tanzania: a case study of the community of Nyakatoke, Bukoba rural district.* Bukoba, Tanzania: Economic Development Initiatives.

Doornbos, M. 1978. *Not all the King's Men: inequality as a political instrument in Ankole*, The Hague: Mouton.

—— 1996. 'Uganda: a Bantustan?' *Review of African Political Economy* 69, 425–7.

Douglas, M. 1987. *How Institutions Think*, London: Routledge and Kegan Paul.

Driberg, J. H. 1939. 'A note on the classification of half-Hamites in East Africa', *Man* 39, 20–1.

Dyson-Hudson, N. 1966. *Karimojong Politics*, Oxford: Clarendon Press.

Edmonds, K. 1988. 'Crisis management: the lessons for Africa from Obote's second term' in H. B. Hansen and M. Twaddle (eds), *Uganda Now: between decay and development*, London: James Currey, pp. 95–110.

Egimu-Okuda, N. 1973. 'The occupation of Amuria and the rise of Omiat' in J. B. Webster, D. H. Okalany, C. P. Emudong and N. Egimu-Oloka (eds), *The Iteso during the Asonya*, Nairobi: East African Publishing House, pp. 159–84.

Ehrlich, C. 1957. 'Cotton and the Uganda economy, 1903–1909', *Uganda Journal* 21, 162–75.

Emudong, C. P. 1973. 'The settlement and organisation of Kumi during the *Asonya*' in J. B. Webster, D. H. Okalany, C. P. Emudong, and N. Egimu-Oloka (eds), *The Iteso during the Asonya*, Nairobi: East African Publishing House, pp. 83–115.

Emwamu, G. 1967. 'The reception of alien rule in Teso, 1896–1927', *Uganda Journal* 31, 171–82.

Engelke, M. 2004. 'Discontinuity and the discourse of conversion', *Journal of Religion in Africa* 33 (1), 82–109.

Englund, H. 2002. 'The village in the city, the city in the village: migrants in Lilongwe', *Journal of Southern African Studies* 28 (1), 135–52.

—— 2003. 'Christian independency and global membership: Pentecostal extraversions in Malawi', *Journal of Religion in Africa* 32 (1), 83–111.

—— 2004. 'Cosmopolitanism and the Devil in Malawi', *Ethnos* 69 (3), 293–316.

—— 2007. 'Pentecostalism beyond belief: trust and democracy in a Malawian township', *Africa* 77 (4), 477–99.

Epstein, H. 2007. *The Invisible Cure: Africa, the West and the fight against AIDS*, London: Viking Penguin.

Escobar, A. 1995. *Encountering Development: the making and unmaking of the Third World*, Princeton, NJ: Princeton University Press.

Fairhead, J. and M. Leach. 1997. 'Webs of power and the construction of environmental policy problems: forest loss in Guinea' in R. D. Grillo and R. L. Stirrat (eds), *Discourses of Development: anthropological perspectives*, Oxford: Berg, pp. 35–58.

Ferguson, J. 1990. *The Anti-Politics Machine: 'development', depoliticization, and bureaucratic power in Lesotho*, Cambridge: Cambridge University Press.

—— 2005. 'Seeing like an oil company: space, security, and global capital in neoliberal Africa', *American Anthropologist* 107 (3), 377–82.

—— 2006. *Global Shadows: Africa in the neoliberal world order*, Durham, NC and London: Duke University Press.

Francis, P. and R. James. 2003. 'Balancing rural poverty reduction and citizen participation: the contradictions of Uganda's decentralization program', *World Development* 31 (2), 325–37.

Gale, H. P. 1959. *Uganda and the Mill Hill Fathers*, London: Macmillan.

Gartrell, B. 1983. 'British administrators, colonial chiefs, and the comfort of tradition: an example from Uganda', *African Studies Review* 26 (1), 1–24.

Gertzel, C. 1980. 'Uganda after Amin: the continuing search for leadership and control', *African Affairs* 79 (317), 461–89.

Gifford, P. 1998. *African Christianity: its public role*, London: Christopher Hurst.

Gledhill, J. 1994. *Power and its Disguises: anthropological perspectives on politics*, Boulder, CO and London: Pluto Press.

Gluckman, M. 1952. *Rituals of Rebellion in South East Africa*, Manchester: Manchester University Press.

Golooba-Mutebi, F. 1999. 'Decentralisation, democracy and development administration in Uganda, 1986–1996: limits to popular participation', PhD thesis, Development Studies, London School of Economics and Political Science.

Goodhew, D. 2000. 'Working-class respectability: the example of the western areas of Johannesburg, 1930–55', *Journal of African History* 41 (2), 241–66.

Green, E. D. 2008. 'Understanding the limits to ethnic change: evidence from Uganda's lost counties', *Perspectives on Politics* 6(3).

Grillo, R. D. and R. L. Stirrat (eds). 1997. *Discourses of Development: anthropological perspectives*, Oxford: Berg.

Gulliver, P. H. 1952. 'The Karamojong cluster' *Africa* 22 (1), 1–22.

Guyer, J. 1991. *Representation Without Taxation: an essay on democracy in rural Nigeria,*

1952–1990. Working Papers in African Studies No. 152, Boston, MA: Boston University African Studies Center.

Hackett, R. I. J. 1995. 'The Gospel of Prosperity in West Africa' in R. H. Roberts (ed.), *Religion and the Transformation of Capitalism*, London: Routledge, pp. 199–214.

Hansen, H. B. 1984. *Mission, Church and State in a Colonial Setting: Uganda 1890–1925*, London: Heinemann.

Hansen, H. B. and M. Twaddle (eds). 1988a. *Uganda Now: between decay and development*, London: James Currey.

—— 1988b. 'Introduction' in H. B. Hansen and M. Twaddle (eds), *Uganda Now: between decay and development*, Oxford: James Currey, pp. 1–26.

—— (eds). 1991. *Changing Uganda: the dilemmas of structural adjustment and revolutionary change*, London: James Currey.

—— (eds). 1998. *Developing Uganda*, London: James Currey.

Hanson, H. E. 2003. *Landed Obligation: the practice of power in Buganda*, Portsmouth, NH: Heinemann.

Harris, J. 1994. *Private Lives, Public Spirit: Britain 1870–1914*, London: Penguin.

Harrison, B. 1982. *Peaceable Kingdom: stability and change in modern Britain*, Oxford: Oxford University Press.

Harsch, E. 1997. 'African state in social and historical context', *Sociological Forum* 12 (4), 671–9.

Hastings, A. 1979. *A History of African Christianity, 1950–1975*, Cambridge: Cambridge University Press.

Heald, S. 1982. 'Chiefs and administrators in Bugisu' in A. F. Robertson (ed.), *Uganda's First Republic: chiefs, administrators and politicians, 1967–1971*, Cambridge: Cambridge University Press, pp. 76–98.

—— 1989. *Controlling Anger: the sociology of Gisu violence*, Manchester: Manchester University Press for the International African Institute.

—— 1991. 'Tobacco, time and the household economy in two Kenyan societies: the Teso and the Kuria', *Comparative Studies in Society and History* 33 (1), 130–57.

—— 2006. 'State, law and vigilantism in Northern Tanzania', *African Affairs* 105 (419), 265–83.

Henriques, P. 2002. 'Peace without reconciliation: war, peace and experience among the Iteso of Uganda', PhD thesis, Department of Anthropology, University of Copenhagen.

Himbara, D. and D. Sultan. 1995. 'Reconstructing the Ugandan state and economy: the challenge of an international Bantustan', *Review of African Political Economy* 22, 85–93.

Hirschman, A. O. 1970. *Exit, Voice, and Loyalty*, Cambridge, MA: Harvard University Press.

Hobart, M. 1993. *An Anthropological Critique of Development: the growth of ignorance*, London: Routledge.

Hooper, E. 1987. 'AIDS in Uganda', *African Affairs* 86, 469–77.

Hyden, G. 1980. *Beyond Ujamaa in Tanzania: underdevelopment and an uncaptured peasantry*, Berkeley, CA: University of California Press.

—— 1983. *No Shortcuts to Progress: African development management in perspective*, London: Heinemann.

Iliffe, John. 1987. *The African Poor: a history*, Cambridge: Cambridge University Press.

Ingham, Kenneth. 1994. *Obote: a political biography*, New York: Routledge.

International Labour Organisation (ILO). 1999. 'Microfinance in post-conflict countries: the case study of Uganda', prepared by John Beijuka for the Joint ILO/ UNHCR Workshop: Microfinance in Post-Conflict Countries, 15–17 September 1999. Geneva: ILO.

Ireland Aid. 2002. 'Programme review Ireland Aid district support in Uganda: decentralisation, local government and donor-coordination', Kampala: Ireland Aid.

Isis–WICCE. 2002. 'Women's experiences in situations of armed conflict, 1987–2001: the Teso experience', Kampala: Isis–Women's International Cross Cultural Exchange.

Jones, B. 2005. 'The church in the village, the village in the church: Pentecostalism in Teso, Uganda', *Cahiers d'Etudes Africaines* 45, 497–517.

Joseph, R. 1999. 'The reconfiguration of power in late twentieth-century Africa' in R. Joseph (ed.), *State, Conflict, and Democracy in Africa*, Boulder, CO: Lynne Rienner Publishers.

Kabwegyere, T. B. 2000. *People's Choice, People's Power: challenges and prospects of democracy in Uganda*, Kampala: Fountain Publishers.

Kagolo, B. M. 1955. 'Tribal names and customs in Teso District', *Uganda Journal* 19, 41–8.

Kanyinga, K., A. S. Z. Kiondo and P. Tidemand. 1994. *The New Local Level Politics in East Africa: studies on Uganda, Tanzania and Kenya*, Stockholm: Nordiska Afrikainstitutet.

Kappel, R. T., J. Lay and S. Steiner. 2005. 'Uganda: no more pro-poor growth?' *Development Policy Review* 23 (1), 27–53.

Karlström, M. 1999. 'Civil society and its presuppositions: lessons from Uganda' in J. L. Comaroff and J. Comaroff (eds), *Civil Society and the Political Imagination in Africa: critical perspectives*, Chicago: University of Chicago Press, pp. 104–23.

—— 2003. 'On the aesthetics and dialogics of power in the postcolony', *Africa* 73 (1), 57–76.

—— 2004. 'Modernity and its aspirants: moral community and developmental eutopianism in Buganda', *Current Anthropology* 45 (5), 595–619.

Karp, I. 1978. *Fields of Change among the Iteso of Kenya*, London: Routledge.

Kasfir, N. 1976. *The Shrinking Political Arena: participation and ethnicity in African politics, with a case study of Uganda*, Berkeley, CA: University of California Press.

—— 1998. '"No-party democracy" in Uganda', *Journal of Democracy* 9 (2), 49–63.

—— 2000. 'Movement, democracy, legitimacy and power in Uganda' in M. Justus and J. Oloka-Onyango (eds), *No-Party Democracy in Uganda: myths and realities*, Kampala: Fountain Publishers, pp. 63–82.

Kassimir, R. 1995. 'Catholicism and political identity in Toro' in H. B. Hansen and M. Twaddle (eds), *Religion and Politics in East Africa: the period since independence*, London: James Currey, pp. 120–40.

—— 1998. 'The social power of religious organisation and civil society: the Catholic Church in Uganda', *Commonwealth and Comparative Politics* 36 (2), 54–83.

—— 1999. 'The politics of popular Catholicism in Uganda' in T. Spear and I.

N. Kimambo (eds), *East African Expressions of Christianity*, Athens, OH: Ohio University Press, pp. 248–74.

Knighton, B. 2003. 'The state as raider among the Karamojong: where there are no guns, they use the threat of guns', *Africa* 73 (3), 427–55.

—— 2005. *The Vitality of Karamojong Religion: dying tradition or living faith?* Aldershot and Burlington, VT: Ashgate.

La Fontaine, J. S. 1959. *The Gisu of Uganda*, London: International African Institute.

Langseth, P., J. Katorobo, E. A. Brett and J. C. Munene. 1995. *Uganda: landmarks in rebuilding a nation*, Kampala: Fountain Publishers.

Laurent, P-J. 1994. 'Prosélytisme religieux, intensification agricole et organisation paysanne' in P. Lavigne-Delville (ed.), *Les Associations Paysannes en Afrique: organisations et dynamiques*, Paris: Karthala, pp. 155–78.

—— 2001. 'Transnationalism and local transformations: the example of the Church of Assemblies of God of Burkina Faso' in A. Corten and R. Marshall-Fratani (eds), *Between Babel and Pentecost: transnational Pentecostalism in Africa and Latin America*, Bloomington and Indianapolis, IN: Indiana University Press, pp. 256–73.

Lawrance, J. C. D. 1955. 'A history of Teso to 1937', *Uganda Journal* 19, 7–40.

—— 1957. *The Iteso: fifty years of change in a Nilo-Hamitic tribe of Uganda*, London: Oxford University Press.

Leopold, M. 2005. *Inside West Nile: violence, history and representation on an African frontier*, Oxford: James Currey.

Lévi-Strauss, C. 1966. *The Savage Mind*, London: Weidenfeld and Nicolson.

Leys, C. 1973. 'Book review: *African Elite: the "big men" of a small town* by Joan Vincent', *American Political Science Review* 67 (1), 288–9.

—— 1975. *Underdevelopment in Kenya: the political economy of neo-colonialism, 1964–1971*, London: Heinemann.

Lipschutz, M. R. and R. K. Rasmussen. 1986. *Dictionary of African Historical Biography*, Berkeley, CA: University of California Press.

Livingstone, I. and R. Charlton. 1998. 'Raising local authority district revenues through direct taxation in a low-income developing country: evaluating Uganda's GPT', *Public Administration and Development* 18 (5), 499–517.

—— 2001. 'Financing decentralized development in a low-income country: raising revenue for local government', *Development and Change* 32 (1), 77–100.

Long, N. 1968. *Social Change and the Individual: social and religious responses to innovation in a Zambian rural community*, Manchester: Manchester University Press.

—— 1992. 'From paradigm lost to paradigm regained? The case for an actor-oriented sociology of development' in N. Long and A. Long (eds), *Battlefields of Knowledge: the interlocking of theory and practice in social research and development*, London: Routledge, pp. 16–43.

—— 2001. *Development Sociology: actor perspectives*, London: Routledge.

Low, D. A. 1971. *Buganda in Modern History*, London: Weidenfeld and Nicolson.

Lund, C. 1998. *Law, Power and Politics in Niger: land struggles and the rural code*, Hamburg: LIT Verlag.

—— 1999. 'A question of honour: property disputes and brokerage in Burkina Faso', *Africa* 69 (4), 575–94.

Mamdani, M. 1976. *Politics and Class Formation in Uganda*, New York: Monthly Review Press.

—— 1988. 'Uganda in transition: two years of the NRA/NRM', *Third World Quarterly* 10 (3), 1155–81.

—— 1991. 'A response to critics', *Development and Change* 22: 351–66.

—— 1996. *Citizen and Subject: contemporary Africa and the legacy of late colonialism*, Princeton, NJ: Princeton University Press.

Marcussen, H. S. and S. Arnfred. 1998. *Concepts and Metaphors: ideologies, narratives and myths in development discourse*, Roskilde: University of Roskilde.

Martinussen, J. 1997. *Society, State and Market: a guide to competing theories of development*, London: Zed Books.

Maxwell, D. 1999. *Christians and Chiefs in Zimbabwe: a social history of the Hwesa people*, Edinburgh: Edinburgh University Press for the International African Institute, London.

—— 2006. 'Post-colonial Christianity in Africa' in Hugh McCleod (ed.), *The Cambridge History of Christianity, vol. 9, World Christianities c.1914–c.2000*, Cambridge: Cambridge University Press.

Meyer, B. 1998. '"Make a complete break with the past": memory and post-colonial modernity in Ghanaian Pentecostalist discourse', *Journal of Religion in Africa* 27 (3), 316–49.

—— 2004. 'Christianity in Africa: from African Independent to Pentecostal-Charismatic churches', *Annual Review of Anthropology* 33, 447–74.

Middleton, J. 1960. *Lugbara Religion: ritual authority among an East African people*, Oxford: Oxford University Press for the International African Institute.

Mirzeler, M. and C. Young. 2000. 'Pastoral politics in the northeast periphery in Uganda: AK-47 as change agent', *Journal of Modern African Studies* 38 (3), 407–29.

Mitchell, J. C. 1983. 'Case and situational analysis', *Sociological Review* 31 (2), 187–211.

Mittelman, J. 1975. *Ideology and Politics in Uganda: from Obote to Amin*, Ithaca, NY: Cornell University Press.

Moore, M. 2004. 'Revenues, state formation, and the quality of governance in developing countries', *International Political Science Review* 25 (3), 297–319.

Moore, S. F. 1986. *Social Facts and Fabrications: 'customary' law on Kilimanjaro, 1880–1980*, Cambridge: Cambridge University Press.

Morgan, A. R. 1958. 'Uganda's cotton industry: fifty years back', *Uganda Journal* 22, 107–22.

Mosse, D. 2004. *Cultivating Development: an ethnography of aid policy and practice*, London: Pluto Press.

Mudoola, D. 1991. 'Institution building: the case of the NRM and the military in Uganda 1986–1989' in H. B. Hansen and M. Twaddle (eds), *Changing Uganda: the dilemmas of structural adjustment and revolutionary change*, London: James Currey.

Mutibwa, P. M. 1992. *Uganda Since Independence: a story of unfulfilled hopes*, Kampala: Fountain Publishers.

Nagashima, N. 1976. 'Boiling and roasting: an account of the two descent-based groupings among the Iteso of Uganda', *Hitotsubashi Journal of Social Studies* 8 (1): 42–62.

—— 1982. 'Bridewealth among the Iteso of Kenya: a further note on their affinal relationship and its historical change', *Hitotsubashi Journal of Social Studies* 14 (1): 14–26.

Nugent, P. 1999. 'A Conversation with Joan Vincent', *Current Anthropology* 40 (4), 531–42.

Nuijten, M. 1992. 'Local organization as organizing practices: rethinking rural institutions' in N. Long and A. Long (eds), *Battlefields of Knowledge: the interlocking of theory and practice in social research and development*, pp. 189–207, London: Routledge.

Ocitti, J. 2000. *Political Evolution and Democratic Practice in Uganda, 1952–1996*. Lewiston, NY: Mellen Press.

O'Connor, A. 1988. 'Uganda: the spatial dimension' in H. B. Hansen and M. Twaddle (eds), *Uganda Now: between decay and development*, Oxford: James Currey, pp. 83–94.

Ojwang, J. B. and J. N. Kanyua Mugambi (eds). 1989. *The S.M. Otieno Case: death and burial in modern Kenya*, Nairobi: University of Nairobi Press.

Okalany, D. H. 1973. 'Mukongoro during the *Asonya*' in J. B. Webster, D. H. Okalany, C. P. Emudong, and N. Egimu-Oloka (eds), *The Iteso during the Asonya*, Nairobi: East African Publishing House, pp. 129–58.

Okidi, J. A. and G. Mugambe. 2002. 'An overview of chronic poverty and development policy in Uganda', CPRC Working Paper, Chronic Poverty Research Centre.

Okidi, J. A., S. Ssewanyana, L. Bategeka and F. Muhumuza. 2004. 'Operationalising pro-poor growth: a country case study on Uganda', http://www.dfid.gov.uk/Pubs/files/oppguganda.pdf.

Olivier de Sardan, J-P. 2005. *Anthropology and Development: understanding contemporary social change*, New York and London: Zed Books.

Olowu, D. and J. S. Wunsch. 1989. *The Failure of the Centralised State: institutions and self-governance in Africa*, Boulder, CO: Westview Press.

—— (eds). 2004. *Governance in Africa: the challenges of democratic decentralization*, Boulder, CO: Lynne Rienner.

Omara-Otunnu, Amii. 1987. *Politics and the Military in Uganda, 1890–1985*. Basingstoke: Macmillan.

Organisation for Economic Cooperation and Development (OECD). 2005. *Statistical Yearbook 2005*, available at http://unstats.un.org.

Orone, P. and J. Pottier. 1993. 'Uganda: report of proceedings of a FSUS/PRA workshop held in Wera-Angole, Soroti District, 15–18 August 1993' in J. Pottier (ed.), *African Food Systems Under Stress*, Brighton: Desktop Display.

Ostrom, E. 1992. *Crafting Institutions for Self-Governing Irrigation Systems*, San Francisco, CA: ICS Press.

Parkhurst, J. O. 2002. 'The Ugandan success story? Evidence and claims of HIV-1 prevention', *The Lancet*, 36 (3), 571–90.

Peel, J. D. Y. 2002. 'Gender in Yoruba religious change', *Journal of Religion in Africa* 32 (2), 136–66.

Pigg, S. L. 1997. '"Found in most traditional societies": traditional medical practitioners between culture and development' in F. Cooper and R. Packard (eds), *International Development and the Social Sciences: essays on the history and politics of knowledge*, Berkeley, CA: University of California Press, pp. 259–90.

Pim, A. 1948. 'Mining, commerce and finance', in M. Perham (ed.), *The Economics of a Tropical Dependency Volume II*, London: Faber and Faber.

Pirouet, M. L. 1978. *Black Evangelists: the spread of Christianity in Uganda, 1891–1914*, London: Rex Collings.

—— 1980. 'Religion in Uganda under Amin', *Journal of Religion in Africa* 11 (1), 12–29.

—— 1991. 'Human rights abuses in Museveni's Uganda' in H. B. Hansen and M. Twaddle (eds), *Changing Uganda: the dilemmas of structural adjustment and revolutionary change*, London: James Currey.

Ranger, T. 1986. 'Religious movements and politics in sub-Saharan Africa', *African Studies Review* 29 (2), 1–69.

Regan, A. J. 1998. 'Decentralization policy: reshaping state and society' in H. B. Hansen and M. Twaddle (eds), *Development Uganda*, Oxford: James Currey, pp. 159–75.

Reid, R. J. 2002. *Political Power in Pre-Colonial Buganda*, Oxford: James Currey.

Reinikka, R. and P. Collier. 2001. *Uganda's Recovery: the role of farms, firms, and government*. Washington, DC: World Bank.

Roberts, A. D. 1962. 'The sub-imperialism of the Baganda', *Journal of African History* 3 (3), 435–50.

Saito, F. 2003. *Decentralisation and Development Partnerships: lessons from Uganda*, Tokyo: Springer-Verlag.

Sathyamurthy, T. V. 1982. *Central–Local Relations: the case of Uganda*, Manchester: University of Manchester Press.

Saul, J. 1976. 'The unsteady state: Uganda, Obote and General Amin', *Review of African Political Economy* 5, 12–38.

— (ed.). 1979. *The State and Revolution in Eastern Africa*, New York: Monthly Review Press.

Scott, J. C. 1999. *Seeing like a State: how certain schemes to improve the human condition have failed*, New Haven, CT: Yale University Press.

Seur, H. 1992. 'The engagement of researcher and local actors in the construction of case studies and research themes' in N. Long and A. Long (eds), *Battlefields of Knowledge: the interlocking of theory and practice in social research and development*, London: Routledge, pp. 115–43.

Shipton, P. and M. Goheen. 1992. 'Understanding African land-holding: power, wealth, and meaning', *Africa* 62 (3), 307–26.

Shore, C. and S. Wright. 1997. *Anthropology of Policy: critical perspectives on governance and power*, London: Routledge.

Sjögren, A. 2003. 'Closing political space in Uganda: the politics of state–society relations under NRM', paper presented at a workshop on Intervention, Local Politics and the State, organised by the Development Studies Institute, University of Helsinki, 14–16 August, Lammi, Finland.

—— 2007. 'Between Militarism and Technocratic Governance: state formation in contemporary Uganda', PhD thesis, Department of Political Science, University of Stockholm.

Southall, Aidan. 1956. *Alur Society: a study in processes and types of domination*, Cambridge: W. Heffer and Sons.

—— 1980. 'Social disorganisation in Uganda: before, during and after Amin', *Journal of Modern African Studies* 18 (4), 627–56.

—— 1998. 'Isolation and underdevelopment: periphery and centre' in H. B. Hansen and M. Twaddle (eds), *Developing Uganda*, Oxford: James Currey, pp. 254–60.

Steiner, S. 2004. *Public Spending on Education and Health in Uganda: do the poor benefit?* Hamburg: Institut für Afrika Kunde.

Summers, C. 2005. 'Catholic action: radical activism in Buganda revisited, 1920–1950', paper presented at the conference of the Africa–Europe Group for Interdisciplinary Studies (AEGIS), School of Oriental and African Studies, London, 29 June–2 July 2005.

Swartz, M. J. 1968. 'Introduction', in M. J. Swartz (ed.), *Local-Level Politics: social and cultural perspectives*, Chicago, IL: Aldine, pp. 1–46.

Teso Relief Committee. 1990. 'Report by the Catholic Diocese of Soroti on the situation in Teso', 12 March 1990, Soroti: Teso Relief Committee.

Therkildsen, O. 2002. 'Uganda's referendum 2000: the silent boycott: a comment', *African Affairs* 101 (403), 231–41.

—— 2005. 'Taxation, prisons and governance in Uganda', mimeo. Copenhagen: Danish Institute for International Studies.

—— 2006. 'The rise and fall of mass taxation in Uganda 1900–2005', DIIS Working Paper 2006:25, Copenhagen.

Thiele, G. 1986. 'The state and rural development in Tanzania: the village administration as a political field', *Journal of Development Studies* 22 (3), 203–31.

Thomas, H. B. and R. Scott. 1935. *Uganda*, Oxford: Oxford University Press.

Thompson, F. M. L. 1988. *The Rise of Respectable Society: a social history of Victorian Britain, 1830–1900*, London: Fontana.

Tidemand, P. 1994. 'New local state forms and "popular participation" in Buganda, Uganda' in K. Kanyinga, A. S. Z. Kiondo and P. Tidemand (eds), *The New Local Level Politics in East Africa: studies on Uganda, Tanzania and Kenya*, Stockholm: Nordiska Afrikainstitutet, pp. 22–49.

—— 1995. 'The Resistance Councils in Uganda: a study of rural politics and popular democracy in Africa', PhD thesis. Department of International Development: Roskilde University.

Tosh, J. 1978. *Clan Leaders and Colonial Chiefs in Lango: the political history of an east African stateless society c. 1800–1939*, Oxford: Clarendon Press.

Tripp, A. M. 2000. *Women and Politics in Uganda*, Madison, WI: University of Wisconsin Press.

—— 2004. 'The changing face of authoritarianism in Africa: the case of Uganda', *Africa Today* 50 (3), 3–26.

Tukahebwa, G. 1998. 'The role of district councils in the decentralisation programme in Uganda' in Apolo Nsibambi (ed.), *Decentralisation and Civil Society in Uganda: the quest for good governance*, Kampala: Fountain Publishers, pp. 12–30.

Twaddle, M. 1983. 'Ethnic politics and support for political parties in Uganda', in P. Lyon and J. Manor (eds), *Transfer and Transformation: poitical institutions in the new Commonwealth*, Leicester: Leicester University Press.

—— 1988. 'Museveni's Uganda: notes towards and analysis' in H. B. Hansen and M. Twaddle (eds), *Uganda Now: between decay and development*, Oxford: James Currey, pp. 313–35.

—— 1993. *Kakungulu and the Creation of Uganda, 1868–1928*, London: James Currey.

Twaddle, M. and H. B. Hansen (eds). 1995. *Religion and Politics in East Africa: the period since independence*, London: James Currey.

Uchendu, V. C. and K. R. M. Anthony. 1975. *Agricultural Change in Teso District, Uganda: a study of economic, cultural and technical determinants of rural development*, Nairobi: East African Literature Bureau.

Uganda Government. 1995. *Constitution of Uganda*, Kampala: Government of Uganda.

—— 1999. *National Household Survey 1999/2000, Socio-Economic Questionnaire*, Kampala: Uganda Bureau of Statistics.

—— 2000a. *Kumi District Report*. Kumi: Kumi Local Government.

—— 2000b. *Review of the Process of Implementation of the Uganda Participatory Poverty Assessment Project*, Kampala: Ministry of Finance Planning and Economic Development.

—— 2002. *Uganda Population and Housing Census: main report*, Kampala: Uganda Bureau of Statistics.

—— 2003. Ngora Sub-County Annual Report 2002/2003, Ngora, Kumi District: Ngora Sub-County Headquarters.

—— 2005. *Background to the Budget*, Kampala: Ministry of Finance Planning and Development.

—— 2006. *Uganda 2002 Population and Housing Census: population composition*, Kampala: Uganda Bureau of Statistics.

—— 2007. *Kumi District Development Report 2006/2007*, Kumi: Kumi Local Government.

—— n.d.. *Ngora Sub-County Three Year Rolling Development Plan 2002/03–2004/05*. Kumi District: Kumi District Planning Unit.

Uganda Protectorate. 1921. 'Census Returns 1921', Entebbe: Government Printer, Uganda.

—— 1933. 'Census Returns 1931', Entebbe: Government Printer, Uganda.

Ukah, A. K. 2003. 'Advertising God: Nigerian Christian video-films and the power of consumer culture', *Journal of Religion in Africa* 33 (2), 203–31.

United Nations. 1998. *Accountability in Decentralized Planning and Financing for Rural Services in Uganda*, New York: United Nations Capital Development Fund.

United Nations Development Programme (UNDP). 2001. *Uganda Human Development Report*, Kampala: UNDP.

Vail, D. J. 1972. *A History of Agricultural Innovation and Development in Teso District, Uganda*, Syracuse, NY: Syracuse University Press.

van Dijk, R. 1998. 'Fundamentalism, cultural memory and the state: contested representations of time in post-colonial Malawi' in R. P. Werbner (ed.), *Memory and the Postcolony: African anthropology and the critique of power*, London: Zed Books, pp. 155–81.

van Velsen, J. 1967. 'The extended case method and situational analysis' in A. L. Epstein (ed.), *The Craft of Social Anthropology*, London: Tavistock, pp. 128–49.

van Zwanenberg, R. and A. King. 1975. *An Economic History of Kenya and Uganda*, London: Macmillan.

Villadsen, S. and F. Lubanga (eds). 1996. *Democratic Decentralisation in Uganda: a new approach to local governance*, Kampala: Fountain Publishers.

Vincent, J. 1968. *African Elite: the 'big men' of a small town*, New York: Columbia University Press.

—— 1976. 'Rural competition and the cooperative monopoly: a Ugandan case study' in J. Nash, J. Dandler and N. S. Hopkins (eds), *Popular Participation in Social Change: cooperatives, collectives and nationalized industry*, The Hague: Mouton, pp. 71–97.

—— 1977. 'Colonial chiefs and the making of class: a case study from Teso, Eastern Uganda', *Africa* 47 (2), 140–59.

—— 1982. *Teso in Transformation: the political economy of peasant and class in eastern Africa*, Berkeley, CA: University of California Press.

—— 1999. 'War in Uganda: north and south' in S. P. Reyna and R. E. Downs (eds), *Deadly Developments: capitalism, states and war*, Langhorne, PA: Gordon and Breach, pp. 107–32.

Ward, K. 1989. '"Obedient rebels" – the relationship between the early "Balokole" and the Church of Uganda: the Mukono crisis of 1941', *Journal of Religion in Africa* 19 (3), 194–227.

—— 1995. 'The Church of Uganda amidst conflict: the interplay between church and politics in Uganda since 1962', in H. B. Hansen and M. Twaddle (eds), *Religion and Politics in East Africa: the period since independence*, London: James Currey, pp. 72–105.

Watson, W. 1964. 'Social mobility and social class in industrial communities' in M. Gluckman (ed.), *Closed Systems and Open Minds: the limits of naïvety in social anthropology*, Edinburgh: Oliver and Boyd.

Weber, M. 1985. *The Protestant Ethic and the Spirit of Capitalism*, London: Unwin Paperbacks.

Webster, J. B. 1973. 'Introduction' in J. B. Webster, D. H. Okalany, C. P. Emudong, and N. Egimu-Oloka (eds), *The Iteso during the Asonya*, Nairobi: East African Publishing House, pp. i–xvii.

Webster, J. B., D. H. Okalany, C. P. Emudong and N. Egimu-Oloka (eds). 1973. *The Iteso during the Asonya*, Nairobi: East African Publishing House.

Welbourn, F. B. 1961. *East African Rebels: a study of some independent churches*, London: SCM Press.

Werbner, R. P. 1984. 'The Manchester School in south-central Africa', *Annual Review of Anthropology* 13, 157–85.

—— 1986. 'The political economy of bricolage', *Journal of Southern African Studies* 13 (1), 151–6.

West, M. O. 1997. 'Liquor and libido: "joint drinking" and the politics of sexual control in colonial Zimbabwe', *Journal of Social History* 30 (3), 645–67.

Whyte, M. and J. P. Higenyi. 1997. 'Writing mourners: literacy and the meaning of mourning in Eastern Uganda', paper presented at the 40th Annual Meeting, African Studies Association, Columbus, Ohio.

Whyte, S. R. 1997. *Questioning Misfortune: the pragmatics of uncertainty in eastern Uganda*, Cambridge and New York: Cambridge University Press.

—— 2005. 'Going home? Belonging and burial in the era of AIDS', *Africa* 75 (2), 154–72.

Williams, F. L. 1937. 'Teso clans', *Uganda Journal* 4, 174–6.

Williams, G. 1987. 'Primitive accumulation: the way to progress', *Development and Change* 18 (4), 637–59.

World Bank. 1996. *Uganda: the challenge of growth and poverty reduction*, Washington, DC: World Bank.

Wright, A. C. A. 1942. 'Notes on Iteso social organisation', *Uganda Journal* 9, 57–80.

Wunsch, J. S., and D. Ottemoeller. 2004. 'Uganda: multiple levels of local governance' in D. Olowu and J. S. Wunsch (eds), *Governance in Africa: the challenges of democratic decentralization*, Boulder, CO: Lynne Rienner, pp. 125–54.

Young, C. M. 1971. 'Agricultural policy in Uganda: capacity in choice' in F. Lofchie (ed.), *The State of the Nations: constraints on development in independent Africa*, Berkeley and Los Angeles, CA: University of California Press, pp. 141–64.

Zistel, S. 2000. 'Successful mediation of armed conflict: learning lessons from a case study of Teso, Uganda', Deutsche Gesellschaft für Technische Zusammenarbeit (GTZ) Uganda.

—— 2002. 'Critical hermeneutics and conflict resolution: an assessment of the transition from conflict to peace in Teso, Uganda, 1986–2000', PhD thesis, Department of International Relations, London School of Economics and Political Science.

Ugandan Newspapers
New Vision
Monitor

Plate 10 The livestock market at Tididiek

The photograph illustrates the strong relationship between men and cattle in Teso society.

INDEX

Abwot, 51
ActionAid (UK), 58n59, 121
adultery, punishment for, 103–4, 124
Aguti Betty, 122
Agwang Angela, 123
aipud, 136, 140, 143, 144
Akello Joyce Mary, 97
Akol Stansilas, 83–5
Akorikin John Vincent, 50n39, 65, 87
Alemu James, 157–8
Alito Fastine, 53–4n49
Amin, Idi, 45–8, 61, 96
Amongin-Aporu, Christine, 79
Amongin Mary, 123
Angatia, 51, 71
Anglican church *see* Christianity
Apter, David, 65n4
Apulugeresia, 85, 129–30
Arionga, 33–4
Aromait, 82
Asians, expulsion by Amin, 45–6, 61
asuban, 140
Atai Helen, 126–7, 150–2, 155
ateker
    and burial societies, 133, 138–9
    justice, 82, 85–7, 105, 129
    land ownership, 14, 126–7, 150
Atekok Esasi burial society, 135–6
Ayeko, Abadi, 49n33

bakungulu, 36–9
Balokole movement, 118–19
Bamalaki movement, 118–19
Banyole, burial societies, 146
Bayart, Jean-François, 25, 67
beer, significance of, 95
Berry, Sara, 8, 39, 73
Besigye, Kizza, 80
Bierschenk, Thomas, 8
'big men'
    murder of, 51, 52, 143, 161
    position of, 18–21, 102–3, 130
    post-colonial period, 44
Bisaaka, Dosteo, 119
born-again Christianity *see* Pentecostalism

Brett, E. A., 41, 46n26, 66, 73n21
bricolage, 27–8, 124, 146
Buganda
    independence, 43–4
    local councils, 66
    morality, 20n17
    pre-colonial role in Teso, 36–8
    pre-colonial society, 35
burial societies
    Atekok Esasi burial society, 135–6
    auditors, 148–9
    borrowing of practices, 147–9
    as break with past, 153–5
    establishment of, 30, 133–5
    influence of Teso Insurgency, 142,
        144–5, 152–5, 161–2
    membership of, 138–9
    payments to, 138, 139
    as proper behaviour, 25, 113, 152–3,
        161–2
    and returnees from exile, 145–7
    social role, 149–52, 155, 162
    workings of, 135–9, 161–2
burials
    Edotun Jackson, 114, 124–8, 149–52,
        154, 155
    practices, 136–8
    pre-colonial and colonial periods, 140–2
    Teso Insurgency, 142–5, 152
Burke, Fred, 43, 72

cassava, mosaic disease, 55
Catholic church *see* Christianity
Cattell, Maria, 107n27
cattle
    cultural importance, 16, 51–2
    raiding, 17, 48–50, 56
Central African Republic, state-society
        relations, 8–9
chiefs
    colonial period, 38–9, 41
    parish chiefs, 67–71, 76
    pre-colonial status, 37–8
Christian Engineers for Development (UK),
        58n59, 121

Christianity
  and burials, 124–8
  Catholic missionaries, 116–17, 119
  charismatics, 122–4
  and civil society, 120–1, 131
  divisions, 128
  in internment camps, 122
  mission churches, 114–21
  Oledai, 91–2, 113–14, 120–1
  and party politics, 115
  revival of, 111–13, 117–20, 130–1
  role of, 91–2, 113–14, 130–1, 160–1
  rules of, 123–4
  see also Pentecostalism
Church Missionary Society (CMS), 16, 37,
    40, 73, 114, 116
Clark, Doris, 141
Cleaver, Frances, 146
colonial period
  administration, 38–41
  burials, 140–2
  legacy of, 67
  local government, 77–8
  mission churches, 114–17
  parish chiefs, 68–71
  social organisation, 41–3
  taxation, 39, 69, 70, 72–3
communities, role of, 7–9
cotton industry
  colonial period, 31, 38–9, 40–1, 61, 116
  decline of, 15–16, 17, 31, 45–6, 61, 70
councils, establishment of, 63–4; *see also*
    village councils
Crabtree, W. A., 33n4, 37n14
customary institutions, development role, 10

de Berry, Joanna, 31, 170
decentralisation
  impacts of, 4–5, 74–6
  policies, 63–4
  studies of, 65–7, 164
Democratic Party (DP), 80, 115
development agencies, role of, 2, 3–4
development projects, politics of, 5–7, 9–10,
    89, 157–8, 164–5
donor funding, 74–5, 89, 157–8
Douglas, Mary, 28, 163

economy
  decline, 31–3
  pre-colonial, 34–5
  'success story', 1–2, 9–10, 59–61, 157
  under Amin, 45–6, 61
Edotun Jackson, death and burial of, 114,
    124–8, 149–52, 154, 155
Egenyu-Asemo, Fiona, 81
Egimu-Okuda, N., 42n22, 69–70
Ehrlich, Cyril, 72–3

Emudong, C. P., 52n44
Englund, Harri, 98n15, 101n17, 109n30,
  131
Epetait, Francis, 79
exile, experiences of, 145–7
extraversion
  churches, 120–1
  governmental, 9, 67, 73–5, 88, 158, 164

famine, 36, 40, 55
Ferguson, James, 56, 88–9
Force Obote Back Army (FOBA), 50
funerals *see* burial societies; burials

'Gandaphilia', 40n20
Gartrell, Beverly, 77
Gifford, Paul, 115
Gledhill, John, 28
Goheen, Mitzi, 26–7
Golooba-Mutebi, F., 66
Gulliver, P. H., 37

Hastings, Adrian, 46n27
Heald, Suzette, 74
Henriques, Peter, 48n30, 170
Higenyi, J. P., 146
Himbara, D., 74
HIV/AIDS, impact of, 17, 145
Hussein, Suleiman, 44
Hyden, Goran, 7–8

Ibuchet Max, 145
Ijala of Ngora, 36–7
income, sources of, 14–15, 22
independence (1962), 43–5
institutions
  bricolage, 27–8, 124, 146
  changes, 25–7, 146–7, 161–3
  role of individuals, 28–30
internment
  and Christianity, 122
  death and burials, 143–4, 152
  Teso Insurgency, 52–6, 98–9
Iteso
  lifestyle, 13–17
  names of, 16–17
  origins of, 33–4
  pre-colonial society, 34–5, 140

John Paul II, Pope, 56
Johnston, Harry, 39, 73

Kabaka Yekka, 115
Kabwegyere, Tarsis, 66
Kakungulu, 36, 69
Karamajong, cattle raiding, 48–50, 56
Karlström, Mikael, 20n17, 47, 66, 91n2
Karp, Ivan, 16, 142

Kasfir, Nelson, 60, 96
Kassimir, Ronald, 119
Kennedy, District Commissioner, 77
Knighton, Ben, 9
Kumi Diocese Planning Secretariat, 121
Kumi District
    district capital, 40, 71, 75
    local government, 88
    population, 53n47

labour, forced, 69–70
land, ownership, 14, 126–7, 150
Laurent, Pierre-Joseph, 103n20
Lawrance, J. C. D., 33, 117, 127, 140
Leopold, Mark, 9, 23
Lesotho, development projects, 5–6
Leys, Colin, 7, 69n10
Local Administration Act (1967), 70–1
local government
    parish chiefs, 68–71
    party politics, 79–81
    state withdrawal, 73–6, 88–9, 158
    see also village councils; village courts
Long, Norman, 29, 110
Lord's Resistance Army (LRA), 56, 143n23
Lund, Christian, 87
luwalo forced labour, 40, 69
Luwum, Janani, 46

Malakite movement (*Bamalaki*), 118–19
Mamdani, Mahmood, 40n20, 41, 65–6, 67
Maxwell, David, 93, 109n30
mayumba kumi, 54, 76, 78–9
Mbale Collectorate, 38
members of parliament (MPs), 79–81
Meyer, Birgit, 97–8, 113, 153
Middleton, J., 109n31
military, influence of, 16–17, 44–5
Mill Hill Missionaries, 16, 37, 40, 116, 117
missionaries, influence of, 37–8, 40
mission churches, 114–21
Mitchell, J. Clyde, 167
Moore, Sally Falk, 7
Movement system, politics, 79–81
Mukula, Mike, 81
Museveni, Yoweri
    and economic development, 60, 158
    government of, 80
    opposition to, 50
    seizure of power (1986), 4, 17, 48–9, 61

Nagashima, Nobuhiro, 140n19, 146–7
National Resistance Army/Movement
    (NRA/M)
    and internment camps, 144
    policies of, 66, 67
    rebel leaders in, 56
    seizure of power (1986), 4, 17, 48–9

    support for, 47
Native Administration Tax Ordinance, 70
Ngora sub-county
    county administrative headquarters, 75
    development projects, 6
    internment camp, 53–4, 122
    Pentecostal churches, 95
    religious activity, 16
    taxation, 72
non-governmental organisations (NGOs),
    58n59, 120–2, 131
Nuitjen, Monique, 26n26

Oberei Fastine, 51
Obote, Milton, 44, 45, 47, 78
Oboth-Ofumbi, Charles, 46
Ogoria burial society, 138–9, 145
Ogwang, David Livingstone, 44
Ogwapit Joseph, 22, 23
Okalany, D. H., 19
Okelai Samuel, 85, 114, 128–30
Okello, Basilio, 47
Okello John, 105–6
Okello, Tito Lutwa, 44, 47
Okodel, Hajji Omar, 56
Okurut Gereson Nairobi, 16–17, 44
Oledai
    burial societies, 135–9, 145–54
    cattle, 16, 17, 58
    Christianity, 91–2, 113–14, 120–1
    committee positions, 100, 101
    cotton industry, 15–16, 17, 61
    economic decline, 57–8, 59
    HIV/AIDS, 17
    household lifestyles, 13–15, 113–14
    local government, 64, 67
    marginality, 15
    parish chief, 76
    Pentecostalism, 16, 27–8, 92, 93–4,
        99–110, 159–60
    propriety, 23–5
    prosperity, 21–3
    seniority, 18–21
    village council, 81–2
    village court, 64–5, 81–8
Olivier de Sardan, Jean-Pierre, 8
Olupot Constant, 145–6
Omadi John Francis, 101, 102–4, 130, 159,
    160
Omagor Alfred, 85–8
Omara-Otunnu, Amii, 44
Omeda, Max, 56
Omiat of Kumi, 42n22
Omoding Justin, 105–6
Ongenge George Washington, 119, 126–7,
    159
Opedun Paul, 82–3
Opolot, Okuni, 44

Oryema, Erunayo, 46
Otai, Peter, 50
Ottemoeller, D., 66, 67
Otunga Justin, 83
overseas direct assistance (ODA), 2; *see also* donor funding

PAG (Pentecostal Assemblies of God) *see* Pentecostalism
parish chief, role of, 67–71, 76
Participatory Rural Appraisal, 167–8
party politics
 local government, 79–81
 religious affiliations, 115
Peel, J. D. Y., 123n23
Pentecostalism
 born-again notions, 97–8
 and Catholic and Anglican churches, 121–4, 160
 development in Oledai, 16, 27–8, 92, 159
 and dispute settlement, 105–7
 incorporation into village life, 99–101, 107, 159–60
 influence on behaviour, 24
 nature of, 93–6
 persecution under Amin, 97
 and political status, 102–4
 Teso region, 96–9
 women, 107–9, 159
Phelan, Bernard, 120, 122n20, 141–2
Pigg, Stacy Leigh, 148
Pirouet, Louise, 91, 117
politics, party politics, 79–81, 115; *see also* local government
Poll Tax Ordinance, 39
post-colonial period, Teso region, 43–8
poverty levels, 1, 13n2
Presidential Commission for Teso, 56, 58–9
propriety, 23–5, 124, 153
prosperity, 21–3

radio, use of, 2, 148n38
Ranger, Terence, 110
Red Barnet (Denmark), 58n59
Regan, Anthony, 66
religious institutions
 development role, 10, 120–1
 influence on each other, 124
 under Amin, 46–7, 96–7
 see also Christianity; Pentecostalism
research methods, 167–72
Resistance Councils, 52, 63n1, 66
respectability *see* propriety
rural areas
 development projects, 5–7, 157–8
 neglect of, 2–3
 state withdrawal, 8, 64, 73–6, 88–9, 157–8

Saul, John, 7
Scott, James, 164
'Send a Cow' International (UK), 58n59
seniority, 18–21
Shipton, Parker, 26–7
Soroti Catholic Diocese Development Organisation (SOCADIDO), 58n59
Southall, Aidan, 74
spiralism, 102–3, 130
Ssali, Jaberi Bidandi, 49n34
state
 development role, 2, 3–5, 9–10, 60–1, 157–8, 164–5
 weakness of, 7–9
 withdrawal from rural areas, 8, 64, 73–6, 88–9, 157–8
Strømmestiftelsen (Norway), 58n59, 121
Sultan, D., 74

Tanzania, peasant communities, 7–8
taxation
 colonial period, 39
 local, 69, 70, 72–3
 payments, 138, 139
Tear Fund (Australia), 58n59, 121
Teso Insurgency, 48–52, 61, 161
 burials, 142–5
 end of, 56
 impact on seniority, 20–1
 influence on burial societies, 142, 144–5, 152–4
 internment, 52–6, 98–9, 122, 143–4
 and Pentecostalism, 98–9
 recovery from, 23, 25, 57, 153–4, 170–1
Teso region
 bakungulu period, 36–8
 colonial period, 31, 38–43, 77–8
 economic divisions, 56–9
 local government, 65, 68–79
 members of parliament (MPs), 79, 81
 missionaries, 37–8, 40, 114–21
 parish chiefs, 68–71
 Pentecostalism, 96–9
 post-colonial period, 43–8
 pre-colonial, 34–5, 77
Therkildsen, Ole, 72
Thompson, F. M. L., 133n2
Tripp, Aili Mari, 66
Tukahebwa, Geoffrey, 66
Tukei Gerald, 49n35
Twaddle, Michael, 36, 115n7

Uganda National Liberation Army (UNLA), 47n28
Uganda People's Army (UPA), 50
Uganda People's Congress (UPC), 44, 115

VECO-Vredeseilanden Coopibo (Belgium), 58n59, 121
village councils
 chairman, 67–8, 81–2, 83–5
 institutional change, 26, 63–4, 77–9
 workings of, 81–2, 87–8
village courts, 76–9, 129
 cases, 82–8
 Oledai, 64–5, 81–8
Vincent, Joan, 15, 18–19, 33, 34, 53, 68–9, 74, 91, 102, 117, 127, 133, 168–9
violence
 Teso Insurgency, 51, 53–4, 61, 71, 161

under Amin, 46–7
Vision Terudo, 58n59

Ward, Kevin, 38, 92n3, 99n16, 122
Watson, W., 102
wealth, 21–3
Werbner, Richard, 28n, 42–3
Whyte, M., 146
Whyte, Susan Reynolds, 9, 23, 60, 145, 152
women, and Pentecostalism, 107–9, 159
Wunsch, J. S., 66, 67

Zistel, Suzanne, 94n8

EUP JOURNALS
Africa

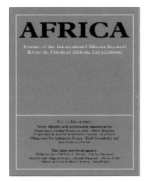

ISSN 0001-9720

eISSN 1750-0184

Four issues per year

Find *Africa* at
www.eupjournals.com/AFR

Africa is the premier journal devoted to the study of African societies and culture. Published as the journal of the International African Institute, editorial policy encourages an interdisciplinary approach, involving humanities, social sciences, and environmental sciences.

Africa aims to give increased attention to African production of knowledge, emerging social and cultural trends "on the ground", and links between local and national levels of society. At the same time, it maintains its commitment to the theoretically informed analysis of the realities of Africa's own cultural categories. Each issue contains five or six major articles, arranged thematically, extensive review essays and substantial book reviews. Special issues are frequent. Edinburgh University Press also publishes the *Africa Bibliography*, an authoritative annual guide to works in African Studies.

More journals from EUP
African Studies
Film, Media & Cultural Studies
Politics and Law
Islamic Studies
Linguistics
Literary Studies
Philosophy and Religion
Historical Studies
Science and Medical

Edinburgh
University Press

Sign up for ToC Alerts at
www.eupjournals.com

EDINBURGH UNIVERSITY PRESS
International African Library

Series Editors: J.D.Y. PEEL, SUZETTE HEALD & DEBORAH JAMES

FORTHCOMING TITLE

THE POLITICS OF RELIGIOUS CHANGE ON THE
UPPER GUINEA COAST
Iconoclasm Done and Undone
Ramon Sarró
Hb 978 0 7486 3515 3

Based on research spanning over 12 years, this book offers an in-depth analysis of an iconoclastic religious movement initiated by a Muslim preacher among coastal Baga farmers in the French colonial period. With an ethnographic approach that listens as carefully to those who suffered iconoclastic violence as to those who wanted to 'get rid of custom', Sarró discusses the extent to which iconoclasm produces a rupture of religious knowledge and identity, and analyses its relevance in the making of modern nations and citizens. This book will appeal to a wide range of readers, particularly those with an interest in the anthropology of religion, iconoclasm, the history and anthropology of west Africa, or the politics of heritage.

Key Features
- Examines the historical complexity of the interface between Islam, traditional religions and Christianity in west Africa, and how this interface links with dramatic political changes
- Offers a detailed ethnographic approach
- Presents a dialogue between the field findings, a long tradition of anthropology and the most recent anthropological debates

Edinburgh
University Press

www.euppublishing.com

EDINBURGH UNIVERSITY PRESS
International African Library

Series Editors: J.D.Y. PEEL, SUZETTE HEALD & DEBORAH JAMES

The International African Library is a major monograph series from the International African Institute.

Theoretically informed ethnographies, and studies of social relations 'on the ground' which are sensitive to local cultural forms, have long been central to the Institute's publications programme. The IAL maintains this strength and extends it into new areas of contemporary concern, both practical and intellectual.

It includes works focused on the linkages between local, national and global levels of society; writings on political economy and power; studies at the interface of the socio-cultural and the environmental; analyses of the roles of religion, cosmology and ritual in social organisation; and historical studies, especially those of a social, cultural or interdisciplinary character.

The International African Library complements the quarterly journal *Africa*, also published on behalf of the International African Institute.

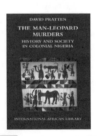

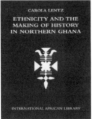

www.euppublishing.com